2012

2012

Crossing the Bridge to the Future

MARK BORAX

Frog Books
Berkeley, California

Published by Frog Books

Frog Books' publications are distributed by
North Atlantic Books
P.O. Box 12327
Berkeley, California 94712

Cover photograph by Dan Heller: *Star Trails*
Cover author photograph by Janet Lee Henderson
Interior author photograph by Murray Rockowitz
Cover and book design by Brad Greene
Printed in the United States of America

2012: Crossing the Bridge to the Future is sponsored by the Society for the Study of Native Arts and Sciences, a nonprofit educational corporation whose goals are to develop an educational and cross-cultural perspective linking various scientific, social, and artistic fields; to nurture a holistic view of arts, sciences, humanities, and healing; and to publish and distribute literature on the relationship of mind, body, and nature.

North Atlantic Books' publications are available through most bookstores. For further information, call 800-733-3000 or visit our website at www.northatlanticbooks.com.

Library of Congress Cataloging-in-Publication Data

Borax, Mark, 1954-
 2012 : crossing the bridge to the future / Mark Borax.
    p. cm.
 ISBN-13: 978-1-58394-208-6
 ISBN-10: 1-58394-208-4
 1. Borax, Mark, 1954- 2. Lonsdale, Ellias, 1947- 3. Astrologers—Biography. 4. Astrology. 5. Prophecies (Occultism) 6. Mayas—Prophecies. I. Title.
 BF1791.B67 2008
 133.5092'2—dc22
 [B]

                                                                2008002140
                                                                CIP

1 2 3 4 5 6 7 8 9 SHERIDAN 14 13 12 11 10 09 08

For Sky and Sky's world.

If you want to change a world, change its story.

—m.b.

(This tale can be read aloud.)

I am certain of nothing but the holiness of the heart's
affections and the truth of the imagination.
What the imagination perceives as beauty must be true,
even if it never before existed.

—John Keats

Nothing is too wonderful to be true.

—Michael Faraday

I am on this journey where I find that I run into myself
all the time.

—Ellias Lonsdale

2012

Contents

Preface

This book depicts my seven-year apprenticeship to the irrepressible William Lonsdale (who later changed his name to Ellias Lonsdale), master astrologer and social visionary. With the help of myself and a handful of others, our provocative headmaster founded a small mystery school in the rustic town of Bonny Doon, California, where we studied the mysteries of our time.

Over the years a few hundred of us attended this school. In a modest, unassuming cottage nestled under the giant redwoods of the Santa Cruz Mountains, next to a rundown old apple orchard, amidst hawks, mice, and owls, we peered into the past and present in order to grasp the future. Led by a reclusive, long-haired cosmic wildman and his soft-spoken wife, Sara, in this rural setting we were taught to paint a captivating soul portrait of our times.

We studied the art of what makes human beings change, and decided that our planet is in the grip of a widespread change, which many now recognize but few agree upon what, exactly, to do with. Using the ancient Socratic method of lecture accompanied by open dialogue, we attempted to decipher this riddle—the mystery of a time many thinkers agree is pivotal, or even apocalyptic in the scope of human events, but which also appears to resist definition by any single tag or *ism*.

Each week our bearded mage brushed aside conventions and clichés of astrology, Western culture and the basic facts of life, firing arrows at every sacred cow to overthrow the old and ring in the new. Beneath the massive trees, this towering man, who literally stood head and shoulders above the rest of us, never stopped pushing our buttons. Relentlessly he challenged our fundamental beliefs about *everything*, badgering us from every angle, mystically and intellectually, to jerk us out of what he calls the Trance of Normalcy and awaken our authentic selves.

In that California cabin we spent many evenings homing in on the course of a new future for the world, connected to the year 2012, a time which the Lonsdales forecast as having something crucial to bring to the human race.

I'm often asked how I've come to do what I do—there are no current schools for wizards that I know of. But from 1987 to 1994 I learned my tradecraft the traditional way, by apprenticing to a stern taskmaster in his workshop in the woods. Ever since, I've been yearning to open the doors of our school to others, and this book is the result of that yearning.

This tale of my mystical apprenticeship lived inside me during the last twenty years beneath everything I did, stubbornly refusing to go away until I committed it to paper. It's a true story of individuals who journeyed beyond the borders where the Known meets the Unknown, and came up with surprising conclusions, which became, for at least one of us, a matter of life and death.

This isn't a novel, a dissection of ancient prophecies, or a list of predictions. Other recent and forthcoming books on 2012 are slanted in those directions and can be referred to for those. I'm not going to tell you what will happen in 2012, because even though I've been known to make accurate predictions now and then, the truth is I *don't know* what's going to happen. I have ideas, but much depends on the choices we now make. Much is riding upon how well we seize the moment. Much depends upon how Big you're willing to dream.

Throughout my practice as Soul Level Astrologer during the last two decades I've listened to the dreams of thousands. I've become a carrier of the dreams people hold in their hearts, helping them build bridges from here to there. I've learned many things about human transformation, what assists it, what supports it, what gets in the way. I've come to believe that some powerful new dream is gestating in the depths of our species. If enough of us catch wind of this dream we may usher in a future that stuns us by breaking the rules of what we think of as everyday life on Planet Earth.

Though astrology was the lure our canny wizard used to draw us into his mountain home, over the years I've found the story to be much bigger than star talk. Astrology is the main channel we tapped to haul up a new creation myth that appears to be bubbling in the depths of our species, a new dream of life on Earth unfolding more fully than before. But if we were correct and that dream is real—then it can be found anywhere. Astrology is a main access route but any path that goes deep enough can take you there. Anything that activates the core nature of a human being will suffice. Anything that ignites the urge to create a blazingly authentic existence during a time of great distortions and lies can tap the same wellspring, fortifying us to sweep away obsolete stories of what we're doing around here and usher in something new.

Though they don't all specifically agree on the year 2012, various cultural prophecies point to our era as a major pivot point in human evolution: the Bible, the Book of Mormon, Hopi, Navajo, Buddhist and Mayan prophecy, sacred Hindu texts, among others. I'm not going to delve into these sources. My goal is to usher you down that private dirt driveway beneath the giant redwoods, and plant you on the couch in front of the crackling wood fire in that timeless cottage, where the mysteries burn bright, and together we can cross a bridge to the future.

—Mark Borax
Harbin Hot Springs
Winter Solstice, 2007

— 1

All Things Converge

Buddhists say it's fortunate to be born during the time of a great teacher. I'm still trying to sort out who Ellias really is, but some facts are clear: he taught me a radical new understanding of the universe. He put a whole different spin on the purpose of humanity. He revealed a magical inner world that coexists with the world we think of as normal. For one shining moment Ellias, who later changed his name from William, stood at the head of our mystery school and led us to truths so steep that, lacking his presence in our daily lives, many of us are still clambering up the slopes to get back on top.

This book is about *how you live* and *how you die* and how you can change the world. It tells the story of my encounter with a remarkable man and woman, and a series of mystical events that came together in such an extraordinary way it has taken me twenty years to sort out.

I could begin this narrative at so many places. Like multiple facets of a single sparkling jewel, each aspect of the story reflects the same image from a different angle; each episode spills into so many others that it almost becomes arbitrary where to start. Out of all the shimmering images though, one giant silhouette rises stark and inescapable. I keep coming back to Mount Shasta, so I'll start there and trust that by placing the mountain in the foreground the rest of the story will fall into place.

But first a bit of background.

In July 1987, at the close of the annual Oregon Country Fair, a friend handed me a pamphlet that diagnosed modern civilization as the end stage of *kali yuga,* a Sanskrit term for centuries of hell the world has been suffering through.

Standing in the giant makeshift parking lot bordered by large bales of hay, while long lines of fatigued vehicles and fairgoers exited all around me like a great hippie dustbowl migration, I opened the pamphlet. I read of a powerful planetary transformation, foreseen in the modern era by José Argüelles *(The Mayan Factor)* and others, who detected parallels among prophecies from many different cultures. Each tradition seemed to point to our time as the culmination of a long tortured darkness, which consists of civilization consumed by distorted values. The pamphlet integrated these findings into a unified theory of cosmic shift called the Harmonic Convergence.

When I got home from the Fair I looked into this matter and found many others doing the same. The closer we got to August 17, 1987, the more anticipation grew. As the Sun, Moon, Mercury, Venus, and Mars headed toward a rare five-way conjunction known as a stellium, in fiery Leo, with three additional planets in fire signs, the Convergence got a lot of air play. Out of ten astrological planets and four elements, to have eight planets in the same element is portentous.

In astrological terms, fire is the explosive release of life force from the repressive shackles that bind it. With four-fifths of the solar system in fire that summer, expectation built wherever individuals gathered to speak about spirit. People began discussing the Convergence on talk shows, and suddenly astrology, numerology and psychic readings were all the rage.

The writers of the pamphlet foresaw a great purge taking place between 1987 and 2012. In that quarter century, I read, whatever is most wrong with civilization *has to come up in our faces* to show us precisely what we need to change. So many divergent cultural sources converged on this augury that the idea of the prophecy itself was near-miraculous.

As with most New Age literature, I spent a great deal of time reading between the lines to sort substance from hype. Contemporary hell, said modern visionaries, comes from life out of balance—what the Hopi elders call *koyaanisqatsi.* We've forgotten who we are. We've lost our ancient connection with spirit. We lack purpose. To usher in a new era our inner and outer paths must converge. No longer can we afford to make money at the expense of the soul. No longer can we content ourselves with unsatisfying, disconnected jobs and marriages. "Now is the time to question our entire basis for living," declared José Argüelles, "... to release obsolete mindsets we inherited from the past."

Leo is the sign of the heart. With five planets closing in on the body of the Lion, our whole galaxy was envisioned as the gargantuan heart chakra of a Metagalactic being. (*Chakra* is the Sanskrit term for "wheel," referring to seven subtle energy globes aligned along the vertical axis of the human body.) Six neighboring galaxies were said to compose this mega-organism's other chakras. It was a beautiful vision.

As the stellium of 1987 approached, groups planned to gather at sacred sites across the world to enact a rite of passage. Even among people unfamiliar with astrology, who hadn't heard of the Harmonic Convergence, something seemed to be up. The San Francisco Bay Area felt fidgety, the neighborhoods of Berkeley plagued with more sirens than I could remember. Each hour, it seemed, another alarm went screeching through the streets.

My girlfriend and I were living in North Berkeley. I was in the city with her to see if we could revive our love, which had self-destructed the previous year on an interminable cross-country trip in a VW bus.

I'd met Elizabeth in Burlington, Vermont, three years earlier while playing acoustic guitar on my front porch. Riding her ten-speed past the corner of Willard and Loomis, she flung a curtain of shoulder-length strawberry-blond hair out of her face and cried, *"Sing louder so I can hear you!"* and I cried, ***"Come closer** so you can hear me!"* She pedaled over and I fell fast and deep for her. Wide sensuous mouth, hungry blue-green eyes, broad cheekbones, freckles, a Burlington College student-dancer with a mad passion for contact improv, authentic movement, art and shamanism—how could I resist?

But we hadn't made love in years. Not really. Not fully. Not like we used to. It was as if our magnetic charge had reversed polarity, and some recalcitrant part of each of us now repelled the other, with an undercurrent of fierce sexual frustration. Talking about this didn't seem to help—it appeared to live somewhere deeper than talk.

Elizabeth's minister father had cheated on her mother for years, moving from parish to parish each time his affairs came too close for comfort. Even though her mother hadn't known about these affairs consciously, the svelte minister's wife retorted by gaining hundreds of extra pounds and walling herself off in her own body. Elizabeth, a Taurus like her mother, took on the elder woman's unexpressed rage. God help me if my head turned at the passing of a cute woman on the sidewalk, or the slightest sign I might not find my lover perfectly desirable. At night if I didn't reach out to touch Elizabeth's breast the moment her head hit the pillow, she often violently yanked her body away and disappeared into a grand canyon of covers, lowering the temperature of the room toward severe frostbite. Who could get aroused on the verge of Taurus bull horns that sharp and relentless? After the hot eroticism of our early days in the Green Mountains, this Bay Area barren tundra felt especially harsh and foreboding.

Each day my girlfriend met with musicians and actors in a creative universe I felt excluded from and envious of, while I toiled at home on editing jobs in the comic book business. My own writing was going nowhere, my lifelong fantasy to have a book published seemed just that—the farfetched longing of a thirty-two-year-old baby boomer who still didn't know what he wanted to be when he grew up.

Lately I'd taken to haunting metaphysics sections of Berkeley and Oakland bookshops, fantasizing about other women, checking their eyes for a sign that the male beast in me was capable of something more than leaping through domestic hoops and reading spiritual literature on my side of the bed. I felt trapped in a life that didn't belong to me but couldn't grasp how to change it. As you can imagine, the idea of global transformation was very appealing to me just then. Feeling thwarted everywhere else, I began to look within.

The summer of 1987 was a confluence of many diverse streams. Ideas about life after death, angels, astrology, UFOs, and psychic phenomena sprang out of the closet into mainstream thought. This encouraged me, not only because it gave me hope that maybe the prophecies were right and the world *was* changing, but also because I'd just begun considering a career in astrology.

For four years I'd studied *Alan Oken's Complete Astrology: As Above, So Below,* faithfully doing his exercises. Following the ancient Greek dictum, "Know Thyself," I was driven through a study of the stars to fathom the depths of my own nature. For four years the only birth chart I looked at was my own.

Could the key to my destiny be found in my chart? Was my nature the product of earlier cycles of energy and design that could be traced to the moment of my birth? Was my unease the result of having stumbled off some clear track in this design?

The natal chart is a circular snapshot of the sky at birth (ideally the moment of your first breath). It depicts a singular pattern of revolving planets distributed in some unique fashion through the twelve signs of the zodiac and twelve houses of the chart.

This planetary mandala portrays the stratified layers of a person's nature *in seed form.* A birth chart has at least as many—probably more— "genetic" codes packed into it as does a seed and requires suitable supportive elements to come to term. I came to see the chart as celestial DNA, an organic blueprint that requires free will and circumstance to flower and achieve its fullest potential.

"As above, so below" was the hermetic axiom of the ancient alchemists, a statement of their belief that each earthly event is reflected by celestial events, and vice versa. Cosmos and we are two sides of the same coin, said mystics, a theory borne out by discoveries in quantum physics that illustrate how human consciousness affects the universe. The macrocosm is contained in the microcosm as well as vice versa. No one is an island. A single human fingerprint recapitulates the whorling galaxy. The whole can be found in the parts, and each part is a whole. The stars don't cause things to happen so much as reflect what's already happening. Astrology depicts this encoded language on the macrocosmic scale of humanity's progression of life on Earth, as well as on the microcosmic level of the course of each individual life.

Alan Oken was particularly good at applying the Ages of the Zodiac to the thrust of history. These "ages" result from the fact that Earth is flattened at the poles rather than being a perfect sphere. Instead of spinning smoothly we wobble, like a children's toy top beginning to slow. One wobble, though, takes about 26,000 years. During that time the north celestial pole of the world, like a huge planetary hand, points to each sign of the zodiac once, as we rotate around the starry dial of a cosmic clock. Astrologers call this 26,000-year period a Great Year, which is divided into twelve ages of roughly 2,100 years each.

During the approximately 2,100-year-long Age of Taurus, ancient Egypt, which worshiped the bull, was in bloom. During the subsequent Age of Aries, Hebrew civilization solidified, with its ram's horn *shofar*. The Age of Pisces followed with Jesus, whose first symbol was the fish. In the Age of the Fishes, mysticism mingled with state affairs. Priests and rabbis held the salvation of the masses in their hands.

Now we stand poised on the cusp of a new era—the *Age of Aquarius*, which many astrologers see us entering in 2012. Thus the origin of the term "New Age"—the vibrant renewal of our species that astrologers have predicted for centuries. Aquarius is the sign of humanity itself, the Water-Bearer, rising out of the darkness of the ages to pour a stream of higher consciousness into the world.

Astrology was the only system of thought I found broad and deep enough to satisfy my lifelong hunger to discover who we are and what we're doing. Because it's not a religion, it leaves room for all religions. Our first science, it passed through many cultures on the way to its current incarnation, picking up and dropping off ideas every step along the way. Meticulous observations of human behavior by inquiring minds down through the ages are encoded into the zodiac (Arabic for "wheel of animals"), which is the band of constellations that the sun, moon, and planets appear to move through in the night sky.

A friend who heard of my four-year study said: "How do you have patience to translate so many miniscule details of technical mumbo-jumbo?"

But I never thought of it as discipline. I just drank it in. A passport to a universe of meaning and magic, astrology drew so many disparate elements together that I couldn't get enough. What else fuses history, psychology, astronomy, myth, culture, and metaphysics?

Einstein was an astrologer, as was Jung. So were a couple of Popes. The father of modern science, Isaac Newton, is known for his retort to Edmund Halley, discoverer of Halley's Comet, who dismissed astrology outright: "Sir, I have studied the matter—you have not!"

Astrology's possibilities for application are endless.

At first it was simply my passion. In the summer of 1987 I began flirting with the idea of it as a career. I was disenchanted with my comics jobs, had a bad case of writer's block and a worse case of lover's block, and wondered if I could make a living reading people's charts.

I'd recently made friends with a grad student of transpersonal psychology, Sita, who had long thick dark hair and a voluptuous body. Though we didn't become lovers, a strong charge of passion fused the air between us, which triggered the hell out of Elizabeth. Despite my girlfriend's discomfort, after assuring her I was not going to act on this charge, I allowed myself to sink into the friendship. Sita and I had marathon discussions of shamanism, psychology, and astrology while taking long walks through the leafy neighborhoods of North Berkeley or staying up late on her living room couch. As summer advanced, our main topic became the Harmonic Convergence.

Elizabeth, Sita, and I chose to drive to Mount Shasta on the morning of Convergence Day and drop acid. We got three capsules from a batch reputed to be very pure, circulating through the hip Marin community. I was impressed by the largesse of my lover that allowed her to expose herself like that to someone who triggered her raw matriarchal wound of sexual betrayal.

I spent the week leading to the stellium fasting, sweating out toxins

2012

in a local sauna, doing yoga and meditating. I hadn't taken LSD in fifteen years and hoped to use it as I had in my teens, as an intergalactic laxative to purge my cosmic constipation. My belly was cramped, my writing stuck, my love stalled. Feeling out of place in the city, I called upon a combination of Convergence and entheogen to open the gates, and silently prayed for the predicted changes to be real.

I drove our brown Honda Civic east on Route 80 out of Berkeley, then north up I-5. Before long we reached the winding highway that soars over Shasta Dam toward the famous mountain, which many people consider a major power point along the Ring of Fire, the geographic circle of volcanoes that includes the Hawaiian Islands. I'd never been up Shasta but had seen it for years from the freeway: sudden, towering, inevitable, rising out of nowhere like a gigantic snow-covered god. It's impossible to drive that stretch of highway without feeling the mountain's pull.

After following road signs to a remote part of Shasta where we hoped to avoid New Age throngs on the other side, I instinctively pulled off the pavement onto a dirt causeway that narrowed to a weed-choked gulley. Ignoring bone-rattling bumps and squawks of protest from both the Honda and Elizabeth, I pushed on through the tangled brush till I could go no farther.

"Guess this is it," I said, shutting off the ignition.

Sita and Elizabeth exchanged a dubious look.

"I'll get us out of here tomorrow," I told them, trying to sound more convincing than I felt as I gathered blankets, water and instruments. Tired of being second-guessed by my lover, I resolved to regain pride and dignity on this trip. *In the city you may be Queen Bull but out here it's a whole new game....*

Daypacks on our backs, canvas bags in hand, we stepped into the wilderness, found a trail and hiked. As we walked I felt a telepathic link with thousands of others. *In Machu Picchu, at the Great Pyramid, in Glastonbury, and on the Big Island, all over the planet we are walking our ancestors home....*

That altered feeling came on that I get from new and full moons, equinoxes and solstices, like tripping before I was tripping. My stomach was fluttery. Realizing I'd outdistanced the others, I paused in the swishing grass and rubbed the hinges of my jaw, which were sore and packed with tension.

At the first flash of Elizabeth's red-gold hair I plunged ahead silent as a cat, and colors and sounds intensified. Part of this was due to the fast, but it felt bigger than that, as if we were being swept into something huge and irreversible.

We began our visionquest sitting cross-legged on Navajo blankets. The silence hummed. We used a method called "talking stone" to establish a sense of ritual. Only the person holding the stone—in this case a large chunk of pyrite—could speak.

Sita and then Elizabeth held the rough-hewn stone and declared intentions of what they wanted to achieve from our quest. Then it was my turn. Enclosing the rock in my fist I said, "I want to evolve. I wanna be free. I want to get out of my own way. I want to break through my blocks and grow into the man I really am. I want to get clear about what Elizabeth and I are doing. *I want to heal my digestion.* I want to find my mission. I want the world to change."

Feeling suddenly self-conscious—*did I ask too much?*—I glanced at the others but spied no cynicism. They seemed silently supportive. We popped the capsules and washed them down with water. Almost instantly the earth became pliant and sinewy, and that telltale taste bubbled in the back of my throat, like tasting my own bodily chemistry of mucus and saliva. *Uh-oh, here we go—didn't I vow to never do this again?*

I reached into a canvas bag, pulled out the calimba (African thumb-piano) and began thumbing the brass tines into a melody that chimed around us like a stream. By pressing fingers on and off sound holes behind the wooden box I bent occasional notes into *wah-wahs* that reverberated through the field skirting the forest. Sita shook a Navajo rattle and added percussive sounds from her mouth. Elizabeth played bamboo flute. The music was sparse and hesitant.

As the acid came on, our environment blended into the song: muted bird chirps, the hush of grass, tiny susurrations of branch, limb and movement. We played the world and the world played us, each *wah-wah* boomeranging our consciousness out and back around in rhythmic waves that soaked us deeper into all things.

Then the acid hit harder as a dull throbbing in my gut. The week's fast had shrunk my stomach. Gripped by nausea—*isn't that why I swore off this?*—I bent a final note that faded as the silence rushed over us like an inland sea.

The women meandered away.

My abdomen growled.

Breathing became aspirating through a wet t-shirt that elongated as my legs were drawn down through flashing layers of soil, while my torso shot up into a sky that strobed powder-blue and cobalt. I was stretched to inhabit some phantom body I seem to possess in another dimension.

Blanched from that peculiar blend of hyper-alertness and debilitating exhaustion common to both fasting and tripping, I levitated above grass spackled with paintbrush and lupine, up and over my cramped life back in the city: Elizabeth and I, two contorted gnomes locked in anger on Rose Street, achieving nothing, touching nothing, arguing nothing. *Nada, nada, nada. . . .*

I was speared by an anguish that went far beyond Elizabeth into some nameless Void that has haunted me since I can remember.

Shivering, I scanned the horizon.

Somewhere were angels.

We were on Earth and I was alive, wasn't I?

The mountain was calling.

What in heaven's name is that guy so worked up about down there?

How could I let myself be lured into the same trap over and over? Why do we fight? Why can't we open our hearts? Why can't we be the people we really are? What gets in the way every time? How had the lusty promise of our early days in the Nest drained to such wasteland?

I licked my parched lips, recalling the cinnamony taste of Elizabeth that

September, how willingly seductive her youthful body had been, the smell of clean sheets below the window propped open to the oaken smoke of New England autumn.

Where does love go when it goes? What demonic force sucks the dreams of lovers who fused in the orgasmic rush of blood and fire that pales away in the frozen breakfast light of morning?

My stomach growled like a trapped beast. The sun hid behind a cloud and I realized with a shudder that I knew this place. Something about it was familiar. I'd glimpsed it in threshold moments, lightning flashes, hypnagogic states between waking and sleeping. This was a place I once inhabited. I'd seen it before. In fact, I'd seen *all* this before, even seen myself on the mountain realizing I'd seen it. . . .

We are so much more than ourselves, said a voice. *So much more. . . .*

I knew this!

I knew better than to get caught in yet another version of the *Who-did-what-to-who Game.*

Hadn't I seen it?

I felt certain I had. I seemed to recall some vow I'd made about it. At some point I'd seen the mechanics of how we shrink ourselves, how we harden our hearts in blame and judgment, how that's a *choice* we can unchoose.

Yes, I was sure I'd broken into this truth with stunning radical clarity at some earlier moment. I dimly recalled sending myself a time-release capsule, an auto-hypnotic suggestion to alert myself the next time I stumbled into the trap. But I couldn't recall the actual message.

Then the capsule released and I remembered: *It's all meant to be—Everything!* Every wrenching convolution of blame and judgment, every retreat into our own corner of the ring, every forgetting to be the love we are, every snarled-up tangle of whatever—*even all this is somehow supposed to be.* We're not meant to remain pristine, virginal, pure—not meant to cling to angels. We're *supposed* to fall off the mountain. I couldn't remember why this was so but knew that it was. *Why don't you ever have pen and paper when you need them?*

My fingers clenched. I jumped up. I had to write about this. I had to tell it. The world needed to know. It would make me famous!

Just then, as swiftly as it came, the epiphany was gone like so many of my brilliant ideas.

A stab of nausea made me retch. Tottering, I coughed and hacked but there was nothing to come up. Some dark vibration pounded down the mountain at me, a sub-audible woof that doubled me over as I grabbed my gut and moaned.

Straightening up, I mourned my now-foggy revelation and wiped my chin. My head spun.

Where was I? I had to get that revelation back. It held some secret I desperately needed. *It can revive your love.* Maybe it wasn't gone, I told myself, mind racing. Maybe I could salvage it.

Squatting, I remembered where I first had the revelation: the sunlit interior of Rose Street with the cherry tree in bloom, oblique rays of afternoon light slanting through the high horizontal window, the Bay Bridge a far-off slash between pink-and-white blossoms.

The tree held the clue.

Yes, it was the tree—I was certain. Obsessed with the impulse to drive back to the city, I strode toward the car and then, realizing what I was doing, laughed it away.

The sun burst through the clouds and made me gasp. Roots and pebbles and grass undulated. I felt I wouldn't be able to anchor my revelation until I shared it. I had to tell someone. I had to find the women.

I rushed to the top of the ridge and spied them, hands and mouths moving like gunfighting marionettes poised on the edge of space, big blobs of rage shooting between them. I realized that behind the wave of acid I'd been subliminally pounded by this rage, psychically jackhammered by whatever drama these hilltop goddesses were enacting. They were deciding my fate and I had no say over any of it.

I broke into the charged field between them. "What—" I said, "is going on?"

"This isn't about you," Elizabeth hissed.

Sita's eyes smoldered. "Give us space, Mark."

I stood too long and lost my chance as a rolling curtain of light swept down the mountain. I threw my shirt off. Veins of creosote and madrone flashed against the leached-green background of sage and lupine. The world became a gyrating organism whose throbbing pulsations mirrored my labored breathing while I strode downhill, picking up speed until I was racing through a dizzying tunnel of green where my relationship splintered to jagged shards. *When will I be loved and when will I be loved and when will I be loved* shot me blindly through the trees. As I ran my heart constricted under some invisible shell of psychic scar tissue that protruded from my sternum.

This wasn't tripping—this was acid as a bloody x-ray of the dark force that consumed me. This was *doppelgänger,* my dark double, the sucking Void that would not let me be, that drew me closer and closer toward its gaping maw and the oblivion to which I'd always known I'd be consigned one day.

I ran and ran and as I ran it seemed I'd always been running to outrun my pathetic inability to do anything that mattered, and the futility of this struck me squarely in the chest like a blast furnace that spun me around and around my endless craving to be loved, until I broke out into a high field and stopped, heart pounding, eyes wild, scanning the mountain from tree to tree, nostrils flared, fingers pawing the ground, sniffing the air like a trapped wolf.

The moon hung directly overhead and the sun perched to my left, suspended on the horizon. The sky was grainy with dancing particles. I knelt, palms to the ground, catching my breath, calculating where I was located in time. Was the moon rising or setting? We'd arrived in late morning, I was sure, but was it the beginning or end of day? How long had we been up here? What were the planets doing?

The sun and moon formed an exact right angle that I was the apex of, with no distance between us. Something very intimate was going on. Energy crackled across the field like heat waves over summer pavement. *It's not just a made-up thing; something really* is *happening!*

Of course, I realized. Aren't I as much a part of the universe as anything? If our local neighborhood of a hundred billion stars was going through galactic renovation, how could it not affect the trillions of cells in my body? Where do planets orbit in plants? How is space stitched into matter?

I sat up, right arm rising until my fingers pointed straight at the moon while my left arm stretched horizontally toward the sun. I was buffeted by a force that anchored me to Earth and streamed through me. I was unbudgeable. Sitting in the alpine meadow like that I laughed, realizing I must've looked like some character out of Hindu cosmology.

The sun and moon fleshed into a roundness that made me kinesthetically aware of Earth's globularity for the first time. The moon grew so round it seemed pregnant and swollen, about to burst. I sat marveling how I'd never noticed such *roundness* before, such exquisite roundness, that I could reach out and touch, as if God threw a ball and there it was: the curved horizon an extension of the freckled curve of the Milky Way, which was an extension of myself. Wheels within wheels within wheels. Everything spiraled in and out of itself like a chambered nautilus. Time bent back around. *Life wasn't separate.* Stars were not distant objects of flame and gas. All things pulsed with cosmic intelligence: creation making love to itself in the serpentine coils of sunflowers and DNA spirals; grass and molecules dancing with meteors like sea plants in a solar wind; quarks and gluinos rushing around a holographic funnel with no beginning or end. The utter curviness of all things made me laugh a laugh that blew away my citified existence of squares and rectangles.

How could I get so heavy when every line's a curve?

If we could just release, the next rung of the spiral is bound to take us back to wholeness. If we could just release. . . .

Then something shifted.

The sun slipped. The moon dipped over the ecliptic. The light changed. Millions of people coupled in ritual mating and I sank to the warm sage-scented grass where I closed my eyes.

Nausea awakened me. I got up stiff and stumbled downhill dry-heaving. *At least no one has to hear me*, I thought, retching. *I can die in peace.* Finally, unable to throw up, I flopped onto a scrabbly incline, lips to the dust, fine thread of spittle leaking down my chin. *Unghhh.*

Despite the nausea, some part of me felt relieved. Trapped like a fly in amber. Whatever demon I'd been running from had finally caught me. The race was over. I mustered a bitter smile. In some tight corner of my soul I'd always known—hadn't I?—that it would end like this. *That was two lives ago, not this time,* said a voice I didn't recognize. Pushing up, I turned and looked around but saw only the sparse and scratchy scrub brush.

I lost ability to distinguish time from space, inner from outer. Sparks revolved in front of my eyes that could have been bugs or leaves or molecules.

The coppery taste on the edge of my tongue, the piney woods, the stark angle of light, vertigo—this saturated choreography had been drawing and drawing me the whole time we drove up the mountain, perhaps from long before, maybe my whole life.

Sensing I was not alone I gulped and suddenly became aware that I had no water, it was blazing hot, my throat was dry, and I was utterly lost. I sank back to the creosote.

It would be easy, I thought, sweat trickling down my neck, so easy to release this world.

Are you ready? said a presence.

The proximity of death, promising the end of all pain, was sweetly seductive, almost sexual, drawing my hips into the ground.

Is that why I came to Shasta? To slip through a cosmic cervix and never be heard from again?

It was tempting. As I leaned in that direction the nausea grew acute, tumbling me into a swirling nebula where everything ceased.

Black infinity....

Then, counter-impulse.

No.

Oh no no NO. You're not ready. It's not time.

You have something to do.

A strain of music wafted down the mountain, drawing me from the Void into some nasal baritone west Texas crooner. A lilting melody. A country song. Underneath it came a tapping that led to a young girl skipping rope in her driveway, radio playing from the shaded crosshatching of an open garage.

I couldn't fathom whether I was seeing something nearby or in a parallel dimension, but I knew she was my ticket back. The dull staccato of rope on pavement and the girl's singsong voice as she chanted a jump rhythm, brilliantly self-absorbed with the devout fixation of a four-year-old, threw me a lifeline. I grabbed it and my chest heaved, eyes leaking salty tears. Then she disappeared, yanking me back to the slopes.

It's not time. An electric current pinballed up and down my spine.

The world needs you. The breath burst back into my lungs.

Yes, I told myself, gasping and clutching the chill night air. *Yes Yes Yes.* I pried my wolf carcass off the hard scrabble and crunched away from my own moon shadow.

"Yes."

You are not alone.

You are not done.

You have something to do.

The world needs you.

"The world needs me."

A good thought.

A comforting thought.

Maybe even true.

We slept in the open that night on the flat of the river bank, and in the morning dove into the icy river before heading back down the mountain to the city with all the rest of the pilgrims who'd come to Converge.

2012

—2

Roomful of Stars

In October Sita told me she'd booked an appointment with master astrologer William Lonsdale, whom she'd heard of through her school, JFK University, where people said his readings soared beyond other psychics and astrologers. When she came back from her session we met at her front door.

"How was it?" I asked. "You're glowing!"

She shook her head slowly. "Mark—I have no words. All I can say is he's the real thing."

"Wow!"

"Wanna hear the tape?"

Huddling on the couch we listened to William Lonsdale paint an in-depth portrait of Sita, via open-ended inquiry, like a scientist of the spirit. His voice was oddly familiar, soft but penetrative, with a subtle New York accent and underlying sense of irony, as if he relished the cosmic jest the universe was letting them in on. There was nothing trite or predictable about his message. Occasionally he giggled and she laughed as some cosmic puzzle piece fell into place.

When Sita stopped to ask for clarification, the quality of the astrologer's focus was palpable. This clearly seemed to be the work of a diligent, sharp-minded craftsman, who treated my friend as an equal rather than talking down to her or hiding behind smoke puffs of cosmic techno-babble. Occasionally he dropped a nugget that prompted us to switch off the recorder and discuss it. When the tape ended Sita said it was even more powerful the second time.

If human nature could be portrayed in such depth and color, then I wanted it done for me. This was the sign I'd been waiting for since coming down from Shasta. When I stood to go, my friend handed me a business card. Glancing at it, I laughed:

Move Your Mountains

William Lonsdale   408 427-0708

The next morning I made an appointment for a session more than two months later, the soonest the astrologer was available. He lived north of Santa Cruz and drove a hundred miles up to Marin every few months to meet with clients in an office he shared with a chiropractor friend. When I asked if there was anything I should bring or any way I should prepare, he said to bring a ninety-minute tape and any questions I wanted answered. Over the weeks I maintained a running list of concerns, which I kept crossing out and revising.

On the December day of my session I woke at dawn, did yoga, dressed and ate in silence. I got in the Honda and took a deep breath before turning the key: *Don't you dare break down till I get back—*

Entering the freeway I realized I'd forgotten my list and pounded the steering wheel, cursing my forward progress of the next few miles until I went too far to turn back.

The farther I got from the city the more my spirits rose. It was a mild northern California morning with a hint of mist in the distance. I cracked open the window while crossing onto the long Richmond Bridge. As I flew over the wide San Francisco Bay, the green hills of Marin opened before me and I wondered if this would all look the same after my mountains got moved. A blast of wind on the far side of the bridge shook the car and I tightened my grip on the steering wheel.

I arrived early at the parking lot of a nondescript building in the town of Ross, a setting so complacently suburban that it undercut my nervous tension; I might've been going to a podiatrist.

I walked the bank of a cheery little stream behind the building, gathering myself. Each time I tried to remember a single item on my list I drew a blank. *Funny.*

At three minutes to eleven I entered the building. A glimpse of long hair, dark eyes and bushy beard peeked out of the back room. "Give me three minutes, then come in," he announced in that slightly nasal, slightly husky tenor which sounded less high-pitched than it did on tape.

"Uh, okay," I said as he shut the door.

After several minutes I knocked softly and entered, with a shock; I hadn't expected him to be so *tall*. We shook hands.

Towering well above six feet, in baggy wrinkled chinos—beige, with worn brown loafers and blue-and-green plaid shirt with one corner sticking out of his pants waist—William Lonsdale struck me as a blend of Merlin, Gandalf and a stuffed teddy bear. Along with his obvious lack of concern for fashion trends, the astrologer's eyes, behind wire-rimmed glasses, were the only hint that something unusual might be going on. Crinkly and limpid, those dark eyes somehow managed, like the eyes of a small animal, to appear both secretive and open at the same time.

He gestured for me to sit on the couch, then closed the door and settled into a stuffed leather chair opposite. A long narrow glass-topped table lay between us, holding a scuffed manila file folder, from which he slid several sheets of paper. A half-dozen large loose-leaf binders leaned against the bottom of his chair in a multi-colored display that made me wonder what was inside.

I gave the astrologer my cassette. He inserted it and clicked on the recorder, then fiddled with the tiny microphone, trying to get it to stay clipped to his lapel, fumbling it a couple times and entangling the wire before he succeeded. "Session for Mark Borax, born 11:17 a.m., October

2nd, 1954, New York City," he said. Then he sat back and steepled his unusually long, delicate fingers. After a moment he looked up at me.

"At thirty-three," he proclaimed, "your whole identity is up. Your work, your ideas, your understanding of all of life, your entire sense of who you are and what you're doing. The totality and the specifics all come up at once." He punctuated phrases with subtle hand gestures, fingers hyper-extending backwards into the arched and tapered hands of a conjurer. His appearance was so mundane, his tone of voice so matter-of-fact, that the impact of these statements had a slight delay effect. Shyly, he looked up, possibly to gauge my response.

"That's true," I said. "Everything *is* up. I've been unable to sleep. All this energy rushing through me, like every day's a full moon. I've got to make some huge change but don't know how."

He tugged his beard while glancing at papers. "Hm. Some of that is due to world timings, not just your own."

"You mean the Harmonic Convergence?"

"Mm-hm. Your personal agitation mirrors a simultaneous event in collective consciousness. We've entered what appears to be an aberration in the space-time continuum. The Thought Police have been caught napping. Things are no longer going their way. We've veered off course, and now the whole world's acting out like crazy."

I laughed, amazed at the colorful sound of his language, which reminded me more of my own than anyone I'd met.

"The result of this combination of personal and collective timings for you is an intensive identity crisis of major proportions." He moved his hands as if playing a harp, and I caught a glint of violet shading his eyes. It took a few minutes for me to realize this was a tint in his bifocals rather than the auras I sometimes see around people.

He examined his papers. "In effect, your question is 'Who am I?' and that ripples into many circles."

I drew my legs onto the couch and folded them in half-lotus.

"Tell me a bit of your current situation," he said, leaning back. "In broad strokes. A few sentences."

"I've been working as editor and promotion director in the comic book business. I broke in three years ago as writer but got sidetracked into management. I've only sold three comics stories after years and years of writing them, though I keep workin' it. All my life I've been a writer. Nobody doubted this future. I wrote poems and stories when I was five, was published at fourteen. I saw myself as a successful author in the Bay Area very clearly by age nine—even though I lived on the east coast. But if it's supposed to happen, why's it taking so long? Maybe it's a bankrupt dream . . . I've written ten books and come close to having two sold, but something inevitably goes wrong at the last minute.

"On the other hand, my comics jobs are the first time I've been hired to be creative rather than stuff my creativity to fit in. All my life I've gotten 'The Talk.' You know: 'Mark—you're a great guy. I really like you *but. . . .*'

When he didn't say anything I went on. "I'm finally getting recognition and respect instead of ostracism for being different. It's hard to let go of this after bouncing from place to place and job to job and woman to woman. I don't know if I should abandon my age-old dream to write, settle deeper into comics, or ditch it all and strike a new direction."

I took a breath. "For four years I've been studying astrology through Alan Oken's book, *As Above, So Below*."

The master astrologer nodded. I paused, gathering confidence.

William Lonsdale's expression betrayed none of his thoughts. He was listening in apparent neutrality, perhaps weighing my words in a remote chamber of his mind, or maybe doing some inner psychic process.

"I've begun to wonder," I ventured, "if I could make a living reading people's charts. . . ." *Whew—it's out.*

When he said nothing I kept going, picking up speed. "I'm not sure if I should stick with chasing my lifelong dream of writing or switch to that. Also," I added quickly, "I'm a fish out of water in Berkeley. I swore I'd never live in a city again but broke that to see if Elizabeth and I could revive our love. We met three years ago, exploded into each other's beds, got frozen out of each other's hearts, and I can't figure out what message the goddess of love's trying to pound into my head.

"This fits an old pattern," I added, "of passionate new love slamming me like a runaway freight train that I can't hang onto no matter how hard I try. Maybe you can look at that. . . ?"

My host still didn't seem to be in a rush to say anything so I divulged the final thing on my mind. "And then," I said, "I had the most powerful experience of my life on Mount Shasta, during the Harmonic Convergence. I've been trying to make sense of it for the last four months. So *yeah*—I guess you could say everything's up."

"Wow. *Whew.*" The bearded mage glanced at a penciled version of my birth chart, scribbled over like a doctor's prescription. He moved his lips as if straining for words. He blew out his breath audibly. He twitched his mustache. "Can you say more about what happened on the mountain?"

"I'm not sure. . . . It was like a death," I confessed, noting the tremor in my voice. " I—I think I might've actually died. . . ."

I flashed on the undulating sage-scented slope with the sun low and moon high above the trapped wolf. "A presence came and asked if I was ready to go. I thought I might be—turned out I wasn't. Just thinking about it makes me queasy."

He got up and slid the window open a few inches, then sat down and crossed one leg over the other. He seemed open to hearing more, so I spilled the rest of the Shasta story in torrents. The astrologer listened without comment from a place of great stillness, nodding slightly once or twice.

When I finished, he squinted his eyes from above the knuckles of that eloquent hand that rested over his mouth. Brow furrowed, he slouched down and studied my chart, stretching his long legs under the table. Then he put down the paper, tugged his beard, and pondered. A moment later he bolted up, grabbed a dark blue binder, and leafed through it. After speed-reading something he laid the book on the table spread-eagled and plucked up his papers. As the silence advanced I began to feel awkward, self-conscious, exposed. *What the hell's he seeing? Why isn't he saying anything?* "What are all those papers?"

He shut the book with a pop that startled me. "Versions of your birth chart. Plus various timing cycles I look at during a first reading."

"And the binders?"

"Oh, all sorts of reference I rarely get to use but keep on hand just in case. Information my wife Sara and I brought through from spirit."

Wow. Who is this guy? I was dying for a look at those notebooks.

He seemed undecided about something, or perhaps all my talk had distracted him and he needed to regain his train of thought. He cleared his throat. "You've got some strange polarities going on in this lifetime," he stated flatly. "Your Libra Sun [he pronounced Libra in a way I'd never heard, with a long 'i'] squares the Lunar nodes, meaning you're basically at odds with yourself."

Great.

"The South Node, or *Dragon's Tail*—in Cancer, as you probably know— pertains to your past, as well as past lives. Cancer—emotional security, issues of home, belonging, family, tribe, placement, finding your location in the world—is a carry-over, more to do with your unresolved past-life history than your current direction. This is the daemon that haunts you, the shaky foundation your entire existence is based upon. You'll need to clear this frequency more than any other to move on to your real work."

I was dying to know what my real work was. I started to ask but he ignored me and kept going. "The basic issue we're discussing is self-mistrust, on a foundational level. This is the karma you've unwittingly carried that makes you a stranger to yourself. On the mountain that chasm opened and swallowed you whole."

I gulped.

"On the opposite side," he went on, "North Node—Dragon's *Head*— in Capricorn is your Destiny Point. You're coming from Cancer and heading to Capricorn, coming from water and heading toward earth. You're fighting to emerge from a sea of insecurity and unbelonging-ness—*stranger in a strange land*—in order to gain solid ground."

I planted my feet. "What would that ground look like?"

"Self-command that can only be won through prolonged wrestling with existence, which is why it's taking so long and has had so many apparent false starts."

"I see," I said. I really didn't but wanted to keep him going; the thought of finally finding my place had got me going.

"I don't think you're as off-track as it seems," he concluded a moment later. "Libra's the best sign for mixing and matching. [It was taking a while to get used to that long 'i'.] It's the only sign whose job is to weigh and balance everything. Libra's a hard-working sign, though, much harder than you'd think given its wishy-washy reputation with most astrologers."

I snorted.

"And Capricorn, your Destiny Point, is the thriftiest sign of all, famous for using *everything*. Little is wasted, little beside the point, though it's hard to recognize this when you're lost in the day-to-day stuff. I have to say, though, that nothing in Capricorn comes quick or easy. It's the sign without shortcuts. You're on a long-term path rather than early success."

I fidgeted. "You're saying there's a method to the madness of everything taking forever? It's all part of some mysterious plan?"

"Yup. There's a design, but you have to implement it. Spirit wants to help but can only meet you halfway."

I ruminated on this.

"You're caught between past and future," he added. "Between an obsolete way to be and something new trying to emerge. So, even though your Libra Sun and Sagittarius Moon and Rising make you extremely fast, the one thing you *can't* be fast in is *life path,* purpose, *destiny.* Purpose is something you have to sweat out manually, intensively, step by step, paying attention, working it, kneading the clay, getting down to it."

"You mean me or everybody?"

"*You.* The gods are testing to see what you're made of. And what you're made of is as tough in its own way as is the test; otherwise it wouldn't be so grueling."

I started to question this but he kept going.

"So, while much of your development is so fast it's almost instantaneous—your wild, spontaneous nature, linked to fire and air—the actual thing that's going to matter most in the long run—*earth*—is a life wisdom you build slowly and gradually, something you *come to* rather than assert."

"Can you say that another way?"

"You can't talk your way in, can't fake or finesse it. You've got to earn mastery the hard way, through long-term diligence. You've got to pay attention to subtle cues that spirit is trying to get through to you, beneath your constant intrigue; cues that you belong to something larger than your own ambition. You've got to settle into a deeper part of yourself, without jumping the gun or forcing the issue, as you often do."

I winced.

He noticed my hesitation and leaned toward me. "Mark—let me say very clearly: you have an abundance of creativity, desire, skill and motivation, enough for at least nine normal people. Like a cat you're living many lives in one."

No wonder I love cats.

"There's absolutely no doubt you're here to do something magical, give something unique to the world. You have a marvelous grasp of how everything relates to everything else. You have an instinctual feel for hidden themes and counter-themes, you're hot on the scent of how life moves in invisible design, how we're all interlinked parts of a whole that keeps changing."

Where does he get this?

"But the two things that come most naturally to most people—a basic ability to inhabit your life, and a clear sense of belonging to the world—constantly elude you."

Shit.

"This is because of a shadow you carry from a past life, more than any behavioral shortcomings. Several lives ago you got caught in a negative tailspin you still haven't recovered from. This shadow poisons the well and makes it hard for you to trust yourself—"

"Is that what's screwing up my loves?" I cut in.

He looked straight into me. "Yes."

As he went on talking I no longer heard his words so much as was battered by the undertow of them. He was spying the spinning Void, where nobody had caught me before.

"If I can put this another way," the astrologer was saying, as if guessing my discomfort, "wherever you go you're a visitor, never the home team, never at advantage, never on your own turf. Everything you're currently struggling with—where to live, who to live with, what to do for work and money—as pressing as these challenges are, they aren't the issue."

"What is?"

"The issue is how to get down to an authentic way to be and stay there from then on, no matter what."

A tightness gripped between my throat and sternum, like something was trying to break out. He glanced at that part of my body. "I must say, the things your Libra Sun is being asked to stretch and encompass in this life involve quite extraordinary stretching! However, as tortuous as this can be, it's ultimately not more than you can handle. You got the precise chart you asked for.

"Oh yes, that's right," he added, noting my puzzlement, "we each get the chart we ask for. We each are born into the exact set-up we need to fulfill our life task."

I sat up on the couch. "What did I ask for? What's my life task? What's the set-up leading to?"

He looked into my eyes. "You're here to be a leader."

I gasped.

"You can't take the normal route to success because you're after a whole different kind. You're intended to be the kind of leader who leads people to *their own truths* rather than getting them to do it your way. Few role models for this kind of authority exist. It requires constant self-struggle. Rather than wielding the false power of ego, you're seeking to free something trapped in the heart and soul of humanity, by simultaneously freeing yourself."

I nodded while wrestling with a concept I wasn't sure I'd heard correctly—something about the word "leader" mentioned in the same breath as me. Hell, I've rarely been sure at the beginning of any month whether I'd be able to pay rent by the end of it. I was the scrawny kid picked last in sandlot sports, kicked out of class to the principal's office time and again, thrown in jail by cops who called me a wiseass, banned from houses of friends by parents who said I was a bad influence. Celebrity, of course, in all my dreams. Outlaw artist, without a doubt. But leader?

"What part of the chart is showing you this?" I asked.

"Sun at midheaven's a good indication. Mostly I'm getting it from overall blend. The hardest thing to grasp when you begin studying charts is *blend.* It's not enough to know planets, houses and signs. Until you get a strong feel for blend you can't gain mastery."

I perked up. "Which is why computer astrology print-outs will never replace human beings."

"That's a whole other subject I can't go into because it'll lead us far afield. But you're right, of course."

"And this is why my writing's taking forever? You sure I'm just not barking up the wrong tree?"

"I don't think there's any problem with your writing. The simple truth is *you haven't found your message.* You don't know what you want to say. You've got to go deeper into yourself."

"But I'm always going deeper into myself! When do I get to go deeper into *someone else*!? When do I get to go deeper into the world? Why's it taking so long? So many writers whose skill seems less than mine are selling books, making money, gaining recognition. I can't understand how—"

"Don't make the mistake of comparing yourself to them," he cut in, "especially without seeing their charts. They're probably not here for such universal reasons. You reincarnated for something broader than personal success as a writer. You're not here to address a narrow issue— you're grappling with the basic fundamental dilemma of existence! You're groping for an artistic way to authentically depict what we all go through, in a manner that's transformative and compelling. That takes time."

"But other artists get on track from childhood and stay there. I saw this future at age nine. I haven't stopped writing since I was five! I'm obsessed. I'll never give up! Yet there's been no breakthrough. *Why?*"

The tall astrologer's chest heaved. "It's not about sticking to plans, Mark. You can't figure it out beforehand. You hardly lack discipline or perseverance, no matter what they told you in school. The normal templates don't apply. Your peculiar destiny is always happening in the moment, immediately, thematically, constantly, not at leisure or in some kind of remote reflection. For you, life happens right in the midst of the action or not at all. You've got to catch it on the fly."

Each time I scrambled atop a wave of his thought, a new one blew me out to sea. I began to suspect that, like a Zen monk, Master Lonsdale might be keeping me off-balance purposely to provoke some deeper revelation of my own.

He paused for a sip of water. I glanced at the hand-scrawled chart that enabled him to excavate such layers.

"And you're sure," I said, staring at my planets, "that I chose this?"

"Yeah, but you still gotta make good on it."

"I don't know what you're able to tell from the chart and what you aren't—maybe you already addressed this and I missed it—but, I need to ask point-blank: Is my writing ever intended to succeed? Would I do better as an astrologer? Or is there a more optimal way to use the next few years?"

"Either could serve you," he stated, "but you have to first find something deeper in yourself."

I fumed. "You're saying it's useless to determine whether I should be a writer or an astrologer?"

"*No.* With your Capricorn destiny almost nothing is useless. Every strange tangent eventually twines back around to serve some greater purpose. But until now you've been at odds with your world because you're at odds with yourself. You've got to go within, and heal the foundational split you've dragged from life to life. You've got to find yourself on a level deeper than you have. You've got to grasp the reins of your own nature and fulfill your soul's vows of why you came here, more than you need to play out yet another scene in the endless karmic theatre farce of unrequited love.

"If you grasp the reins of your nature, then everything of the most divergent kind makes sense, connects, fits together, feels like it always *has* been together, always *will* be together, may *look* like it could never connect—but of course it can! It's perfectly right-on. Until then it doesn't seem to add up."

"All right. All right! You're saying I came into this life with a backlog of self-mistrust, an emotional wound of not belonging, from past lives. You're saying I've got to stay super-alert to what's unfolding each moment rather than have a fixed plan, because I have an improvisational path. You're saying if I do this I'll break through lifelong cycles of dysfunction in love and money. You're telling me I'm here to be a leader who shows people a new way to be, where they find their own truth. And—most of all—I have to heal my inner split before I can do this. Okay, fine. *How?* What practical steps can I take? What must I *do?*"

"Finish the initiation begun on the mountain. Stop looking outside yourself for answers!

"Mark, some part of you died on Mount Shasta so another part could be born. You crashed headlong into an incomplete death from two lives ago, which has been easy for you to confuse with this life."

What?

"Until we win a place in ourselves deeper than the roots of past-life karma, our existence is not fully our own. Despite your noble intentions, you end up sabotaging yourself time after time.

"On the mountain you encountered your dark double, a rite of passage mystics call *Meeting the Beloved in the Dust.* Shasta's a cosmic portal. You slipped through a hole in the time-space continuum and met a dark part of yourself that's the internal root of every external dysfunction you've ever drawn. Half of you is in one time zone now, half in another. Your karmic patterns are morphing. Your pasts are invading your future. But the process is unfinished and needs to be furthered before it releases you."

"How do you know all this?"

"I see it clairvoyantly."

So he's clairvoyant as well.

"This metamorphosis needs to complete itself, which it can't do in your current situation. With all the other factors you're juggling you haven't been able to carve out space. Your task is to get somewhere you can.

"Look. You're very bright, Mark. You don't have to have everything spelled out for you. You just need to give yourself benefit of the doubt. Take the depth journey to heart rather than giving it lip service. Stop running from yourself. Sink into things. Don't get snagged by fascinating distractions, as you often do."

My jaw clenched—how did he know this?

So much energy was buzzing through me that I couldn't see straight. I was beginning to feel that each answer he gave raised ten questions. He wasn't going to make this easy. Yes, I wanted to believe everything has a purpose. Sure, I wanted to be a leader, but could I trust him? Was it truth or ego? Maybe instead of being the greatest astrologer who ever lived, he was the greatest flatterer, ratcheting the art of ego-boosting to a whole new dimension—the Jimi Hendrix of flattery. Maybe he used psychic ability to crawl in my head and suss out what I most wanted to hear, then couch it in clever cosmic terms he knew I couldn't resist.

Or, maybe he actually *was* calling up a future that I couldn't afford to ignore.

I took heart from the fact that his rap sounded much different than Sita's reading. He wasn't dishing out rote enlightenment to everyone. But I felt raw and empty and unable to gather my thoughts. The tape clicking off jolted me out of reverie.

He looked at me curiously. "Was that the first or second side?"

"I—I don't remember . . . think it was the first."

"I have the oddest sensation," he confided, flipping the cassette. "I've completely lost track of time. Hm." He pressed buttons and we waited for tape to clear the leader. "Let's shift gears to your relationship."

I groaned.

After reinspecting my chart he said, "Relationship turns out to be your 'Keep-You-Honest' arena. Everything you'd rather not deal with keeps coming up and coming up and coming up to meet you there. Relationship presents all the things your ego would rather stay away from. And you have considerable ego."

My cheeks grew hot. "Are you suggesting I stick with Elizabeth because she has something to teach me?"

"Not necessarily. But until you resolve your underlying split, every love will turn out the same."

I flushed with anger. I really didn't want to hear that. I fished for something clever to rebuff him with but he kept going. "The danger with you, Mark, is that *everything could be anything* and something could be nothing. Your Libra Sun and Sagittarius Moon and Rising get lost in a myriad of possibility that isn't necessarily the same as *life*.

"Your four planets in Libra and four in Scorpio get saturated with such a volatile psychic charge of emotion that you think you're getting somewhere when you're not! So much is constantly moving through you that it's hard to tell what's yours from what's the world's. You're never just basically sure, in a very simple sense, where your life is. It's always here, there, sideways, in-between, all around, up for grabs. An odd, goatlike way to climb the mountain!"

I was half-relieved and half-pissed he could see this far into me. He didn't seem to care what I thought, though. He was on a roll, picking up steam and not about to stop.

"So, periodically you've got to reassess everything, reevaluate everything, throw everything up and see how it lands.

"In effect, at this time in your life, everything that used to be is over. Your sojourn on the mountain makes that clear. The past is gone. You have that raw, haunted look. So, while you're dripping amniotic fluid, what do you do now? What do you do now that everything's over? Do you reconstitute it? Do you go somewhere else? Do you change everything? Do you change only some things? Who's doing what to whom? Is *anybody* doing anything to anyone?

"You've gotten a woman to throw up in your face everything you could possibly not want her to! Now you have to find a way to deal with it. Do you take that relationship situation further? Do you get the hell out? Is she trying to destroy you? Is she trying to save you?"

"I—I really don't know," I stammered. "My bias is always toward relationship. Love is my God. I'm a sucker for the Goddess. I've been this way since I was four."

He smiled.

"I like to assume we can tear down the old version of ourselves and start over. I never want love to end," I mused in a way that seemed to alert him. "Maybe that's not such a good thing. . . ."

"Thirty-three starts to tap a certain energy of life task," he explained after a moment. "You're beginning to come of age. It's the age Christ was crucified. Between thirty-three and thirty-five is the major pivot point of the soul, when you get crucified by living outside-in, giving the world what it wants before learning what *you* want.

"Mark—you're being crucified. I can't stress this enough. This is your *understory*—the drama beneath the drama. Everything you've created that isn't yours has come back to nail you. You can't take one more step in that direction. You've run around and around something you now have to tackle head-on. You're being pinned to the world. The beauty of this is you have nowhere left to turn."

"Oh, that sure is beautiful!" I quipped.

He relaxed his tone of voice. "You've got to stand your ground now, which is always problematic with Libra because everything is checks and balances and constant readjustments."

I sighed.

His eyes narrowed. "Look, Mark—your former self is dying. Ego dies hard. You've got a good strong one and it's squirming. This is the source of your intensity, your frustration, your outrage, your sleepless nights. You're on death watch. The worst thing you could do is ease off before the process completes itself. Instead of running to safety, go the opposite way: Dive further *into* the intensity. Get some place you can midwife your own death. *Take this seriously!* Don't you see? It had to reach this level of crisis to get your attention. Otherwise you're all over the place!"

I was jumping out of my skin.

He bulldozed on. "You've got to overcome your own resistance and get to the core of yourself. The job of love is to impel us to become more of who we are. The dark side is when you get caught in downward spiraling, endlessly repeating karmic drama."

"What karma's going on here? Do I owe Elizabeth a debt from a past life which I'm being made to pay for?"

His pause was long enough to make me wonder if I was trying his patience, but his voice was gentle when he resumed. "We don't work out karma the way you might think," he said. "It's not that someone did something to you in *that* life, so now you've got to do something to them in *this*. It's not that you slaughtered someone before and now have to slaughter yourself."

"How *do* we work karma?"

"By getting down to the core of a repeating pattern and this time bringing more awareness to it. By expanding in the very place fight-or-flight instinct forces you to contract. By injecting freedom of choice into the places you seem to have none."

I nodded, knowing I was going to have to listen to this tape more than once to parse its meanings. I could scarcely remember what we'd talked about two minutes ago. I had no idea how long I'd been in the room. My head was swimming and I gripped the edge of the couch cushion.

"The daemon you're up against now grew out of a darkness spawned ages ago," the astrologer continued. "You have to find a will to live that's stronger than the death grip. This is beyond the mind. You're in need of breakthrough more profound than modern consciousness allows."

He tossed his papers aside. "I have to say to the part of you that has a very panicked look on its face that charts like yours, with such fierce karmic components, also contain the most potential for growth. You're a bow whose gut string gets pulled back and back and back until the wood's about to split, then fires directly to the kind of freedom that can only be won by such pressure."

"So when do I fire? What's my target?"

"You need to clear away the disruptive element and give yourself psychic space to breathe into the new part of you that's busy being born. Otherwise you'll never believe in yourself. With Dragon's Tail in Cancer, it's your main danger. You started something on the mountain that you've got to finish." He removed his glasses and rubbed the bridge of his nose.

"So that's where psychology goes wrong," I interjected.

He raised a bushy eyebrow. "Eh?"

"Psychology would work better," I postulated, "if it recognized reincarnation."

He looked into me as if for the first time. "Precisely." His eyes glittered. "Which is the reason siblings will be completely different. It only makes sense when you consider they had different past lives. Along with environment and genetics and astrology, you have to factor in reincarnation or you miss the key piece of the puzzle."

I nodded, filing this away.

"Without past lives," he continued, cleaning his glasses with his shirt, "psychology falls short. In certain cases—yours, for example—nothing you go through between birth and death is as drastic as the deep imprint of what you carry from before. This is what haunts you, and what needs to be cleared for you to go on."

He slipped his glasses on and skimmed through a large brown looseleaf binder until he found what he was looking for. He perused a page then glanced up. "You were born with a deep emotional wound that goes way beyond whether your mother breast-fed you."

"She didn't."

"I know, but that's just the tip of the iceberg. The more important part is that you carry an unconscious past-life recall of a drastic battle with existence. That's the source of your dread. It's what's haunted you since before you were born."

Jeez.

"When you enter a current situation that even slightly replicates this earlier karmic wound, you get sucked into a whirlpool. The past takes over the present. Intimate relationship turns disproportionately severe, plunging you into a heavy sense of fate that makes it hard for you to think straight. You lapse into a toxic mindset, difficult to dislodge, because you don't even know you're doing it. They don't tell you these things in school."

I snorted.

"The blessing of so much karma is that no matter where you go you'll keep running into yourself. So instead of shifting once again—which you've become a bit too good at—you've got to stand your ground and sink one stage deeper than the nightmare to unhook it."

Working this out to mean he was telling me to hang with Elizabeth, I relaxed.

"You've got to give death the chance to break down your old self to compost," he added, "and free up the real you. Which places a high priority on where you live. To tell the truth, I don't see you staying in Berkeley."

"Why not?" I said, neck muscles tensing at the implication.

"Because more than most people, you're a reflective vessel of what's going on in your psychic space. You're not a self-contained individual so much as a walking Collective, Incorporated. You're Everyman. Like Charlie Chaplin or Buster Keaton, your highly visible pratfalls illustrate the archetypal journey of the fool.

"What with all the flack flying through the world at this point, it's a bit too much to ask you to play Cosmic Fool while you're busy dying, though. You're too raw and vulnerable. You'll get back into things later if you first remove yourself from them." He looked straight at me. "You're probably going to have to let go of your life in the city with Elizabeth."

So that's what this is leading to. The end of yet another love. Well, I wasn't going down without a fight. "But I've been letting go of things forever! All I do is let go! When do I get to *hold on?*"

After a tense silence his features gentled. "When I was a child I had a profound set of dreams that to me then were nightmares.

"We had an elevator in our apartment building in New York City. Nothing fascinated me more than this elevator. It went down to the cellar, which was an amazing place. In my dream I went further to a sub-basement that was even more amazing. Then there was a sub-*sub*-basement, and a sub-sub-*sub*-basement. I would dream of going down one more level and risking everything. And when I finally got to the bottom there'd be this incredible world where anything at all could happen."

He paused as a breeze ruffled the curtain. I'd followed each descent through my own New York City childhood apartment building that I hadn't thought of in years.

"And this scenario," he concluded, "from a child's point of view, is pretty much how it is. For a long time it seems endless. Relentless, the work of clearing karma, *the hardest thing you'll ever be asked to do.* But what you're clearing is your resistance to being full-force alive here in the living moment as a free being *now!*" He snapped his fingers and I started.

"Mark, if you remember one thing from this reading, remember that if *you use the very pressure bearing down on you to crack into your core, you'll free the rest of your life.*

"You're at the main karmic crossroads of your existence, right up against something you've been on the verge of forever. Everything has conspired to drive you here. You can't back off, can't bungle this opportunity. You've got to penetrate your own resistance more than solve anybody's anything, Elizabeth, *Shmelizabeth;* comics, *shmomics.*"

"Okay. Okay! I think you're finally getting through! But, practically speaking, what can I *do?* How do I cross the crossroads?"

"Take yourself seriously enough to honor your own process. Grant yourself the benefit of the doubt that your crazy meandering path actually has a reason for having led you to this impasse. Even if you have no idea—though you do—what your next step will look like, you've got to get yourself in a position where you can stay alert enough to recognize it the moment it arrives.

"Get vigilant. *Wake up* each morning clutching your truth before you get sidetracked. Grab existence by the throat and demand that it come through for you. Get real about this. Be absolutely honest with yourself. Lust after transformation more than you lust for wealth or success as a writer or to be with the most beautiful woman."

Whoa. Lust after transformation more than the most beautiful woman—?!

"Each external choice you're facing—'Should I stay with comics or go back to writing or move to astrology? Should I stay with Elizabeth? Should I stay in Berkeley?'—is designed to peel away everything but raw fusion with your own soul, so you can finally claim the ground that's been allotted to you.

"Every outer drama reflects your inner need to return from karmic exile and be a part of this world in the way you long for. Get into a lather about this. Get pissed enough that you stick with it rather than falling for the Libra trance of equivocation and compromise. Air signs confuse the act of thinking about things for the things themselves."

My eyes were burning. The pause after this statement dragged on so long I began to think we were done and it was time to go. But I was grafted to the furniture. My forearms trembled. *This is more than a reading. . . . He's doing some occult practice beneath the words.*

"Are you aware of what's happening in the room right now?" the wizard asked.

We were on the edge of space anchored in chairs that swirled around and around the revolving floor. Books and papers and pens rotated like star trails. *Crack through the core. Lust for transformation more than the most beautiful woman. Come back from karmic exile. Comics, shmomics. Crucifixion. Leadership.*

The air poured through stained glass. *Is this really happening? What's going on? How can pages of scribble open such intimate gateways to the soul?*

Where does chart-knowing end and magic begin? And, most of all I wondered, *can this be taught?*

At that moment the master astrologer nodded.

Then he shifted in his chair as if some burden had released. He closed his eyes and exhaled a long ragged breath. When he opened them he seemed much lighter. The room relaxed to its former shape, star trails giving way to furniture that was trembling and luminescent.

"There's one more thing," he mentioned. "I think you'd make a great astrologer. Your chart has a lot of factors to enable you to see how everything connects with everything else. You'd be superb at getting blend.

"To be *real* in astrology, though, I have to say, is not easy. I ought to know something about this," he added with a glint in his eye. "It requires one thing above all, which few astrologers seem to get: *You have to be willing to change your mind every day.* You have to never think you know anything. Every fake astrologer thinks they know what Geminis are like. To me, the idea I should know what Geminis are like is awful! If I did I'd go around like a robot, with my head saying: 'Gemini . . . Gemini . . . Gemini . . .' It wouldn't mean anything!

"There seems to be a tremendous temptation in this field—therapy, psychic readings, astrology, numerology—for people to fake it rather than do it real. To do it real, every time a Gemini comes to you, or a Cancer or a Taurus or anything, you have to be willing to find out what that sign means all over again, through their eyes.

"If you go into astrology *that* way—and, with your chart that's really the only way you'd be able to do it—you'll be put through the most fascinating changes. The cosmic truths you tap will have to get used on you more than any of your clients.

"After fifteen years at this I've been pushed through more things than I could've imagined. You'll be motivated, of course, by the need to help others, and that's true—that's a real thing, and a good thing. We need visionaries to guide us back to ourselves because society is no longer set up to do that. But the demands spirit will ask of you will far outweigh what you offer others. It has to be like this. Do you see?"

Swallowing dryly, I nodded, distracted by the dawning recognition that I'd just been initiated into some unknown realm of mystic awareness.

"You're going to be ramped up the conveyor belt of your own evolution to be able to offer that same capacity to others," the mage continued. "This shamanic dimension of the work can be relentless at times. Helluva way to make a living!

"That's the cosmic side. Here's the mundane: First, it'll take three years for your business to solidify. Second, don't expect to make much money. Third, if you stick with this, your practice will become one of the most rewarding things of your life. If you decide to go into astrology you'll rise to the top, you'll become one of the world's greatest astrologers. But you won't be satisfied."

Whoa—

"Your whole chart is bristling with a need for self-expression which I myself don't have. Born with Sun directly overhead at the apex of the chart, you won't be content just interpreting others. Your own nature will have to shine. And (and this'll be the final thing—even the world's longest reading can't go on forever) I don't see you in the city. The only place in the Bay Area I see you, in fact, is the Santa Cruz Mountains, where I live."

The tape clicked off and the room went quiet but for the muted hush of vehicles in the street and birds warbling in the trees. A soft breeze streaming through the window mingled the scent of suburbs with the sea.

I once read that every second, somewhere deep in the universe, a star explodes into a supernova that flashes with the brilliance of a *whole galaxy.* At that moment I could believe there was a place where such things happened. I was drenched in light, and it was going to take a long time for whatever had just happened to make sense to me.

William Lonsdale opened the recorder, rattled out the cassette, replaced it in its case, and handed it over. I took it then pried myself off the couch. We shook hands. He was even taller than I remembered. He walked me to the lobby as a woman with dark hair and piercing eyes looked up from her briefcase.

"Susannah," he said, "I've just met the most amazing thirty-three-year-old!"

The dark-haired chiropractor took my hand and stared into me for a long moment, scrutinizing the effects of the reading. She looked from me to the astrologer, then back again. "Wow," she said. *"Wow."*

"You may want to transcribe that to make the best use of it," William Lonsdale added, pointing to the tape.

I nodded, then stepped out and made my way through the parking lot to a small bridge above the creek where I stood at a rail. The planks beneath my feet and rippling currents below gradually made me aware there still was a world out there, a world that seemed stretched around its curvature like a freshly gessoed canvas.

In the diffuse suburban light I found myself having to squint. I looked back at the building as a woman in a camel-colored coat walked in. *How many times can he cross these waters in one day?*

An amber dragonfly swooped over the stream, circled, then landed on a stone. I put my hand to my face and was startled to find wetness. I looked down. My shirt was soaked. I was drenched in tears.

2012

—3

Crossroads of the Soul

A few days later it became apparent Elizabeth and I were breaking up. It wasn't choice so much as *recognition*. Even if we'd wanted to push on we couldn't, because the organism of the relationship was dying. I began to think of love as a triad more than a dyad—you, me, and the shared entity formed between us.

Like a dying human being, break-ups seem to have their own biological rhythm: death-defying forward surges, heart-stopping caesuras and implausible turnarounds until the thing finally expires. This organic entity, this Vermont-bred, Taurus/Libra, strawberry-blond/brown-haired, Russian-Jew/Welsh Love Being, that had risen from the cotton sheets of a New England autumn three years before, was going to a watery grave in the San Francisco Bay.

Although the break-up seemed inevitable it still hit me like a blow to the chest. As my love ended, a part of me, I knew, was obliviating along with it, and I fought to free myself from the suction of that memory-whirlpool and clutch instead to whatever piece of me could be salvaged to go on.

Lost in a funk, I moved through the world but the world didn't move through me. Caught in crescendos of pain that no one else could see (can the world be so *blind?*), I wandered the city raw and aching, hoping for a miracle. However, in the throes of death and dislocation I also sensed dim promise, a budding awareness that some membrane around me had snapped and might even now be exposing me to a future that could somehow be better than the one we'd dreamt of.

Every woman in Berkeley had her own way of walking, her own rhythm, her primal scent. Each as she bent in or out of her car became a question mark. When you're without a lover anyone can be your mate. Suddenly the Goddess was everywhere. She couldn't be so cruel as to send me woman after woman, and when I reach out to touch, slap my hand every time, could She? Intrigue loomed around every corner but I needed a way through the numbness.

As Elizabeth moved into a friend's house, just for something to do I packed my things. While I was stacking boxes my old friend John called, whom I hadn't heard from in seven years. His father had died and left him a five-thousand-acre ranch in the Santa Cruz Mountains in La Honda. John could trade me rent for helping him fix the place up. With no rent I could ease out of comics and launch a career in astrology.

Would things have gone this way if I hadn't met William Lonsdale? Would I have landed the same future? Would I have become an astrologer? How could he have seen this move to the Santa Cruz Mountains in advance? How much of where we're going can be gleaned before we get there? Is there another way to conceive of time than how it gets parceled out by clock and calendar? What percentage of what he said was clairvoyance versus lucky guess?

The promising view of my future the master astrologer foretold, however, was hard to swallow during gray days on the ranch when my heart sank and cosmic concepts shriveled to *blah blah blah*. The notion of me as leader, writer, astrologer or even whole *human being* was laughable on chill mornings when my limbs were so heavy I could barely get out of bed, and I seemed to be suffocating under the weight of my mountain rather than moving it.

The ranch turned out to be Eden with a snake, and the homestead I'd agreed to help fix, a mausoleum for a dead drunkard. John's father had drunk and chain-smoked in front of the TV so many years that I had to haul off stinking truckfuls of beer bottles, and scrub layer after layer of nicotine-stained grease off wood paneling, dishes, and ceilings, just to be able to breathe. Fabric was hopeless, curtains and rugs toxic enough to be trashed. The house felt sickly and haunted.

And my benefactor, to my horror, seemed to be playing out the same karma. During marathon afternoon drinking sessions he had a charming habit of tossing empty beer cans in the yard, while declaiming worldly-wise philosophy over and over in a voice that was a demented *nyah-nyah* caricature from a childhood with that same father. With little income I felt no choice but to soldier on until some other doorway opened.

In the spring woods I contacted a pain so deep and raw it seemed endless, catalyzed by present circumstance but rooted in an anguish that had boiled since Adam. How could man ever be whole, I raged against heaven, when his first act is to break out of the wholeness in woman's womb and then spend his life fighting his way back in? Woman could be whole, I reasoned, with the fecund power to recreate the sacred circle inside her, while man seemed doomed to tear in and out of that circle forever.

Ammonia, beer cans, swollen-hearted rage, and great empty stretches of field marked my days on the ranch. At night I took solace in the stars, scouting the Hunter and his Dog and the Seven Sisters, wondering if I was ever going to be happy, ever going to find my own starry sister or be dogged by endless love ruptures till my penis shriveled and testicles shrank.

Through weeks of scouring powder, sheep shit, and baling wire I somehow mustered the self-belief to launch a career. I came up with the name Soul Level Astrology to distinguish my method, which now had become primarily influenced by Jeff Green's *Pluto: The Evolutionary Journey of the Soul.* This new book outlined a visionary method for uncovering the reincarnational arc of each chart, karmic issues to be resolved, hidden themes that perpetuate dysfunctional patterns of behavior.

William Lonsdale seemed to know much about this under-layer of life that few others directly addressed, and each time I listened to the tape of my reading I puzzled over how he came by this knowledge.

Fortified with the master astrologer's soul portrait of myself, bolstered by four years of self-studying Alan Oken and now Jeff Green, I marched to the printer's and ordered business cards and flyers, then made the rounds of New Age bookshops and health food stores within a fifty-mile radius. I offered my first astrology class, in Half Moon Bay, and recruited enough students to maintain a weekly study group, which brought in slight though regular income, but more importantly helped me conceive of myself as real. *Maybe he was right. Maybe I* am *going to be a leader....*

Even though Northern California was rife with metaphysical practitioners, the social climate in the Bay Area just then seemed ripe for admitting new ones. Shirley MacLaine's metaphysical memoir *Out on a Limb* had recently popularized the mystical element in mainstream thought, and Joseph Campbell and Bill Moyer's *The Power of Myth* had just delivered a new spiritual catch phrase to collective consciousness: *Follow your bliss.* The Harmonic Convergence was still being discussed, and the scent of change was in the wind.

Many times I felt the urge to call the master astrologer and ask his advice regarding both my budding career and the deeper meanings of my chart. I fought this urge, though, because I didn't want to annoy him. Sensing he placed a high priority on his privacy, I kept a growing list of queries toward a time we might reconnect.

Whenever I listened to the tape of my reading I was swept away from the thudding reality of the ranch. Though I was uncertain what to make of some things Lonsdale had told me, I was bowled over by the simple fact he could even say them. He seemed to inhabit some inner dimension that coexisted with ordinary existence, yet was more potent, vivid and so real it appeared surreal. The mythopoetic version of astrology he practiced cut deeper than the few previous readings I'd had. Nothing I'd come across in books sounded like him, either.

The more I listened to the tape, the more I marveled at the mechanics of what allowed him to see what he saw. Where'd he get it from? What sources did he tap? What underworld window on existence did this wizard have at his disposal? How had he come to know what he knew? I recalled him saying he and his wife Sara brought information through from spirit—what was *that* about? What arcane forces enabled him to do what he did?

I had to know.

I became obsessed with those secrets.

I needed to pick his brain. I needed to study with him. With him in my corner I could claim a path, gain a mentor, forge a life out of the constant flux. Maybe I could be his apprentice. *Wouldn't that be something?* But would he take a gypsy misfit who barely kept his shit together?

Several times when John was out I picked up the phone, dialed the mage, then hung up. *Make sure you exhaust his advice before asking for more. Do your own work first or you'll come across as the boy who cried wolf.*

So I transcribed the reading to a thirty-page document that I fretted over as if it were the Rosetta Stone. Along with gaining self-insight I extrapolated subtle astrology lessons from various things Lonsdale had said, scrutinizing every sentence for hidden meanings.

Yet as life darkened on the ranch I sank into cynical disbelief of cosmic concepts, offset by desperate clinging to this brilliant future I supposedly had in store.

I called my folks in Florida. They were supportive as ever but couldn't follow me into the depth zones where I so needed to be reached. I felt ashamed to call the wizard and admit I'd run from one impossible situation to another. Plus, I didn't have money for a second reading. If I phoned, what would I say: *Make the monsters go away?* He'd get sick of me before he even knew me. So I taped his card to my mirror and kept it there as days of digging holes, pouring cement, setting posts, and washing windows slogged by.

In La Honda one afternoon I stumbled upon a loose-knit tribe of artists, activists, musicians, and healers, which gave me a lifeline. Taking heart from my new friends, I ducked out to the barn to use the extension phone and mustered courage to call.

As I dialed, horned imps poked their fingers into my ribs: *what makes you think you're so hot? everybody wants to study with a master . . . of course he'll say no. idiot!—astrology's a bunch of malarkey . . . how can you believe the stars are gonna change your life? there ya go again, chasing a mirage, looking to someone else for answers. . . .*

Just when I was about to hang up, Lonsdale answered and seemed open to hearing from me. We chatted about things in general (me doing most of the chatting). I learned we both started life in Queens, New York, then moved to southern New England; northern Vermont; Willamette Valley, Oregon; northern California and the Santa Cruz Mountains.

"We're on the exact same mystic highway!" I exclaimed.

"Yes," he replied. "Not for the first time."

He said this so offhandedly it brought me up short and I blurted, "I've been listening to the reading and realize your work's on a whole other level than everybody else and feel the need to study with you. Is there any way I can hire you for private tutoring? Or—do you teach classes?"

The pause stretched to infinity. I held my breath.

Finally he replied, "Sara and I recently completed a cycle of classes. We're moving in a new direction. We have no plan to start teaching again. And I'm really not set up for private instruction."

"Tell you what," he added after another interminable pause, "why don't you come visit our cottage in Bonny Doon?"

"Okay."

"How's next Friday?"

"Fine."

"Bring your sleeping bag."

Oh my God, I thought, replacing the phone. *I did it.* He said no to the teaching but I did it. *How could he say no?! Didn't he read the end of the book? How could it go: 'And then he met his teacher and his teacher didn't'?*

Maybe he'll change his mind. There's always some test the apprentice has to go through to prove himself in these kind of stories, isn't there? At least he didn't laugh at me. He did seem genuinely glad to hear from me. Unless he's being polite. But why would he invite me if he didn't feel some connection?

The following Friday afternoon I packed my sleeping bag into my newly acquired 1963 Volvo 122S and drove the winding rural highway through the mountains, south along the Pacific past Pescadero and Davenport to the turnoff for Bonny Doon.

Following directions, I turned onto Comstock Lane, a private gravel road heading west through the mountains back toward the sea. Then I turned right onto a dirt driveway, which, as I approached the homestead, narrowed toward a grove of giant redwoods. The massive grove towered above the pine and madrone forest, casting a shadow over the house that stained it deeper than the shade of nightfall.

I pulled to a bumper log, got out and walked the short footpath through the rundown apple orchard. Nervously, I strode up the rough-hewn stairs, pausing at the top as I remembered my Tolkien: *Be careful when meddling in the affairs of wizards for they are subtle and quick to anger. . . .* The screen door opened, and there was the front-porch mage in a tan flannel shirt with the tail rumpling out of baggy blue jeans.

He said a shy hello and we shook hands. It was three months since we had met. I followed him in and the door banged. A small woman with frizzy straw-colored hair and upturned nose smiled at me while stirring a pot. "Mark!" she announced as if I were a long-lost friend.

"Sara!" I replied, taking her hand, which was warm and responsive.

"How was the drive?" she asked, holding onto me longer than I expected.

"I hadn't realized how desolate the Coast Highway is," I said, noting faint freckles on her cheeks and subtle smile lines around her crinkly eyes. As we let go of each other I added, "It felt like Appalachia."

"It does, doesn't it?" she said, turning back to the stove. From a small bowl she picked a pinch of something that she rubbed between her fingers and sprinkled into the pot. "Have you eaten?" She indicated one of the captain's chairs at the round wooden table.

"No," I said, taking a seat.

"There's not much, soup and bread," she offered apologetically.

My host went to the living room to put a log in the woodstove, while his wife ladled pumpkin-colored soup into wooden bowls then set out dark bread and butter. As we ate, no one said anything. It didn't seem like an awkward silence but one they were accustomed to. I wondered if I were intruding.

During the meal I glanced furtively at Sara Lonsdale a few times and got the feeling she'd been doing the same to me. Our eyes met, but, too self-conscious to hold her gaze, I turned away and studied their home instead, wondering about the kind of life they lived, the kind of relationship they had.

My astrologer's wife wouldn't have been considered classically beautiful, and might not have been called sexy, but she had some alluring elfin depth, some mischievous spark, a mystery, an inwardly potent energy I found visceral and compelling.

I couldn't perceive any overt romantic link between the couple; as they ate, each seemed self-contained and shrouded in thought. Could I be witnessing the deeper passion of some new version of relationship? A subtler wavelength than the sex-and-drama-driven loves of my own? Then again, I thought, sipping my soup, who knows what happens behind closed doors?

The main thing that struck me about the cottage was *books*. Wall shelves, crammed with hardcovers and paperbacks, mounted to the ceiling. Book stacks blossomed willy-nilly like magic mushrooms, rising precariously from the clutter. A deep storage closet, with louver doors partly open afforded me a glimpse of inner darkness stretching to books. Further volumes lined the dusky hall to the rear of the house. I recognized many titles and noted some abstruse classification of subject matter, which ranged from high literature and metaphysics to pop psychology and science fiction.

The ceiling had a thick exposed crossbeam that ran the width of the house, like a medieval cottage, and a large rectangular skylight through which a sprinkle of bright winter stars shone. The living room floor was covered with a frayed rug. The lighting was warm and dim. An upholstered couch that had probably been green once sat across from the woodstove, next to two stuffed chairs and a leather-backed wooden rocker with matching hassock. There was no TV. A deck of tarot cards lay next to a large geode. Boots and drinking glasses and jackets and pencils were strewn about. Paintings and posters adorned the walls. A turquoise futon lay folded into a portable couch below the porch window, with magazines and catalogs piled on one end. Clearly, life at Comstock Lane revolved around something other than neatness.

When we finished eating Sara slipped into her jacket. "Sorry to walk out on you, but I've gotta go to a meeting. I'm sure we'll be seeing more of you," she added tentatively, glancing at her husband, who nodded.

I stood to see her off, extending my arm to take her hand, but she slipped inside my reach and hugged me.

"I'm really glad you're here," she said, as our cheeks grazed. "Next time maybe you can explain New England to me," she added, breaking away. "William says you have a soul link to that part of the country, which I still just don't get, even though it's a big part of his life." She threw her hands up in exasperation.

"The key to New England," I said, inspired by one of my favorite subjects, "is autumn."

"You ought to know something about that," said the astrologer.

"Yeah, since eight of my planets and my rising sign are in Libra, Scorpio or Sagittarius—the three autumn signs. I guess I should know something about it since I'm mostly autumn!"

Sara laughed. At the door she glanced back and this time I held her gaze. After a moment she arched her eyebrow: *I'll leave you wizards to your meddling.* Then she walked out.

"Let's go in Sara's massage room," William suggested, drawing my attention back from the porch, as his wife's footfalls died into the night. A moment later I heard the car start and felt a bit let down that she was going.

By lantern my towering guide led me down the hall, stopping to don floppy slippers. I followed him to the far room on the right, which had two huge black wooden stereo speakers rising from a long counter. This room was much neater than the rest of the house, adorned with a glass-fronted oak cabinet showcasing hardcover classics of metaphysics: Rudolf Steiner, Yogananda, Ouspensky, Krishnamurti, Sri Aurobindo, Madame Blavatsky, Anne Re Colton. As I walked by, the collection seemed to tug on me, making me yearn to be left alone there months on end. *What have I stumbled into?*

My host tossed a log into the fire ebbing in the fireplace. It looked as if this offhand gesture might just as well extinguish the flame as rekindle it. I waited a few smoky minutes—he didn't seem to notice—then I prodded logs free with a brass poker, releasing the blaze.

After settling onto the floor he said, "So. Things have changed for you since we last met."

I sat on the dark braided rug, knees up, clasping them, leaning back into the couch. "As you predicted, I moved to the Santa Cruz Mountains, though I'm not sure how long I'll last at the ranch. But it's given me a new lease on life. I hadn't realized how trapped I was in the city."

"And Elizabeth?"

"Gone, separate ways, as you indicated."

He nodded. "No second thoughts?"

I started to shake my head, then caught myself. "It's funny. There was a moment . . . in the rain," I mused, "under a shop awning in Berkeley, we got struck by the revelation that neither of us was gonna project that way again. That we'd spent more than three years frozen in anger caught in some infantile projection of unmet emotional needs, which prevented us from seeing each other clearly or finding each other sexually. That our choice to part—my first mutual break-up, by the way—marked the end of a long bitter road, a whole unconscious way of loving."

He stretched a long leg in front of him, and I recalled that quality he had, of active listening, and how it made me feel that, as long as I had his attention, I better make good on it.

"I think I've been caught in projections of love all my life without knowing it," I admitted haltingly. "And," I added, fighting a gush of emotion, ". . . I can't believe what that's cost me—"

Nobody said anything for a long moment.

"I'm beginning to see how my fierce desire for love drives it away," I said, getting hold of myself. "I don't know why this should be. It doesn't make sense to the little kid in me who just wants to be loved...."

He smiled.

"Under the awning—Elizabeth felt it too—our projections dissolved and we *saw* each other, for the first time in a long time. We really saw each other, as free beings, vibrant, erotic, alive. She turned electric-hot and stunning, like an erotic dream in the flesh." I shivered as another rush went through me.

"Wow," he said.

"Then something funny happened," I remembered, suddenly feeling sheepish. *What the hell.* "The rain became all silvery, and she shone with a light that pierced me and gave me the strongest erection I ever had— suddenly I craved her more than ever—at the very moment we broke up!" I shook my head and laughed nervously. "And another strange thing happened. Along with getting horny I felt stricken by anger. I mean, we were breaking up—I had no reason to hold anything against her."

"Mars rules both anger and passion," said the mage after a moment.

I nodded.

"Sounds like your male force has been violently suppressed, perhaps for years, so the full-force virility of your Mars desire couldn't flood back into your body without bringing the rest of Mars with it."

"*Ahh,*" I reflected, recalling my basic astrology. "Yes, that feels right. Yet," I added, throat tightening, "the thing we realized, simultaneously, was that without our projections—there was nothing left to keep us together...."

Through welling tears, I saw that moment in the rain and felt a tremendous heart-surge for this passionate artist who'd been frustrated with me so long that she pushed me deeper and deeper into my inability to make love with her the way we used to.

"Being that close to where her nipples protruded from her shirt and doing nothing about it was like holding five wild wolves on the end of two-foot chains," I said.

My host rounded his lips and uttered a sound somewhere between admiration and sympathy.

"I was struck with an overwhelming sense of what it must've been like for her to be so hot for me all those years, and me unable to burst the barrier and come through for her. Now the tables turned and I wanted her so bad that I couldn't take a step toward her—or away. My lust swelled to its peak, and there was a moment when I think both of us sensed the possibility of some reversal of our decision." I heaved a sigh. "But it wasn't to be."

"And then she filled with a rose-golden light that seemed to radiate from her vulva and draw us into an astral chamber apart from the wind and rain. I saw the golden goddess that she was, which had been veiled from me for so long.

"And the iceberg of frozen passion that had kept us apart for years thawed into a deluge of weeping and sobbing that wracked our bodies till we began to laugh and laugh. We clung to each other like we had in the early days, and laughed and cried and breathed in the strange familiar scent of these creatures we used to be, and of those we were becoming." I sniffled. "It was the most incredible goodbye—" I said, tears streaking my face.

"You haven't spoken since?" the astrologer asked after a moment.

I shook my head.

"Our break-up seemed to catalyze the rest of my death on the mountain. I'm still in it, though I think maybe the worst is over. I hope it is. I've been escaping into the woods, pounding the earth and releasing a pain that seems bottomless."

I waited for a response, but none was forthcoming. He sat there much as he'd done during my reading, with an alert passivity I found both curious and unsettling.

"It feels like pain is scraping away gunk that clogged my cells forever. I'm hoping a whole way of love is dying along with it. I don't know what I've been doing wrong all my life. No matter how I try I can't seem to make love work."

"What, exactly, isn't working?"

"My loves start out with the most incredible poetry and promise and night-long lovemaking to Van Morrison." I smiled wistfully. "What happens to all that when love dies?" I shook myself back to the present. "I just can't understand. One moment we're in Eden, and the next I'm blinking like a dumb dog. I just don't get what I'm doing wrong."

"Hm." The mage slid a paper off the end table next to him and glanced at it.

I wondered if beneath those long silences, psychic gears were turning. I'd never met anyone with the rich quality of attentiveness William Lonsdale had, which made him seem both much nearer and farther away than most people.

"You have a leading asteroid," he observed, "as the sole planet in your seventh house, house of love, which is very tricky. I've seen that before and it always makes it peculiarly hard to sustain long-term relationship, without some radical rearrangement of what the whole thing means. It's as if you have to exhaust every possible version of what love *isn't* before you find what it is."

"*Great,*" I said in a way that made him laugh, "so that's what I've been doing all my life."

He giggled a surprisingly high-pitched giggle. "That's not such a bad thing, in the long run," he said. "If you have to make every mistake in the book on your way toward gaining something as complex as love, you're bound to end up a master."

"I should live so long."

He cackled.

We talked deep into the night, he lying on his stomach, brow creased in thought, or springing up impassioned as a schoolboy; me curled near the fire. We spoke of music and politics and astrology and sex and love and Santa Cruz and New York and Oregon and Vermont and books and movies and the sixties, and the difference between east and west coast, which got us going for a long time. He spilled a few astrology tips that I carefully jotted down. It seemed that along with picking the master's brain I was also making a friend. At least I hoped so.

"I don't want to take advantage of your professional nature," I confided during a lull in conversation, "but I've been wondering what you make of all this talk of 2012? Is there really something going on beneath the hype and projections?"

He considered. "I've been asking myself the same thing."

I waited.

"Too many prophecies point to this time," he continued, "for me to write it off as New Age delusion. I don't think this is something we're all imagining. Regardless of the hype that crops up around these things, I believe something significant is happening. It has people edgy, alert, even if they don't know why. And I think it's going to become even more so between now and then."

"What's it all leading to?" I asked.

He thought for a moment. "We seem to have entered the accelerated school of human development."

"What makes it accelerated?"

"You mean, astrologically, what planetary factors am I looking at?"

"No, I just mean what's it all about."

He scratched his beard. "We get to live many lives in one now. Get to go through every bit of our karma from previous lives in *this* life."

I waited for more.

"It's not a sudden thing," he added. "We've probably been gearing up for this since the first third of the twentieth century, since we split the atom and released the collective nightmare of our time.

"The acceleration's been coming on since then but now seems to be emerging as the key signature of our times. It's the main reason many of us reincarnated at this specific point."

"What's the reason?"

"To *evolve*," he said. "To face our fears and undergo a planet-wide initiation into something that works better than the sham. To bring people out of their stupor and to wake up to the truth of what's possible around here.

"The other day," William went on after a minute, "I noticed that some major planetary cycles are going to occur around 2012. Taken separately any one of them would be powerful. But together, a tremendous series of events will catalyze the most massive energies between 2009 and 2013. *Basically, the world will end and begin again.*

"That's why we're accelerating now, in preparation for what's coming. Karma is quickening to bring our disowned shadow to the front of our screen where we can no longer ignore it. The gods are no longer content to bide their time and mind their own business. The stakes are being upped all around the world."

The fire popped and crackled, and I rearranged it with the brass tongs.

"So," I said, "we're either at the beginning of the end—or, the end of the beginning. . . ?"

"After 2012, 2013," my host said, "we'll be in a completely different orientation. Everything happening now is the set-up for that. When we look back at now from then it will become obvious this was the last gasp of a rabid culture that had to be put out of its misery."

I swallowed hard. I started to comment but stopped myself; I didn't want to pry all night for free advice, didn't want to wear out my welcome.

Long after midnight he announced, "I'm going to have to go to sleep," after which we gabbed another half hour or so until he stood up stiffly, rubbing his left shoulder. "I really do have to go now—I've got readings in the morning."

"I can't get over how we lived in the same places in the same order," I said, reluctant to let him go.

"Yes."

He looked like he was going to add something but instead yawned and shuffled out. I went to my car and got my sleeping bag. A few remote stars shone through high cloud cover. Everything was damp and fresh, the redwood grove shrouded in gloom like a vast chamber of secrets soaring skyward.

In the morning Sara was still away. Standing on the porch William and I hugged goodbye, and I felt like a hobbit hugging an Ent. Feeling as if I'd gone on a much longer trip than forty-five miles, I got in my old Volvo and drove back to the ranch.

Things deteriorated rapidly there, and I moved to a tiny studio a few blocks from the rustic center of La Honda. After my final shuttle I sank to the floor and wept to have a place all to myself. *What kind of karma keeps me getting all bound up with everything I'm not?*

The move was a leap of faith, because even though rent was modest, my comics income had shrunk and I was becoming dependent on astrology, which forced me to shake off the Dead Love Blues and face financial reality, something I tend to put off as long as I possibly can.

Readings arrived sporadically. I might go weeks without, then get two in a row. In those seminal days of my practice it took sixty hours to study a chart, three hours to do a reading, and I got twenty-five bucks, which made me proud as a peacock.

I was able to squeak by laying bricks, doing rush work in comics, and hanging sheetrock. *Are you out of your mind to think you're gonna make a living from the stars?*

Lonsdale does.

Yeah—he's a giant. Where has each of your great starts gone?

He seemed to think I was something.

That and two bits'll get you on the A-train.

Since I couldn't study with the master I enrolled at the Berkeley Psychic Institute's nearby branch in Palo Alto. This had little direct bearing on astrology but taught me basic psychic hygiene, daily tools to develop my clairvoyance. I came to feel that everyone is psychic, though some more than others, and in most of us it remains dormant.

One afternoon while meditating in my studio I saw fairly large colored spheres vertically aligned inside my body. It took a moment to realize I was looking straight at my chakras: translucent balls of slightly different size and very different colors, which I saw so lucidly it made me gasp. The vision lasted maybe ten seconds. I was thunderstruck.

Previously I'd thought of chakras the way I thought of God—as a fascinating unproven idea. But now I'd seen them exactly as you'd see bouncing balls stacked in a wire basket in the local pharmacy. The substantiality of this vision is impossible to articulate. It could not have been more concrete. There was nothing hazy or ephemeral. Just as I see the desk in front of me, so I saw chakras. It seems as if layers of matter that normally obscure this view suddenly vanished, revealing organs of a different sort down below. In that moment the absolute truth behind mystical ideas walloped my entire worldview out of me. The universe changed and never went back, because it led me to wonder how many other things I took as symbolic were *actual*. How many meta-physical ideas are *physical*, but on a subtler wavelength than we're taught to perceive? What blinders are we given at birth that block our ability to see what's really there? How many planes intersect with the supermarket and post office?

With no warning, an inter-dimensional curtain swept open and ushered me to a secret realm I'd heard whispered of since childhood. The pivot point of the soul described in my reading pivoted. I crossed the crossroads. At least a big part of me did.

From then on my lifelong love for fantasy and science fiction gave way to a deeper fascination for ordinary existence. Instead of relegating magic to the imagination as I'd done since childhood (I'd never believed in Santa Claus or the Easter Bunny), my imagination became harnessed to *finding the magical in the mundane.* Reality itself became juicier than all but the most brilliant speculative fiction. Life became so much more than it was.

More than ever I sought someone to ask the dozens of questions that arose. I phoned the astrologer twice but got his answering machine and hung up without leaving a message, then plowed deeper into my studies. I bought astrology texts. I checked a book out of the library on anthroposophy, Rudolf Steiner's science of the spirit. I skimmed channeled material. I interviewed clients about their supernatural experiences. I asked tough pointed questions of my teachers at the Psychic Institute but was dissatisfied with their answers. They seemed to have their own pat idea of how things worked, or to be bound by some agreement to reveal only vague glimpses of the thing I sought which was so much bigger than that.

The summer after moving to La Honda I met a local herbalist named

Alison, a sharp-minded, willowy, dark-haired Capricorn who'd recently broken up with the father of her three-year-old daughter. I'd spotted the winsome herbalist a few times around town and at the Half Moon Bay health food store. "Ah, the local witch," I said the first time we talked. She responded with a fetching gleam in her eye that prompted more than a few sex fantasies in me.

After days of deliberating, I phoned and asked Alison out. After she hemmed and hawed, and steered the conversation everywhere but, I repeated the question.

"So, you wanna see me?" she asked, adding barely audibly, "*Why?*" ... "Oh all right!" she finally blurted, as if telling some part of herself to shut up.

She invited me on a long hike through the hills above the ranch in San Gregorio where she lived in a small trailer, with part-time care of her daughter.

My relationship with Alison was launched on lust and intrigue. From the outset we had gripping sex and fierce existential debates. She started breaking up with me the day we met (!)—something we joked about but the joke had an edge. Like a nimble Nubian goat, dark-haired Alison danced at the edge of my vision, luring me on while shying away, her Gemini Moon pushing me out and pulling me in, daring me to dive in and claim her to put her out of the misery of indecision.

Instead of taking the hint and backing off, I bit the bait, of course, telling myself I'd finally found the woman I'd been searching for. I always tell myself that. *This one's different. This'll last. I've never felt this way before. . . .*

I channeled my frustration with her indecision into a fury of poems, stories, songs, and love letters. Her constant ins and outs had the effect of making me never able to stop thinking about her, which probably was exactly what some part of her wanted.

Romance felt like my natural state. My parents stayed in love their whole lives, flirting around the kitchen where dad would pinch mom's butt while she cooked. I grew up thinking that's the way it was.

Yet, underneath those reams of writing I offered to this lusty and exasperating goddess of indecision, I was unable to wholly repress the creeping fear that, like previous loves, my love for Alison would end disastrously and plunge both of us into the Void.

Even so, I reckoned, what could I do but push on? With the gods dangling that eager body (subtle rhythm of her hips as she hiked in front of me, beckoning. . . .) then snatching it away, then dangling it, despite every permutation of conflict and contradiction—or maybe *because* of it—what could I do but thrust myself into the musky center of this Goddess, and pray for deliverance?

The beauty of Alison was that she had a brilliant scientific mind but was so randy that she appealed equally to the lover and metaphysician in me. She led me on long hikes through the Santa Cruz Mountains where we humped like rabbits and then lay discussing astrology and herbalism. She was a casual student of the stars, and in that first blush of love we spent many hours lying side by side on our bellies with our legs folded behind us, studying charts and laughing at sexual innuendos, occupying our minds while giving our bodies time to recover for another round.

In the autumn of '89 Alison decided to relocate from La Honda to Santa Cruz for acupuncture school. We rented a log cabin in Bonny Doon and moved in together. The new home turned out to be a mile west of Comstock Lane.

I was excited about Santa Cruz because of the metaphysics scene on the rise in that quirky university town. Much less isolated and more populous than La Honda, it seemed the perfect place to launch my career. On bulletin boards I saw more spiritual events posted each week than one person could possibly attend (or even ten people going to separate events simultaneously). Buddhist schools, Hindu schools, yoga studios, meditation centers, chakra classes, Osho study, a plethora of bodywork all gave me the sense of enrolling in a Northern California University-of-Life specializing in metaphysics.

But I was even more jazzed because the Lonsdales lived there. During the year and a half since visiting them I'd never let go of the idea he'd become my teacher. Though I hadn't been to their home since, we'd spoken by phone a couple times and when we ran into each other at the Santa Cruz farmer's market.

From the community, I gathered that the master astrologer had a reputation as an eccentric hermit genius who emerged from his dusty bookshelves once in a blue moon to give unforgettable cosmic weather reports on the state of the universe. When people learned that I'd been to his home I was pummeled with questions that made me feel as if I'd been admitted to a secret inner sanctum, and wonder if I'd get to go back again.

In September I found a small bookshop on the outskirts of town specializing in Celtic literature and gifts, Avallone. The owner, Renee, and I hit it off as soon as we learned that we were both poets, and I arranged to present my first public astrology talk there. I chose to speak on the coming Earth Changes. The date scheduled for the talk was October 19, 1989. Little did I know how prophetic that date would prove.

On the morning of October 17, after Alison drove her daughter to Santa Cruz, I sat in our cabin to study for readings, pulled the first chart, and no matter what part of it I inspected, drew a blank and grew strangely tired. *Hm.*

I looked out the window, then back to the chart, making cursory observations that went nowhere. For the first time in trying to interpret a horoscope I came up empty. After pushing for half an hour, I yawned and set the first chart aside, then picked up the second and drew another blank. *What's this?*

My inability to decipher the astrological script made no sense. There was so much resistance I could barely keep my eyes open. But as usual I needed money, so I bent back to the task. Hours later I was in the same position, exhausted, until I surrendered and uncharacteristically curled in bed for a midday nap.

The next thing I knew the cabin was shaking like a roller coaster, catapulting me from deep sleep. *It's that secret missile base at the end of Pine Flat—thank you for this life, thank you for—*a glass jar fell off the kitchen shelf, conked, and rolled around the floor boards.

I went out relieved to see the world still there.

Minutes later the phone rang. Alison. "We're downtown—we saw the buildings collapse—people died! It's awful!"

"What?"

"Don't you know? *Earthquake!*"

If you haven't lived in a populous area during a major quake, it's difficult to fathom the extent of disruption, like an atomic blast spreading dislocation in waves that last for years.

The Loma Prieta quake was on a Friday, with an epicenter very close to Santa Cruz. On Sunday I presented my talk. Because the topic was Earth Changes, Avallone was packed, with standing room only. As I was about to begin the lecture William ducked furtively into the shop then lost himself in the crowd—no mean feat for someone towering head and shoulders above everyone. Our eyes met for an instant; I smiled and he nodded.

From then on my career took off. I began appearing on radio a few times a year, on *Seeing Beyond,* a new AM morning talk show that introduced spiritual ideas to the Bay Area rush hour commute. The hostess of the program, Bonnie Colleen, a school teacher who'd quit teaching to launch the show when she realized she was psychic, was particularly interested in my take on the Harmonic Convergence and the year 2012. Bonnie considered *Seeing Beyond* an open classroom that could raise the consciousness of commuters between their homes and their jobs. I thought it was a brilliant idea.

I loved sitting in the control room, beneath the overhead boom mike, foam-padded headphones on, delivering the current cosmic weather report to inspire listeners and promote my work.

Bonnie and I had a spicy, flirtatious chemistry that seemed to put people at ease enough to call in for piggyback readings, as we dubbed them. While she warmed the caller up with a minute of psychic insight, I'd hastily look up birth times in my astrological ephemeris (book of planetary positions) and rattle off intuitive astrological observations to take the radio listener home. When my comments struck pay dirt, and we recognized that telltale gasp on the other end of the phone, I was proud but also puzzled. Without doing much I seemed to really *get* to people. The sincerity of their responses was unmistakable. *How can a Cosmic Fool who barely has his own shit together keep so many others on track?*

I began to realize the need of the world for someone to step in and claim responsibility for things. Even though I was new at it, people seemed to recognize a depth of insight in me, and in my own quirky language I was gradually developing for metaphysics. I could feel confidence building in me throughout the greater San Francisco public, which strengthened my self-belief and made me want to do the best job I could. *Your work's going to put you through more changes than any of your clients.*

From radio, public talks, classes and word-of-mouth regarding my readings, my reputation spread. Readings became more frequent, and I raised my rate, reduced study time and sharpened my skills as both the radio show and I grew up together, establishing our presence in the Bay Area.

Looking at the ups-and-downs of my income in those years, it's hard to see how I afforded to live in Santa Cruz, with the highest cost of housing in the U.S. Somehow I got by. But I was conscious of the huge gap between my skill and the master's. It wasn't that clients were dissatisfied. Most readings were pure magic. Still, I felt I was dwelling in the huge shadow he cast. A part of his aptitude, I knew, could only come from years of training he'd put in. Another part was due to his native genius. But a third part, I was convinced, could be taught.

After almost two years of breaking up with Alison we finally broke up. Of course this came as no surprise, and I turned out to be pretty good at it after all that practice. It was a good clean ending. As with my previous break-up, with Elizabeth, this didn't seem like something I had control over so much as simply had to acknowledge. This one was less tearing, though, and came as a great relief to the part of me exhausted from pushing that boulder uphill. To be that hot for a woman impossible to live with had worn me down.

Along with the sting of lost love, I felt an exquisite lightening of my earthly load. I mourned the death of our sexuality, but the release of Alison was like taking off a fifty-pound backpack after a two-year hike. I tried to see her once as friends, but neither of us could make the conversion, probably because our bodies had been arc-welded to each other. Once more I was flying solo.

—4

The Sorcerer's Apprentice

In the winter of 1990 I got news I'd been waiting three years for: William and Sara Lonsdale were starting a class! To test information from the new book they'd begun writing—or that was being written through them—I was invited to join others at Comstock Lane the following Wednesday.

That evening seven of us gathered in Sara's massage room, along with our teachers. There was no fanfare to mark the start of our class. People stretched on the floor or chatted casually until William clicked on the recorder. I did not chat; I was too wonderstruck.

"Our new book," said the mage, calling the room to order, "is called *Inside Aspects* and is about the aspects (or angles) between planets, which have never been explored with any depth to my way of thinking. *Inside Aspects* is the first of a series of volumes we're going to produce on 'inside astrology.' Inside astrology happens when you approach cosmos as if it's already a natural part of you, rather than something remote—a part of you, though, that's linked to all things in such a way that you have to stay very, very alert to track with.

"Sara and I have been working this way for years but hadn't gotten far enough to talk about it. Tonight we're ready." The two compatriots exchanged a knowing glance that said much about whatever they'd gone through to get here. Then William handed the reins to his partner.

Sara's feisty little body sprang to attention and her face shone. "I can't tell you what a relief it is," she blurted, "to finally be talking about this stuff! It's just been building and building for years, until it was either going to break us apart or finally make it out to the world. I'm just so thankful to be sitting here with all of you discussing these things. You don't know how much it means to me." Her enthusiasm spilled through the room.

"It's easy to see," William picked up the stitch, "why the aspects haven't been excavated with any adroitness. At first glance they don't seem as juicy as planets, houses and signs. After all, what are ninety-degree squares between planets, hundred-and-eighty-degree oppositions, conjunctions, trines, sextiles? There's nothing there! They're just *measurement*. It's just space.

"But *space*, it turns out, is everything. When you look at a chart, or a living being for that matter, if you really want to know who they are, you can't just be guided by what's there. You need to know even more what's *not* there."

He plucked up a sheaf of loose-leaf paper with neatly penciled handwriting. "I'd like to begin by sharing our most recent tap-in: 'The planetary aspects,' he read, 'move through a star dance impenetrable to time-bound awareness. They split time open into many simultaneous streams of unfoldment. If one were able to step out of time, one would observe wheels within wheels, geometric patterns of every description, all at once driving through upon their own unique course. Thus the cosmic picture of the aspects is vast, intricate, and multidimensional.'"

I flashed on the universe as a gigantic clockworks with solar systems, cogs and spring bars clicking and whirring at different speeds. Some movements were the revolution of planets, others the eccentric orbit of comets and the infinitesimal swirl of galaxies. Numerical dials were lit by the stars. Everything meshed and moved in a way that meshed and moved with everything else.

I wondered if my fellow students experienced this subdimension underscoring the overt lesson of the class. But all eyes were fixed on the mage, including Sara's.

He spent the next hour applying Saturn's twenty-nine-year cycle to his autobiography, referring to a system of timing known as "transits." Between your twenty-eighth and thirtieth year, Saturn passes over the exact point it was at when you were born, forming a conjunction with its birth position, known as Saturn Return. This conjunction between Saturn of the present and Saturn of the past summons us to get real about who we are and what we're doing.

Our first twenty-nine years, the Lonsdales explained, inscribe a karmic circle. Much of what happens then is a necessary reinstatement of patterns from previous lives. This is the set-up we need to launch the second twenty-nine years, when we can gain independence and authenticity by carving a path of purpose more suited to the present life. And so the stage is set for clashing forces of karma and destiny (past and future).

When Saturn returns, all life structures not based on the inner needs of the soul can get prickly or unbearable. Many people experience death or divorce or loss or accident or pregnancy or some such intense disruption at this time. Others get the more drawn-out version. In either case, circumstance tends to press in on us like the rings of Saturn, urging us to commit to something more authentic.

To personify the aspects Saturn makes as it revolves around the wheel, our teacher exposed his personal history: his dreams, fantasies, loves, losses and blunders. At every juncture he explained how choices made during earlier aspects set up these later events, and how it might've gone otherwise.

He peppered his tale with brief excerpts from his journal. Every night for decades the mage has made copious notes about whatever he's going through that day, and how it pertains to the planets, assembling a rich source of experiential star knowledge.

It was like witnessing intimate performance art replete with Greek chorus, as the class was propelled through the trapped underworld, egotistical high jinks and disastrous freefall of William Lonsdale's youthful follies. The chorus came via the view from the planets, which lifted my perspective toward a grand irony of the complex dimensions at work in a single human life.

Now that I had a brilliant mind to guide me I began to grasp the intricacy of the celestial arts. That first class confirmed my career choice to be an astrologer, teaching me how astrology and life were more inseparable than I'd thought.

"The point of my sharing," concluded William, bringing his Saturn story up to date, "is to illustrate where cosmos lives in me, in Sara, in you—in all of us. Whether we know it or not our lives are utterly woven in with the stars."

Now it was our turn, as our teachers encouraged us to apply the Saturn cycle to our own lives. Everybody who wished was given free rein to step into the spotlight and speak. I was touched by the confidentiality that arose. People spoke thoughtfully, often from the heart. In bits and pieces a greater tale began to emerge from each individual story, a tale of how we run from truth while craving truth, how we seek and push away love, how the face we had before the world was made keeps calling and calling us to persevere through every challenge, and get real. *If we're beginning at this level of candor,* I thought, *where will we end?*

As the first month of classes elapsed we were led into the charged spaces between planets by guides who, I began to realize, spent so much time there that the unknown territory off the edge of ancient maps— *Hyre Thyre Be Monsters*—was at last becoming chartable. I got my first major answer to the many questions that plagued me since my session: the reason William Lonsdale can do what he does during readings is because he *lives* there.

Most astrologers have their normal life, then do astrology. William and Sara were opposite. They lived each moment in a primal realm of clashing forces, which they occasionally took a few baby steps out of only to hold the door open for the rest of us.

We weren't just learning astrology, I realized. The Lonsdales were blazing a trail to an invisible inner realm that seemed to undergird all existence. They weren't alone in this; as their prodigious library indicated, they were breaking into territory previously surveyed by powerful minds through the ages. But they were making original discoveries. They had their own unique way of seeing metaphysics, as a basic inescapable fact of life, and also something vividly magical and mesmerizing.

More than some slapdash New Age theory wrapped around reality to make it palatable, there was a breathtaking elegance to their vision. It made sense. It didn't feel like a made-up scenario so much as something that had always been. Similar to what Tolkien did when he created *Lord of the Rings,* I felt as if the Lonsdales thrust aside some heavy curtain that had previously kept the world back from a fundamental dimension of existence, which already vibrated somewhere off on its own until people began to notice.

Some students in our class had been hiking the spirit path for years, others were novices. Some seemed more or less familiar with astrology, others not at all. We often had to pause to clarify some metaphysical concept or astrological idea. There were many comments throughout the first weeks that began, "Excuse me if this is a dumb question everybody already knows the answer to, but—"

As is common in the Bay Area, few people in the group were native to California. There was a wide span of incomes and ages. Apart from the Lonsdales, and Renee who owned Avallone Books, and Rob, who worked there, I hadn't met the others before.

As the light of autumn days eclipsed toward the dark solstice, our class solidified into a weekly discussion group to dig into the growing material of *Inside Aspects,* the book Sara told me they'd been retrieving as "tap-ins," straight from spirit. They didn't call it channeling. William said channeling implies a state of unconsciousness, whereas he remains awake during tap-ins—in fact, he said, more awake than ever. Unconscious channeling, he explained, is atavistic, a throwback to a primitive clairvoyance humanity had in ancient times that we need to grow out of.

"Don't get me wrong," he told us one night, "it's a magnificent thing to contact spirit beings. It's the most exquisite thing I know," he added, glancing at Sara. "But we only evolve when we do it consciously. Otherwise our own development gets lost in the bargain, which is what happened to Edgar Cayce, who burned himself out channeling that way for others. Spiritual beings don't need that of us. In our day the best way to contact beings who vibrate on a more refined level is by becoming *more* present in your own nature, not less. If we humanize the connection this way, we ground cosmic voltage rather than abandoning Earth for the higher planes and flitting off into the blue.

"The Aquarian Age, beginning in 2012, is the full flowering of the human being, which only happens when we show up as fully human as we are—a whole subject in itself which we'll get into later."

Twice a week, for hours, in private, the Lonsdales "tapped into" spirit and William spoke words that Sara transcribed. The result was the growing body of colored loose-leaf binders I'd glimpsed in Ross.

One day while gathering dried flowers in the garden, Sara mentioned that these manuscripts were heading toward publication. I asked if they had a publisher and she said nothing had been signed, but William had been talking to someone. Like many things Sara ended up telling me through the years, this casual comment brought me up short. *Can publication be so easy? . . . Then why's it taking me so long?*

As class progressed, my notebook filled with notes. After each session I went home and carefully recopied the material, adding my own observations. With my new guides I made rapid progress, and my thirst for knowledge grew acute.

The comments of my classmates made me realize that everyone seemed to be getting something different from the class. Even though I held back the larger percentage of what I always had to say, I still tended to ask the most questions and make the most comments, something I felt sheepish about but couldn't restrain. I didn't want to hog the show but felt ill and shaky when I kept my words corked. *Something rare is happening. You may never get this chance again.* So I became the pesky hobbit dangling at the wizard's sleeve, badgering him for the names of everything under the sun and many things beyond it. Before breaking new ground I wanted to make certain I understood the ground we stood on.

I was driven by a need to bring the stars down to earth, to make metaphysics real. The east coast cynic in me wasn't going to move into a house without first banging on each door, wall and window to see what it was made of. The built-in enigmas of the supersensible territory we explored were a necessary evil in themselves, I reckoned, without having additional vagaries of communication. So when people got that blank look on their faces, I took it upon myself to play devil's advocate and press William to nail what he meant instead of just intimating it. At such times I found Sara glowing, as if she appreciated having someone else rein in our resident cosmic wildman.

I'd been generally familiar with some metaphysical ideas since adolescence. I grew up in Queens, New York, and Stratford, Connecticut, in the late fifties and sixties. I had a pretty conventional middle-class upbringing, except that by seventh grade I'd gone to five schools, lived in four homes, and had had to make entirely new sets of friends every few years because of my dad's job selling Exercycles.

Whenever I asked why we were moving I was told the landlord was selling and we couldn't afford to buy. This set up my lifelong pattern of wandering. Early on, I learned not to depend on anything that was here today still being there tomorrow.

My father worked ceaselessly to make ends meet. Our family wasn't poor but rarely had extra, and I felt burdened by an underlying tension in the house, which was our family's white elephant in the living room that no one mentioned. Dad never hit pay dirt as a salesman, probably because he was too honest and incapable of faking it. He was a Cancer with a great sense of humor but no friends, no one he could phone for a beer. My father was the strong silent type who kept his own counsel, whereas my mom—Libra like me—was gregarious and effervescent.

By age nine I sensed my magical existence to be an endangered species that needed protection from whatever had stolen the same thing away from my parents and other adults. *They've forgotten,* I said to myself, over and over, in a secret passageway between rooms in my Old Colonial home on Warwick Avenue in Stratford. Huddled in the musty tunnel, I vowed this would never happen to me: *They've forgotten. They've forgot-*

*ten the magic of childhood. No matter how old I get, I will never forget. I will never forget the magic of this moment. I will always remember. **Always!***

I grew up with open minds and distant hearts. It was very easy to talk with my family about things that didn't matter. I don't remember being hugged or told "I love you." It was a household of well-meaning strangers with much dependability but little intimacy.

Not until I was twenty-four and had a spiritual awakening in the presence of the medicine man of an Indian village in southern Oregon, did I realize my parents had always loved me but had trouble showing it.

Within this shaky ground I immersed myself in science fiction, fantasy, comic books and the supernatural. I often had insomnia. Long after midnight, especially in autumn, with the sugar maple branch tips creaking against my second-story window in Stratford, I read under covers with a flashlight and wrote the poems and stories that kept my soul alive.

My curiosity was insatiable. Books were friends I turned to more than I turned to human beings. I felt more kinship with the Great Wide World of Literature than the mainstream suburban WASP society all around me. Never content to remain exclusively within my own age group, from fourth grade on I sought out unemployed actors from the local Shakespeare Theater and other odd and marginal characters for friendship. I loved playing Chinese checkers with the retired merchant seaman down the block and listening to his tales of far-off places.

I read voraciously and wrote the same, spending hours ensconced in the hulking granite library in the old part of Stratford, where I blazed through every mythology and astronomy book I could find, as well as Ray Bradbury stories and books on reincarnation and UFOs.

I recall lying in the grass at the top of Highland Avenue with Stacey Loop and Mary Ellen Horsely, the summer after sixth grade, contemplating the nature of existence. By eleven it was quite clear to me that scientists, for all their wisdom, are blind. How could anything like a Big Bang have started the universe? *Something* had to start whatever it was that banged! Something had to provide energy and context for what we thought of as life.

Science without spirit always falls short, because regardless of how small the particles you break matter into, *something* had to create that first particle! It amazed me then and even more now why everyone doesn't realize this. How can a particle create a particle? How can matter spring to life without some x-force? How can conscious beings not only act but come to know they're acting?

Obviously, physical creation has some metaphysical force behind it. Not necessarily a God, but some kind of higher design. By my teens I noticed that things tend to move in patterns; disconnected forces resolve into some greater whole. I would've never called myself psychic or spiritual at the time but was in the neophyte stages of both.

While hitchhiking from Connecticut to Florida at seventeen I met an older southern girl who taught me remnants of astrology and mystical thought. She didn't train me in anything specific, but on hot Tampa evenings and later in the Smoky Mountains of Sylva, North Carolina, we had heartfelt all-night discussions that initiated me into a general realm of metaphysical awareness.

She told me Edgar Cayce said we sail from life to life in karmic pods, like dolphins, reconnecting with others we've known before. Podmates, she called them.

"When y'all find each other," she explained in that soft southern drawl, drawing a hit off the joint before passing it to me, "y'all get to continue working on something begun ages ago."

This made a kind of incomprehensible sense to me and explained the feeling I get about certain people—like her—that I know them intimately the moment we meet. I couldn't break down the deeper mechanics of how these things actually work, but her ideas struck me as more sound than the big bang or random chaos theory of existence.

In William and Sara's class I was able to draw forth strands of knowing from these earlier periods. And there was a practical side to our studies. As my astrology practice grew I had ample opportunity to apply class material to my chartwork. The Lonsdales tested out information fresh from spirit on us, and I tested it on others.

I began teaching a basic astrology class in downtown Santa Cruz and relayed insights from Bonny Doon. I picked my teacher's brain whenever I caught him with a free moment. A few times I drove to Comstock Lane and got private time with the wizard, which I valued as a rare opportunity to ask whatever my heart desired. At these moments I either recorded him or took careful notes, grateful to have gotten in with him. Other times he seemed aloof, preoccupied and off-putting, and nobody wanted to approach.

In class Sara Lonsdale spoke less than her husband, but she had a way of bringing cosmic concepts to earth in one fell swoop, with a kind of rural canniness, like Will Rogers of the soul. Nothing she said was superfluous. I began to wonder if she was the power behind the throne.

One night I sped from Santa Cruz through the mountains, racing to class long after they'd started, late for the first time. I squeezed in next to Sara. A moment later I felt a force on the base of my spine like a warm lead weight, instantly grounding the nervous tension rushing through me.

My breathing relaxed. My thoughts calmed. My whole being anchored into the firmness of that point—the flat of Sara's hand, steadily, unobtrusively pressed into the small of my back. I glanced at her but she remained focused on William.

The incident went unmentioned. That this wisp of a woman could have such profound effect made an unforgettable impression on me. I felt her telepathically teaching me to ground energy and get a handle on the wayward cross-currents of my impulsive nature.

I saw further into the nature of Sara when we traded astrology for massage. I gave her a reading and she gave me the most unusual deep-tissue work I'd had. She put me on her massage table, blasted a Beethoven symphony from those huge wooden speakers until my organs shook, and dug her strong Virgo fingers into the base of my spine, reaching under my coccyx and pulling on me as if boning a fish, to lengthen my body.

When I got off the table and went outside to meet Sara's adolescent daughter from a previous marriage, Amy, who spent part of her time in

Bonny Doon, I felt like a sailor thrown from a shipwreck. I excused myself and collapsed on my back in the redwood grove.

The thrust of our study group, and what distinguished it from other astrology, was the vividness with which we were led to inhabit cosmic forces and become intimately acquainted with them. Instead of Saturn in Pisces or Jupiter in Gemini representing some abstract concept, we were taken on a guided tour directly *inside* each planet. We were introduced to planets as vital living beings with as much outward inconsistency and inward sameness as the most fascinating person or animal. I came to see the stars not as faraway objects that stood for psychological qualities, but living forces with their own nature and agenda, which sometimes clashed with our own.

From science reading I knew we were made of stars. Literally. Life on Earth, I'd read, had been seeded by nitrogen dumped by comets passing through our solar system from deep space. The iron in our blood originated from exploding white dwarf stars. The sun itself is a star whose life-giving rays awaken the world each morning and nourish the plants that enrich our atmosphere. Every human being and all rocks and plants are composed of star matter, so even at the most earthy level this new cosmology struck a deep chord in me.

Sara and William Lonsdale, I recognized, were pushing the envelope of all that astrology had been. She with her no-nonsense tactile orientation to things, he with his penetrating intellect, had evidently been at this for years, on a track of their own, tapping in, assembling manuscripts, constructing a vast body of work that, through our class on aspects, was being exposed to the world.

Someday everyone's going to get in on this, I realized during many class moments when a shroud seemed to lift upon some new view of spacetime that came rushing in. Other moments I glimpsed a life where we'd studied the mysteries in the ancient air of a lemon-scented garden. I was living a waking dream, I realized, long dormant in me, and, like Sara, was more thrilled than I could say at the mere fact of being able to meet with others week after week like this.

As trust formed, class became challenging emotionally as well as intellectually. We confronted thorny issues that arose when we strove to apply the material. Sometimes group veered toward therapy, when a class member who resonated strongly with the night's material stepped into the spotlight and divulged her story. These sessions were especially moving because I felt the realness of them. They placed cosmic theory squarely in the convoluted history of people striving to untie Gordian knots they'd inherited from parents with their own knots.

One night William told us, "True astrology, contrary to the pop version, is the *art of identifying a person's uniqueness.* That everyone is unique is a truism so commonplace as to be cliché. But authentic star work pinpoints the *precise ways* each of us is a distinct one-of-a-kind being.

"The typical way to understand someone else is by imagining what you'd do if you were in their shoes. *Star Genesis*—the name Sara and I have just been given for the new astrology—reveals what they would do if *they* were them. Because most people nowadays are busily consumed with *not being who they are.* Modern society seduces individuals to betray themselves and opt for an artificial life. Star Genesis provides a route back."

As winter gave way to spring, with so few students we were able to plow into the aspects and apply them to each of our charts. Little by little I began to fathom what William said at the first class—that the charged field between planets is a force of its own, a wedge of sacred geometry that indicates as much or more of a person's nature as do planets and signs. And that you can learn so much by what's not even there.

I came to see astrology's basic units in terms of my theater background. (Since age four I've been on stage and later went to college for acting and directing.) Planets are actors. Signs are roles. Houses are plays. This simplified things. My Sun in Libra in the tenth house means: Who's trying to express? The Sun. How? Through Libra. Where? In the tenth house.

My Sun (basic nature) in Libra (one-to-one partnership) in the tenth (public recognition) indicates that my basic nature expresses itself through partnership linked to the public. That fits, since my astrology practice is based on one-to-one encounters, and my whole life, for that matter, can be construed as little more than a strung-together series of partnerships. For me, *everything* boils down to relationship. I can't imagine being any other way (but if I were Virgo or Aquarius I'd probably say something different).

"The aspects are the most cosmic layer of astrology," taught William. "They're the celestial mechanics of the chart, the underlying blueprint you'd have if you stripped away the human side of the equation. What we're doing in this class is making abstraction real."

I never knew who was going to show up in Bonny Doon, and we rarely had the same attendance two weeks in a row. A handful of us could be counted on to be there most nights. There were no entry restrictions or fee. At our small mystery school in the hills, bolstered by an occasional private meeting with the mage, my apprenticeship began in earnest.

For the first time I had a mentor I could follow along a clear course of development. I suppose at some point in childhood I must've felt this way about my father, but I did not grow up believing my parents' world was solid, or even that they themselves were firmly rooted within it. Most of my school teachers couldn't match the hunger for knowledge I pursued intimately in the public library. And when I came of age, precociously, during the Summer of Love, and three years later hitchhiked from Stratford to San Francisco at sixteen, who could believe anything we'd been told by the Establishment?

And so, William and Sara Lonsdale became my teachers, guides, and to some extent, role models, seasoned sidekicks on weekly excursions down the mystic highway. I now had a group of cohorts to regularize my cosmic studies. I felt welcomed into a mystical kinship, and no matter how much I got I wanted more.

As a kid I'd absorbed huge quantities of *Doctor Strange* comic books and other fantastic tales of mystic apprenticeship, which thrilled me with the idea of secret powers locked in the heart of ordinary human beings, and magic codes from ancient days that could somehow be revived. Beyond all expectation I found myself not *writing* one of those tales, but *living* one, and I knew with prescient clarity I was onto some-thing that was going to change the course of my life.

I looked forward to years of study with the Lonsdales. I imagined a moment when instead of just being their student I could rise to be their colleague, forging my own trail alongside theirs. Maybe I'd write my own book some day. Maybe I'd be invited to speak at prestigious events. Maybe I'd make a name for myself, start my own college of wizards.

The wayward gypsy that had wandered the world in search of love and meaning now found a home on Comstock Lane. I could scarcely believe the good fortune that had brought me to the one place on Earth where a new approach to astrology was being born. Day and night this mystic highway revealed its curves and contours and increased its pull on me.

So it was to my great disappointment one Wednesday when William announced class would end in a couple weeks. He and Sara were going summer traveling and also had personal business to attend to.

When we protested, he said group might reunite for one or two spe-cial gatherings, or could possibly pick up in a new form in the fall, but for now we had to quit.

There was an awkward silence. No one wanted class to end, but we suspected William had his reasons. *Okay,* I told myself, *if you learned any-thing this year it's that all things are part of a grand design, so this must be too.* I forced myself to grin and bear it, even though I felt like jumping up and shouting *we're just getting started!*

Two weeks later at the last class, just as at the first, there was no fan-fare. For a professional magician William Lonsdale seemed the least rit-ualistic man in the entire New Age. No incense, no invocation, no opening moment of silence, no burning sage, no candles, no liturgy, no glam. But then, I don't think anybody thought we were done for good.

—5

Dark Karma

Three months went by with no sign of the Lonsdales. Spring turned to summer.

In July I got word from Renee at Avallone there was to be a special full-day gathering at Comstock Lane on the date of a powerful solar eclipse which William said had far-reaching consequences. Many more people attended the gathering than had come to the class—close to thirty, most of whom I didn't know. It felt ceremonious.

The early part of the day was celebrational. We sat on a huge parachute spread on the grass with potluck feast and musical instruments. I'd rarely seen Sara so happy and alive. She flowed through the grounds in a mid-length cotton dress, fielding conversation, nibbling food, beaming in the fresh mountain air. Somehow the addition of food made everything different—tribal, communal, villagey and *real*.

Beneath food and music, though, something tugged on me. It had to do with the rhythm of conversation and the cast of faces; with tone and texture of some underlying psychic symphony each small word or phrase was a part of. This dimension drew me as far down as the invisible tops of the redwoods shot me up. Similar to my mountain experience during the vast Convergence, Harmonic forces seemed to be coming into alignment, like the synchronizing of a cosmic clock. Where Shasta had been horizontal, though, this felt vertical, like a grandfather clock rather than a sundial. Without smoking or drinking I entered an altered state. Even new people seemed so familiar that I couldn't fathom if I was seeing them for the first time or somehow forgot that I knew them, until I lost track of who was who and the afternoon became one big *déjà vu.*

Not everyone stayed for the next phase. After dark the remaining fifteen or so of us headed for the large empty yurt newly erected in the backyard. One by one we crossed a narrow plank over a ditch into the round nomadic canvas dwelling, where we sat in a circle on pillows. The cavernous area was lit with flickering lanterns.

As we got settled, conversation lulled. The yurt fell silent but for the far-off hoot of an owl. The mage raised an eyebrow as if rolling up his sleeve for some formidable task. I thought I saw Sara squeeze his hand.

"For centuries," our teacher began, "this species has been struggling to overcome something that happened way back at the beginning. Today's solar eclipse in Thirty Degrees Cancer is a direct link to the ancient kingdom of Atlantis, where something went very right and very wrong."

A rumble shook the yurt and lanterns jiggled, sending a ripple of goose bumps through the room.

William nodded. "Precisely."

After an outbreak of nervous laughter, he continued. "When the Atlantean flood struck, as you can imagine, there was tremendous despair, apocalyptic anguish. What did they do with that?

"They found something somewhere to cling to. They latched onto something to put their whole being into. And they clung to it with main strength and have been clinging ever since, life after life.

"The flood shocked our nervous systems. To the extent that we haven't come back yet. The normal human state now is to dwell in frozen emotion. We've become frozen inside ourselves. It's hard to notice this because it's become the common condition. It's now the norm. In fact, when someone breaks out—someone over the age of seven, I mean—*they're* the ones who seem weird by comparison. We've become acclimated to living a great shutdown that must be exposed in order to move through it."

William paused, surrendering the class to a chorus of chirping crickets which underscored the mounting buzz of the eclipse. Then he straightened on his cushion. "To understand the impact of the flood," he continued, weaving the story with his hands, "you must know that at the time of its demise, Atlantis was the center of a thriving world culture. Even though it was small geographically, it was highly differentiated, refined and multiplex, more than any culture since. Understand—I'm saying that the most cosmopolitan, sophisticated, wide-open society we've had was in the very beginning. Many people have carried the memory of this and been aching to get back to something like it ever since."

Our teacher's eyes got a far-off look, as a cool breeze trickled in through the screened window behind me. I wondered about people new to the circle, how they connected to the Lonsdales, what they were making of this, the first I'd heard anyone speak of Atlantis.

"This buried sense-memory," continued the mage, "is one reason many of us are frustrated with the limited way people relate to each other nowadays. The experience of a much different way to be is trapped inside us.

"Have you ever had dreams of flying? The kind where, for an instant when you wake, no part of you questions it's real, and it takes a kind of sharp jarring motion to bring you back to the present?

"Many of these dreams are memories of a technology we once had, a mystical science that harnessed this planet's energy fields in ways we haven't been able to duplicate.

"The Atlanteans knew the great secret that Earth, like the human body, is a fluid medium, awash in tides of electromagnetic force, composed of invisible meridians, energy frequencies that weave together matter and can be manipulated for various purposes. *Everything* here is energy. Earth is really a water world. We're completely swimming in seas of subtle fluid. Thoughts are energy. Matter is energy. Nothing's as solid as it seems. Our forbears learned the code of this primal fluid and did amazing things with it.

"The main idea behind their technology was the freedom to move through space unbound by normal laws of physics. We could have a whole session on this alone, but for now I want to mention one critical aspect: Compared to the modern state, the consciousness of even the most common Atlantean was greatly expanded, greatly aware of physical reality as an intersection of many different planes of existence. The universe they inhabited was bigger than the one we do. They were not outcasts in their own world, as we have become. The main technological achievement of the Atlanteans was to align human beings with cosmos. This was their passion, and they succeeded wonderfully with the project for a few generations. They found a way to unlock secrets of time and space and draw vast powers into being." My teacher's tale was underscored as his face strobed in the guttering light.

"But after this peak period, the Atlanteans turned a dark corner and became deluded. Our field of awareness shrank. We reduced. We withdrew from identifying with a cosmically expanded state, and shrank to identifying with limitation, with fragmented aspects. We clung to these aspects and then couldn't get out of them, and kept repeating that motion, life after life, repeating and repeating it, until the reduced state became the norm.

"Since our first civilization we've greatly diminished, become isolated, cut off from self and cosmos. Our wholeness splintered. We view everything through a lens that cracked when Atlantis crumbled. The extent to which this fragmented state has taken over is difficult to grasp—because we see *everything*, even the idea of wholeness, from the viewpoint of fragmentation.

"In our first civilization, in the early period of Atlantis, we didn't know we were whole, because we had no idea in any way, shape, or form there could possibly be any other way to be. At this point the situation's reversed: it's hard to see how reduced we are, because we have little example of anything *but*. We go through the motions of life never realizing we're only tapping a fraction of our inheritance, a fragment of our greater awareness.

"Most of us have been caught in these syndromes of fragmentation for so long that we've had to hide the patterns and keep them back from the light of day. This is history's shameful little secret. You see, we would've been immobilized if we'd allowed ourselves to see how far we've fallen. So we stuff it and go along with the dominant paradigm. We don't remember wholeness. But our deep bodies remember.

"To remedy this we have to find who we are in the depths. We have to unlock the story in the shadows. This is the glaring error of most New Age philosophies. We need to claim our shadow to release our light. We need to go *down* more than up. We need to find our feet. We need blood, bones, and ankles: Pisces, Capricorn and Aquarius. We need to extract late-winter wisdom from this late-winter passage of humanity, to bring on Spring of the Soul."

I said, "How?"

In the half-light William turned to address me. "We have to conquer our phobia of going deep. This phobia—a species paralysis, really—is enforced by ancestral codes. Ancestral codes are hidden messages passed down in the blood—karmic programmings that bubble beneath genealogy, taboos buried in the muck of your family tree. These karmic prohibitions tell you that you must not make waves, must not take matters in your own hands, must not delve beneath things. 'Don't get so worked up.' 'Don't sniff the rotting elephant under the rug.'"

Somebody laughed.

"And so our fears encase us in a predictable territory of circumscribed experience," William continued, "and frighten us that if we risk going into the depths, we'll experience what our ancestors did—humiliation, devastation, shock, banishment, exile. Therefore, don't ask questions. Stick with the program. Better safe than sorry.

"This force hinders the awakening of humanity more than anything: visceral, reflexive, subconscious, irrational terror and distrust of anything deeper, on the supposition that there are all these horrible things down there—*stay away*. Don't go down the creaky stairs to the cellar!"

Nervous giggles tittered through the yurt. William paid no attention. "This taboo has been exploited to the *nth* degree by pop culture— you know, all those movies where the person is both terrified of and *drawn toward* ignoring common sense, contradicting gut instinct, and going down to the cellar—but it nonetheless has a very powerful truth behind it.

"The truth is there *are* things down there that'll curdle your blood. You *do* have to beware. You very much need to have your wits about you if you decide to take the plunge, because you'll be catastrophically unprepared for all you will meet, and you most assuredly will not return.

"The you who goes down—if you go all the way—will not be the one who comes back. The whole point of going down is to reconnect with something that got left down there, something that scares the hell out of you, that you need to find more than you need to do anything in this world.

"If you persevere in this quest, if you don't jump out of this level of experience when you're actually faced with it, if you don't sneak to the side of it, if you stay in the midst of it—something happens that we've got to get in this group tonight *that is the single most powerful learning experience we can ever have on this plane of existence.* Something happens when you stay in the place of 'I don't know' long enough to know, or to find out, or evolve.

"What happens when you're down-under in this deep body place? You meet someone you left behind. Whom do you meet?

"Many of us are familiar with the idea that part of oneself dwells in higher worlds, but few of us are familiar with a companion idea which states that another part of us dwells in the depths.

"I will characterize this being as the one who died before. There's a being in us who's died different times. And every death speaks in us and lives in us and doesn't fade and doesn't go away and doesn't dissolve.

"And these deaths—and all that's involved with them—live on in each of us as a kind of death-body, deep inside, that's waiting to be met, and is full of grief, loss, despair, and especially one overwhelming emotion: that when you died previously, you lost the Earth. When you had to leave the body and go to this other non-physical world, you lost the Earth, but a part of you couldn't lose the Earth and fell back into the Earth and lives on there.

"If we persevere in the depth-journey, then, we enter communion with our previously dead selves that has a power few people realize, because they have something to teach us. What do our past dead selves have to teach us?

"They teach us how to die again! *Our past dead selves teach us how to die.* We don't learn this from teachers or from other people's experience—we learn how to die from our own experience. And we have to learn this in the depths, and also learn how to be reborn in the depths. And we only learn because we've been there before.

"I'm suggesting there's a lost piece of you, a fragment which haunts you and will not let you be, and won't go away until you meet it, and isn't because your mother did something to you, and isn't because there's something wrong with this world, and isn't because there's something wrong with you, but *is* because you've been through the single most radical experience any soul ever goes through, which is to die, so many times that it's made a deep impact on your being, and you're never going to forget it even if you don't consciously remember it.

"But our cells remember. Your deep body remembers and holds this memory in your body, which is weighed down by previous deaths, and by the fact it's going to die again.

"You're going to die," stated the mage, opening his hands to the room. "I'm going to die. Sara's going to die. Everyone in this circle has died before and will again.

"Death is the most absolutely basic fact of existence, yet is the one fact our society ignores and casts aside as if it only happens in books and movies. When you live in a culture this ignorant of death, you can't ever understand life.

"Nonetheless, our bodies understand. Our bodies remember. Our deep body comprehends death, after having lived through it. What your deep emotions remember and try to get you to do with this memory is to inhabit your body at such a profound level that you *die before you die,* and then are reborn.

"It may sound farfetched or impossible, but that's actually our deepest desire in this world—to die to death, and learn to be ourselves always, in all worlds."

That's what happened on the slopes of the mountain, I realized, recalling the haunting sense that Shasta had been calling me long before I got there. At the time I thought it was my love for Elizabeth dying, but now I knew it was more.

Maybe that was the purpose of love—to slay the me that rises up each time reborn through the eyes of my lover. *Maybe love gives me death in order to destroy my illusions and purge my clingy attachment. Maybe that's why love kicks my ass. Maybe the reason each break-up slams me like bad acid is to break my heart over and over until I get to something that can't be broken. . . .*

"Unless we gain this kind of context," continued William, "unless we confront ourselves in the depths, we don't even know what we're doing in this world. So we have to go down, down, down before we go up. Have to contradict blood fear and ancestral taboo and past-life trauma to claim our authenticity in this life. Otherwise, we never initiate, never break from the herd, never become who we are.

"This depth journey has been called various names in various cultures, but the basic ingredients are the same. Joseph Campbell spoke of it as the Hero's Journey. It's something most primitive cultures are aware of but we're too civilized to notice.

"What enables us to complete this journey?

"How can we win freedom in the most un-free place of all? What motivates us to transgress common sense and go into the cellar?

"Because we feel in the deepest part of ourselves there's something down there for us.

"What's there?

"It's something that we've lost, you see, something particular we left behind once upon a time—*we ourselves are there.*

"You're down there, but you're not alone. You find others are there with you.

"You meet the person you were in your last life down there. You meet the shadow-reflection of your greater self, living under the earth, waiting for you to develop courage and vision to meet them. And you meet the ancient tribal elders, saints and wise ones in and out of the body, who summon you to council.

"Until we go down, our shadow-self pulls on us, constantly. Our depth-nature is always trying to get through to us. Our soul is forever calling us. The air these days is filled with so many false signals, so much static, though, that we fail to hear the lost cry of our own nature. If we had high cultural initiation, a tribal rite-of-passage common to the Western world, we'd reach a point in life where we'd know instinctively when it's time to leave everything behind and go down. Society would look much different then." William pressed on. "But, because we live in a Junk Culture instead of a High Culture, we medicate ourselves with TV addiction, junk food relationships, artificial standards, and avoid confronting ourselves on a deep enough level to win freedom and authenticity.

"Most of us, most of the time, remain unaware of our lower nature, but it remains very aware of us. Most of us erect a life far away from this under-realm, but it's an impoverished existence, a half-life.

"And so we lack a foundation. We lack roots. We project our shadow everywhere. Remaining blind to our darkness we never grasp the nature of our light.

"We refuse the call of the soul because it seems too much, and because we have no cultural map for this journey. Our soul calls us to a place and we don't go. We fail to fulfill our incarnational promise. We fail to come alive while we're alive, and so fail to die when we die, and when we reincarnate, start the whole thing all over again.

"Meanwhile, the people we used to be in prior lives go on haunting us from the depths because they died without making good on their promise, either. As did many of our ancestors. At this point we're trailing a chain of hungry ghosts. And so we never come alive at the root."

"What would it be like to come alive at the root?" I asked.

William closed his eyes for a long moment, then opened them. "It feels like you're being engulfed and submerged and carried away by dark forces."

The room grew very still.

"How can we complete the soul initiation at this time?" he continued after a pause. "How can we bear to hold steady in a space that's so intense, so heavy, so drastic, that our culture never even talks about it?

"This is what we've got to know. This is our mission. That's the point world culture is stalled at now—the point at which we cannot go on, cannot take one more step toward anything resembling an authentic living future for the human race, until we gain the courage to find who we are in the depths."

The ring of faces, by lantern light, seemed to contract in misty dimness. Ages ago in some bright world we'd eaten together and played music on the lawn; I remembered Sara floating through the orchard as if in a dream, but now we were in a baleful pressure chamber at the bottom of a karmic sea. The owl hooted, closer this time.

William looked out the window into the darkness. He appeared to have gone through some transformation since I'd last seen him teach. Previously he'd taken his time, coming at a subject from a variety of angles, coaxing it along until it gradually took shape. Tonight he was driven. The group entity had been harpooned, and I was being buffeted by waves of psychic backlash released from the impact. Any doubt that may have remained in me after Harmonic Convergence that planetary events have a direct bearing on us was dwarfed by the weight of what was unfolding under the eclipse.

"If this shutdown has become the norm," I ventured, breaking the taut silence, my words sounding strange and waterlogged, "what was it like before? How did we get shut down in the first place?"

William regarded me. "Atlantis was an incredible place, an amazing place, one of the greatest stages in human development so far. But at a certain point, toward the end, a small sub-group of elite became drunk with power. The forces they'd unleashed backfired. Over the brief space of a couple generations, members of this priest-scientist caste grew inflated. They forgot they were serving the high gods and began to think they *were* the high gods. They went crazy with their own mystic technology. Their cosmic awareness took a dark turn. They set themselves above everyone. They puffed up like balloons and eventually popped. The memory of that lives on in our cellular consciousness.

"The resulting impact set in motion the primary downfall of the species. This is the main karma of humanity we've been repeating in various ways ever since: *the chosen few lording over the many.* Corrupt leadership. Media manipulation. Abuse of power."

"How do you know all this?" said Nancy, my music partner from La Honda and a close friend who'd joined us earlier that day.

"I was there."

"Oh."

"Have you ever stopped to ask yourself," William picked up momentum, "why most of the world's cultures all point to a flood myth? How can that many civilizations so far removed in place and time tell the same story?

"Hidden beneath the outward progression of the ages lies this dark trauma of our species, which we have to get further *into* before we can get out of. At this time in history we're poised between worlds, hanging on the edge of a cliff, being offered a path of light which we can only take if we claim our shadow."

"If this story's been lost to the ages," said Nancy, "why's it coming out now?"

"Because during the Harmonic Convergence of 1987 to 2012 a great purging is taking place," said William, "in which the current world drama is intended to replicate what went wrong in Atlantis so we can make it right. The main karma of the species is being torqued as far as it can to crack apart and release something deeper than the trauma.

"The reason the story's coming out now is because you can't turn around an entrenched karmic pattern until you sufficiently recreate enough of it to have something to work with. The whole thing has to heat up again to give us fuel to burn. Until then it's too slippery to get a handle on, too down-in-under—the elephant under the rug."

William turned to Sara and some unspoken comment passed between them. Then he turned back to the circle. "The world's becoming neo-Atlantean," he said. "Mystic technologies are back. The sense of apocalypse is back. And the drama of blindness and corruption is back. We've entered the alchemical crucible where lead can turn to gold. Humanity's worst traits are infused with its best. Our greatest aspirations and darkest nightmares are bubbling in the karmic stew.

"The future hinges upon the main soul drama of our species: will humankind awaken in time to claim its bright inheritance, or repeat the mistakes of the past and vanish in the muck?

"The riddle of our time is figuring out how to keep ourselves busy while the old drama of corrupt power plays its final scene. Underneath business as usual, though, the world's becoming pliant and volatile, clay-like, raw, newborn, filled with danger and possibility.

"And it is to this under-layer we must address our actions. We have to take up existence with a fierce force of love lodged deep inside us that can crack the whole thing open. We have to dig down to release the vast soul force of humanity. We have to plant new roots at the bottom of things and claim our true place at the center of creation."

"Are you going to mention the two worlds?" Sara asked after a moment.

William nodded. "We recently learned there's more than one Earth here. The world we think of as the world can be understood as a kind of shell-world, a papier-mâché construct plastered over the Living Green Earth that's trying to emerge.

"As civilization plunges into end-time, the construct is tearing apart. Earth is shedding. She periodically goes through these things, the fermentative chaos that accompanies death and rebirth.

"When Earth dies, a part of us dies with her. I can't overstate the intensity of this. All over the world, underneath business as usual, the human soul is writhing—and needs to—and we have to stop repressing this fact and just get on with it so we can shed the skin of the past. But snakes are blind when they shed, so a great darkness is rising to consume the world."

William scanned the room. "Let me be clear: We are in crisis. *The world is dying.* The world we think of as the world is dying. This dark underlayer of humanity has to be exposed in order to slough it off. The False World we've created from living outside ourselves is speeding up, because that's what life forms do when they die.

"At the same time, a new force is rising; a new planet being hatched within the sloughage of the old."

In the center of our circle I envisioned a blue-green planetary embryo crowning through the crust, pushing up from beneath the yurt into the energy matrix that linked each of us with filaments of light.

"Outside of today's eclipse," said a big bearded guy with dark hair and barrel chest who looked like a lumberjack, "what's linking us to this ancient karma? Surely there's been eclipses in Thirty Degrees Cancer before tonight?"

"The simple answer, Jade," William called the newcomer by name, "is *we've finally become lost enough to be found.* The world is reversing polarity. In the very places there's been the most strife and bickering and discord, now comes the greatest opportunity for something new."

"I'm sorry," said the woman next to me, "but I'm finding it hard to believe we're so special. Doesn't everyone want to think their time is special at every period in history?"

"We couldn't return from exile," said William, "until we'd gotten sufficiently lost.

"Let's face it—this is a lost world. Everybody goes about business as usual, as if living without love, truth and meaning is acceptable! As if there were nothing wrong with everything being a sad joke. Normalcy has now become a very toxic state of denial, caked over by the drugged media of a phony culture. We're rushing around putting on make-up and parting our hair on a sinking ship." Outside the yurt the wind rose, pelting the canvas with dust and debris.

"But it's hard to stop a pendulum in mid-swing," continued the mage. "It usually has to reach its extreme before swinging back. That's the point we're at now in world culture, and we have to realize the most extreme period of all is much closer to breakthrough than any former point in the arc.

"At this pivot point of the ages we have a rare chance to guide the course of the future. Our passion must be to reclaim basic existence as something sacred and real. Though I'm making it sound ultra-dramatic for purposes of illustration, this task is actually more of an extended project than a moment's choice. It's the underlying purpose of the twenty-five-year period from 1987 to 2012: to get so fed up with living the great lie that we bust out of it.

"Humanity's going to get very confused in coming years and will need help as the new clashes with the old. Priestesses and yogis and shamans must rise from the ranks of secretaries and salesmen. Mundane life must split open its sacred core. We can no longer pretend to be normal. We're entering crisis, and everybody's recruited to dig for something deeper."

William stopped talking and the yurt grew silent. A shadow seemed to pass overhead, which made me think that just then the moon was blotting out the sun in some part of the world. I shivered as I felt the rush of all that had been said stream through me. I felt the swell of summer air pushing in on us. I felt the immense power of the redwood grove like a great sentient creature out there, keeping watch, bending its will toward some inner decision we were being asked to make.

Not for the first time I wondered how my teacher came by his knowledge. Tonight it was as if he single-handedly rolled up his sleeves and took on all of history. *Where does he get this?*

Some part of me was resisting this theory of Atlantis, but I couldn't tell if it was healthy skepticism or denial.

Group has changed, I realized.

"Can I ask a question?" said a woman with a thick golden braid, breaking the silence.

William turned to her.

"One thing about astrology always bothered me," she confessed. "I'm trying to understand the conflict between predestination and free will. If these world changes have been predicted from ancient times, and if they're true, won't they happen whether society catches on or not?"

William considered this. "Changing the world is volunteer work. It won't happen if you don't do it. Despite predictions regarding 2012, prophecies rarely force themselves upon us. The job of prophecy is to empower, not enslave us. The whole point of reading the stars is to equip you to choose a wise future out of all available futures—not give up free will. You can choose to say 'No thank you,' and the gods will let you be. *Mostly.* Though things are quickening in ways that will become harder and harder to ignore."

"But what about people who say, 'If it's already going to happen then I don't have to do anything about it'?" the braided woman persisted.

"They're missing the point," Sara chimed in. "The purpose of spirituality is to make you pro-active rather than disengaged. Disengaged spirituality is a carry-over from the Age of Pisces, when you had to give your power away to all these authority figures like kings and popes. In the Aquarian Age, when you find a truth that works, you have to test it and test it and test it to see what it's made of instead of following it blindly. You have to find your role in it, make it your own. Don't take anything William and I say at face value. *Try* it."

Thoughts I'd had about Sara lingering in her husband's shadow were eased by this comment, which led me to think her quietness might be more due to the strength of her own conviction than any timidity. I wondered about her past, what led her to this life of tap-ins with a giant bearded wildman in the hills.

"Yes," William agreed. "And there's something more. If prophecies of *kali yuga* are correct and the long hell of humanity *is* finally ending, then we have to face the fact that the old is also rising to assert itself one last time before giving up the ghost. That's what life forms do when faced with imminent destruction.

"This will mess with your head because retrogressive forces all over the planet, sensing their demise, will act out more than ever. We cannot allow ourselves to be distracted by this. You can't bite the poisoned apple one more time.

"Yet, I will say this to you over and over in coming years, and you'll go out and get snagged by another—by twenty other—rounds of illusion, because that's your privilege. Humanity always reserves the right to refuse spiritual help. That's the blessing and curse of free will. We resist change mightily, even when for the better.

"In truth, there's no guarantee we'll make it. I get snagged by all that's in the way of change every time. I grow disconsolate—and then I remember."

"And if we don't refuse spiritual help," I put in, "what can we do with it? How can we change in a way that sticks? How can we sustain the higher forces this time? What can we do to avoid making the same historical mistake all over again?"

"More than anything," replied William, "we need a new way to be; we need a *how* more than a *what*. We need a new mode, a new manner, a way of life that satisfies the soul. We need to jerk ourselves out of the Trance of Normalcy to see what's really going on."

"How do we do that?" said a husky voice in the shadows.

"Inspiration and enthusiasm open the channels," answered William. "Creative imagination is key. You've got to bust through numbness and isolation and fire up the soul. We have a lot of help for this, because the creative force locked in human beings is sick to death of being marginalized while machinelike drones take over the world.

"It's really a matter of presence more than anything. We don't need super powers or a magic ring. Full waking presence is the only way we're gonna do it. No bright idea of the mind, no team of experts, no technological marvel invention will ever turn around the nightmare until we first find a way to show up in the depths, and show up and show up and *keep showing up,* regardless of what we find, and never stop."

When the Lonsdales opened the class to questions the yurt exploded. The whole idea of Atlantis and past dead selves spun us around and around. This revolution my teachers were advocating struck me like a torch in the night, plunging us into fiery debate long after any previous class would have ended. Even though part of me felt wary of this story and didn't know what to make of it, it nevertheless got to me.

Hours later, as if we'd been pummeled, we staggered out of the yurt and over the plank like dazed veterans of The Karmic Wars, to stare mutely at the stars. As I walked down the long dirt driveway toward my car, I realized the earlier part of the day had marinated us for the soul blast we'd just gotten.

That foxy wizard. And high priestess. What are they after? What ancient mystery has been stirred here? Where will this story end?

For weeks after the eclipse I couldn't get Atlantis out of my head. The haunting tale thrummed in a wordless part of me that made me feel psychically linked to everyone in the circle. In some subterranean layer of my blood, perhaps, the truth of a time before time silently bubbled.

During these weeks I befriended two classmates: Jade Redmon, the lumberjack, who turned out to be a Tarot-reading astrologer from Bend, Oregon; and Rob Callahan, a lanky musician-astrologer whom I'd met when he clerked at Avallone Books. We three formed a casual friendship based on bumping into each other around Santa Cruz.

In parking lots and on sidewalks, Jade, Rob and I speculated upon how William had gotten to be the way he was, what dimension of the universe the Lonsdales were tapping into, and if their growing collection of manuscripts would ever see the light of day. It seemed selfish to be keeping these things to ourselves. One Friday night in downtown Santa Cruz we made a roisterous Three-Musketeers-of-Consciousness vow to someday bring the material out to the world. *One for all and all for one— GO, WIZARD!!*

When I ran into Jade and Rob or Renee and the others, I saw they also seemed to be carrying the talk in the yurt in some place too deep to dredge up. Already that night had acquired the patina of legend. During the July eclipse Atlantis had risen like a breaching orca, then plummeted back beneath the waves.

But not entirely. In August I had a fantastic dream, the kind William mentioned, of flying. Soaring above a summery landscape of bushy green deciduous trees, I rose like a human kite. When I willed my body to tilt just so, I caught invisible energy currents and swooped off in a new direction.

This felt more sense-memory than dream, a memory of using the planetary energy grid like a cosmic trampoline. When I tilted my head I shot through a netting of energetic force fields that hold our planet in place.

As I flew, the landscape dissolved to a bone-colored city laid out like a crescent moon along an aquamarine sea, and I became a gigantic, cyclopean, winged white whale, soaring majestically above domes and minarets. Fresh sea air streamed past as I sailed above the city on a mission.

I was record-keeper.

It was a recording mission. I was using my great frontal eye as a camera to preserve the scene in the Akashic Records, the Book of Soul mentioned by Edgar Cayce and others, said to contain the story of everything that's happened on this planet, and everything that will. I recorded psychic impressions as well as visuals. My vast body stored the data in deep layers of cellular consciousness. When I awoke I could still feel the wind on my cheeks.

Years later at the Berkeley Art Museum I saw colored sketches Rudolf Steiner had made to accompany his lectures from the early twentieth century. I got a full-body rush when I spied a drawing of a winged cyclopean whale next to a note Steiner had made regarding Atlantis.

In September I went to a three-day singing-for-power workshop on the outskirts of Santa Cruz, taught by master voice teacher Mouna Wilson, where we learned to sing from the inside out. Just as the Lonsdales taught inside astrology, Mouna taught inside singing. Instead of stressing vocal technique, I learned to inhabit the place sound is born and to track that impulse through wherever it has to go to stream up and out of my throat.

This work was terrifying and therapeutic. Standing in front of others singing, especially a cappella, without the distraction of instruments, raised so many repressed feelings that it seemed a continuity with Star Genesis, and an even more direct link to the soul.

When my turn came, a buried memory surfaced of a fourth-grade end-of-year school concert when I closed my eyes singing "This Land

Is Your Land." When I opened them at the song's conclusion the whole schoolyard was staring at me and I froze, never learning if I blew the words or what I did wrong, then stopped singing for ten years.

Of course, it wasn't enough to share this story with the group. Mouna made me sing the song again.

Feeling dubious *(it won't work)*, I haltingly began singing *(am I on key?)*, and my voice burbled up from a hollow chamber *(why is she making me do this?)*, sounding young and fragile.

When I made it to the end Mouna asked why I thought they were all staring. I shrugged.

"Class?"

A beefy guy with dreadlocks raised his hand and Mouna nodded. "Dude. Maybe they were blown away by your voice."

I started to protest. *No*, I was going to say, *no, no!—you don't understand.* Then it dawned on me, maybe *I* was the one who didn't understand. All those years I'd been carrying something that might never have happened. Some uncertain trauma had stranded me on the flimsy perimeter of my voice rather than my inhabiting its liquid center. With Mouna on her knees in front of me, stiff-armed hands driving her weight into my thighs, forcing me to stay in my body, she had me sing the song again. As I did, with her tiny powerhouse will anchoring me to the earth, the stone weight in my chest dissolved in the warm sunbeam of group support, and I broke down crying.

I began to sense a pattern, the morphogenesis of a cultural movement emerging in the world, of which Star Genesis seemed to be one branch. Later I came across this in Emilie Conrad's Continuum bodywork, and Standing Wave yoga as well—a teacher who taught only two poses in ninety minutes, focusing on the micro-movement of energy through the body more than how exactly you position your limbs.

From different disciplines the same urge seemed to arise: an urge to release the semblance of what we'd been given and get down to the substance; the need to shed outmoded structures of the past and carve out a life that honors inwardness and authenticity. A world ensoulment seemed to be taking place. In the stars, in the voice, in the healing arts, in the deep energy body of the world, some original impulse was flickering.

To stay faithful to it I became a tracker. My music became a practice to get out of my own way and track the song rising within me. My readings became a way to track soul through the welter of contradictions that is each human life. I became a psychic sleuth honing in on the reasons each of us is born. Everything outer became filled with inner. Everywhere I turned led to the same place. I now had a clear path to follow, but it was a path that didn't exist until I took each step in that direction. It was a magic path.

Calling the Circle

During the singing workshop I bonded with a cute, impish-faced musician named Val, who had a mass of thick dark hair spreading past her waist, and a pretty, rounded, vulnerable, childlike face that took on the look of a Muppet whenever she mugged for the imaginary camera that followed her through her life, which was often.

Val had asked me out a year and a half earlier, but I was with Alison and declined. After Alison and I split I'd asked Val out, but by then *she* was with someone. Now we were both single, and behind the rousing chorus of our workshop I thought I heard the Relationship Train clattering once more down the tracks in my direction.

We went home together that night to Val's studio apartment in downtown Santa Cruz. In bed, my new lover's hair was like a third presence, a creature of mass and scent and history, a thing alive. Val and I had known each other casually for two years and crossed over to lovers in a moment sweet and tender. We held each other after and fell asleep.

Val was well-versed in astrology and knew Sara and William, though she hadn't gotten a reading from William or come to class. She perked up when I showed her my Star Genesis notes. As we discussed our charts we joked around and settled into an easy camaraderie of wit, which had something to do with our Jewish backgrounds, no doubt.

Val had a penchant for puns and mimicry. I had one for situational satire/human folly. In those first weeks, we twisted Santa Craze life around to extract humor from its chameleon-like nature, ever-changing cast of characters and fabled transitoryness. I dubbed Santa Cruz the Almost Town, where everything was always almost about to happen, but somehow few things ever got around to actually happening.

Like my father, Val was a Cancer and had that sign's reputed sensitivity. She seemed to dwell in some remote watery chamber that captivated more of her allegiance than the constant barrage of activities she juggled throughout Santa Cruz.

Compared to my hot bond with Alison, our sexuality was much cooler. Sometimes we seemed more friends than lovers. Instead of getting exhausted by the constant debates I'd had with my goaty girlfriend, though, I had an easy meeting of the minds with my new Cancer lover, and took refuge in the warm familiarity growing between us. Even without superheated passion, however, my will-to-love kicked in: *This one's different. This'll last. I've never felt this way before. . . .*

In early October I heard through the grapevine the Lonsdales were launching a new class. Rob heard this would be different from previous groups. Jade heard we were supposed to bring recorders instead of take notes, because our teachers didn't want note-taking to distract from the direct experience they were now after.

The following Monday, in my old Volvo I drove Val along the winding roads through Bonny Doon onto Comstock Lane, around back near the yurt where I parked. I grabbed my recording equipment and strode through fallen leaves to the cottage. I knocked, walked in and saw we were first to arrive.

Sara hugged me. "We're going to be meeting in here tonight," she said, referring to the living room. "I think we have a few more people than before," she added, shrugging her shoulders and looking at me almost in apology, which alerted me that something was up.

Spotting William's recorder on the wooden tray table in front of the rocker, I claimed a seat on the end of the couch to the right of his seat, inserted a cassette in my machine, and set the microphone.

Little by little, cars pulled up. More and more people arrived, and

Sara was soon busy clearing clutter and making extra room while I went to the inside back porch and found collapsible chairs to put out.

Students drove down from San Francisco and the East Bay. Susannah, the chiropractor from Ross, was there. Contingents came over the hill from Palo Alto and San Jose. Others drove up from Monterey and Carmel until the room was packed.

Loud bursts of talk rose and fell in the din. One young drummer stashed her African djembe and sleeping bag on the porch. The age range was from early twenties to sixties, scruffy hippies alongside well-groomed professionals. Latecomers had to content themselves squeezing in on kitchen counters. Suddenly the sleepy cottage was transformed to Grand Central Station Metaphysics.

Shortly before seven o'clock William emerged from the back hall with a black loose-leaf binder tucked under his arm. Moving half-gracefully, half-awkwardly, as if the crowd fit too tightly for comfort, he shuffled through the room slightly hunched, averting his eyes, talking to no one, looking straight ahead.

Taking his seat in the leather-backed wooden rocker, he arranged his papers, checked his watch, then clicked on the recorder. In a soft but clear voice he said, "Okay, we're gonna do it in about ninety seconds. Ninety seconds, everyone." A battery of recorders switched on. Val and I exchanged a humorous glance: *a symphony of clicks.*

For a long moment our teacher surveyed the crowd. Murmuring died down. He glanced through the living room and kitchen, where more than fifty people were crammed in. The aroma of crackling logs suffused the cottage.

"I find myself right now in a strong place of inward dwelling," he began. "There's a way to live *out* and a way to live *in*. You can live out by being very very alert to everything around you. You live *in* when you're deeply attuned to yourself and the inner worlds of all that's going on behind the scenes. That's the place Sara and I have been in for many days now, and that's the place we're going to be sharing from.

"I want your cooperation, especially in one particular way. I tried to make a few phone calls in this mode and found that to chiropractor's secretaries and people like that, I wasn't coming across. Because I didn't have that ego-voice we're supposed to have. You know that voice?

"The one *RADIO ANNOUNCERS HAVE SOMEHOW COME TO BELIEVE THEY NEED TO USE TO GET THROUGH TO US?*"

My jaw dropped—I'd never seen him shapeshift like that before. The imitation was so spot-on it struck me as more obnoxious than funny, though it produced a roar of laughter from the class.

"I don't have that ego voice tonight," he said, relaxing into his customary self. "So I'd like you to really try to listen, from your inside to my inside. *Brrr. . . .*" He shook off the persona.

"I have a lot to say but can't say it in that harsh, strident manner we seem to think is necessary in order to come across to each other nowadays.

"Especially with all the people packed in here, I want to be quiet. Not really quiet, but quiet in a way, like in a meditation group, or when you're really trying to get somewhere that's important to you. *Please pay attention.* This happens to have everything to do with what we're talking about. It's not just that I'm sort of in this state."

In the long silence that followed I glanced around the room, struck by the diversity of appearances—there seemed no obvious common denominator.

"There's nothing better in life than if you can really listen," said the mage. "Listening is a lost art we must regain. It's the greatest thing in the world. If you want to be a therapist, you really listen. If you want to be an artist, you really listen. If you want to be a human being, or a relationship person, or alive in this world, you really listen. You really listen to the other. You really let them be there, as who they are and what they are—man, woman, child or animal."

William closed his eyes for a long moment. The silence wore on. A burst of wind scattered leaves across the porch. "From now on we're going to enter a new phase of the work," he said, opening his eyes. "A deepening. A mutual discovery process. We'll have to stay inwardly alert to what's unfolding moment by moment in order to track with it."

He tapped the spine of the binder. "These are the Destiny Classes, and they change everything. The book Sara and I have just begun writing is *The Book of Destiny.*" He held the thick notebook up, then opened it and leafed through the pages. "It's different than all our previous work," he noted, "different than all astrology books, different from anything we've seen.

"Everything we've produced for years has been building to this, but this is the thing itself. We've alluded to the new astrology before without bringing it all the way through. Tonight that changes." He placed the book on his lap.

"The first thing I have to say is astrology is a body of thought that bears only a slight resemblance to what we're now doing, which is Star Genesis. Star Genesis is finally presenting itself in full living color, and I can't hold back anymore."

I gave the power sign to Jade and Rob: *Go, wizard!* Rob grinned. Jade gave me thumbs-up. Val rolled her eyes: *you boys.*

"Since we're breaking ground tonight—bringing a whole new system into being—it's helpful to define terms. There are three principles that complement each other: fate, karma and destiny. Fate happens when you follow unconscious patterns without awakening from them. Your inner nature remains asleep, taking a back seat to peer pressure and cultural conditioning. It's the state most people dwell in most of the time. Fate circuits are adaptation-and-compromise strategies that keep things predictably in place, with little room for innovation. External events drive you without you realizing you're giving your power away to institutions and thought forms that have little to do with who you really are. Fate lubricates the World Machine.

"Karma is when you begin to take up your own individual path and walk it, when you first separate from the herd and encounter the law and continuity of your being. When you start to recognize that some pattern other than randomness is at work, that there's a flow and design to things. Going with the karmic grain is far easier than going against it, but there's still another stage.

"Destiny is the most powerful activation of your potential along a coherent, directed path. Destiny happens when you follow—like a projectile toward the future—the rocketing arc of your greater capacity. Destiny is the full-on activation of your creative drive, the pressurized release of your hidden potential shot from a bow like an arrow.

"I know people don't generally use 'destiny' in this sense, but I do. *Destiny is proactive.* It's up to us to activate our destiny. That's the whole point. Destiny's coming to meet you, but you have to meet *it.* Destiny is co-creative. If you don't take up your future, it won't happen. I know this sounds crazy but is nonetheless true.

"The three levels exist concurrently. It's up to us which to tap. Events can be seen from the viewpoint of any of the three, and life will look much different. Most people spend more time in one than the others, but we shift frequencies from time to time.

"By learning to free our destiny from fate and karma, we not only activate our potential, but free up the whole thing for everyone. When one person claims her optimal future, it accesses a channel others can use. Destiny is contagious, the most contagious force there is.

"The object of these classes is to spring our shared future." William hunched at the forward apex of the rocker like a big cat stalking its prey. "We're entering Millennial times. The world's in crisis. The future's endangered." He searched the crowd. "So we're calling the circle. We need your help like never before. We're groping for community. We need to move. We need to hustle. We need to act. We need to bring this material all the way through, and everyone here is the first stage of that. We're launching our mystery school for real now.

"The eclipse class some of us attended three months ago was the stepping stone to this new dimension. We're stepping beyond former codes, strictures and taboos. This is going to be a rigorous class, more rigorous than any we've taught, and quite demanding. It's already asking a lot of Sara and me."

William glanced at his wife, who seemed rock-solid as she sat there receiving his gaze, poised as a yogini. *A sumo wrestler in disguise,* I thought, marveling at this petite woman's ability to ground and center the room. Without appearing to do anything, drawing no attention, she somehow defined the group: the smooth stone in the Zen garden, the solid object contrasting with the flowing dynamism of the raked sand.

The sand-raker turned back to the class. "Tonight we begin a nine-month journey, the typical human gestation period," he said. "The goal is to birth not just a new form of starwork, but a whole new future trying to come into the world, which can use each of us to bring it all the way through."

Val took the cue. "In what sense do you mean 'the future'?"

William regarded her. "Interestingly, the future can be understood as a *place* as much as a time. Paradoxically, the future's a place that *already exists but won't fully materialize if we don't go there.* This is hard to grasp by modern consciousness, which has become too literal. Too jaded. It takes a leap."

"Can you say that some other way?" asked Val.

"For a long time," answered William, "humanity's been busy fending off its destiny, saying 'No thank you' to its greater experience. We've spawned a whole world culture, in fact, whose main job seems to be to prevent the actual optimal living future of our race. That other future, the one we dream of, has gotten stalled at the gates, and all of Sara's and my work is devoted to getting it going again. Each of us has the power to loosen up that stuck future by claiming our own destiny."

"Is destiny an entity?" said a male voice in the back of the crowd, by the kitchen counter.

"Destiny is a force," replied William, "a beingness that's bigger than us, that speaks to us in terms we understand when we're ready to, and is the most powerful thing in the world."

"Is destiny love?" someone asked.

"Love is a messenger of destiny," said the mage. "Love gives destiny its signal strength. That's love's power—it has a way of penetrating jammed circuits of the mind to speak to us in ways we can't ignore. Destiny uses many messengers to get our attention. Love is one of them. Synchronicities of various kinds are another. Inner signal is the way I usually tune in."

Hands shot up across the room. William brushed them aside. "My main point is that destiny is fully co-creative. *At any given moment the future is streaming toward you, but you have to become present enough inside yourself to notice and engage with it.* Otherwise it streams right past you and goes somewhere else, and you fade back to karma and fate, which keeps the false world in place."

After this introduction to *The Book of Destiny,* the Lonsdales revamped astrology from the ground up via the birth chart, which they presented to us as a multidimensional sphere more than a circle. The circular diagram with twelve houses on a sheet of paper, William explained, is the two-dimensional representation of a mystical globe that's actually even more hologram than sphere. They led us on a guided journey through this magic globe that took up the rest of the evening. It was a command performance, and I sat back at the right-hand seat of the wizard and let the tale wash over me.

Sara described the reincarnating process as a serpentine journey the soul takes from the higher, or etheric, dimensions, spiraling down into denser and denser vibration until embodying in the womb.

William talked of light-filled realms we come out of. He said that even after we incarnate back in the body, a part of us remains suspended in those realms—our higher nature.

Sara told us much of our work on Earth is to stay open to those light-filled realms, which constantly offer the muddled parts of us operating instructions on what to do next to align with destiny. She said we can remain in touch with this dimension via intuition, instinct, vision and inspiration.

William pointed out how this incarnational journey is mapped out in each of our charts. He spoke of how the birth chart is a globe entwined with spiral coding of past, present and future; how even the empty chart itself, with no planets in it, can be entered and known by feel rather than just intellectually.

I began to see the chart as a fascinating world of its own, containing past lives, future incarnations, and our optimal path of destiny through all the vicissitudes of life.

William said the left side of the chart is the domain of inwardness; the right side, outwardness. The top, spirit; the bottom, matter. He called the left the Inbreath and the right the Outbreath; the bottom, the Earthly Root, and the top, the Heavenly Crown. He said he was using new names to spring astrology from its mind-heavy, overly mental overlays and turn it into a visionary art.

A forceful planet like Mars, for instance, on the right side or Outbreath of someone's chart would become more so. A person with Mars on the left, or Inbreath, would have a "softer" Mars. Someone with Mars at the crown would have a call to spiritualize their forceful urges and energies. And a person with Mars at the bottom (like me) would have an inner warrior yearning to anchor all the higher forces of the chart fully into the material realm.

Top, Bottom, Left and Right now became Crown, Root, Inbreath and Outbreath, which gave us an innovative compass for charting everything that was to come, and a new language of Star Genesis, both elementary and elegant. Suddenly the age-old science of the stars became simplified into a fourfold paradigm that a child could understand.

For the first time I grasped astrology as a creative art akin to visual arts or sculpture, something I could get my hands on and craft in order to unlock its secrets. An art that, like music or painting or poetry, could be accessed immediately but would take years of soul-wrestling to master. Thus, the most remedial element of all—the birth chart itself—was recast into a crystal ball that could powerfully render the full dimensionality of a human being in a way both utterly simple and profound.

I was glad I didn't have to take notes, because what was unfolding felt so spontaneous it seemed to require the group's full presence to help our teachers bring it to life. But I was distracted by the cacophony of recorders switching on and off throughout the evening. So as class dispersed I approached the Lonsdales.

"What if you and I have the only recorders," I proposed, "and each week I transcribe the tape of the previous class to a printed chapter, which we make available for a small fee? That way everyone can follow our journey, even if they skip a class, and those who can't be here at all can subscribe by mail? That would enable the work to go out to a broader audience."

"Hm," said Gandalf, stroking his beard. "I'm not sure. I've tried things like that before, but the results didn't reflect the actual experience. Something gets lost in translation."

"You didn't have me then," I replied. "After years editing *Comics Interview* I've become adept at breathing life into taped interviews. The only thing I'll need is to speak with you once a week, at least by phone, after copying the raw transcript, to help edit."

"Interesting," William mused, "a book within a book."

"Yes," I said, catching his meaning. "Spirit gives you this *Book of Destiny*. You give a chapter of it to us each week, while I transform the lectures to a whole other book, accessible to a wide variety of readers."

Sara nodded enthusiastically. "This could be the missing link we talked about."

"Okay," the cantankerous wizard agreed after a moment. "Let's try it and see what happens."

As I headed toward the door Sara caught up with me. "I have a good feeling about this," she confided, grabbing my arm. "I have to tell you I think you're going to do something with our work that we haven't been able to do ourselves. William may not know it yet, but don't be put off by his standoffishness."

My curiosity was piqued by her confidentiality. This was the first time she'd broached the subject of her husband's personal nature. "Okay," I said, accepting the challenge. "I'm a writer without a book. And you've got books with no readers. Maybe we can put it all together."

Sara lowered her voice. "William made some vow of poverty in a former life," she confided. "I'm not sure it always serves him."

I waited, wondering where this was going.

"Anyway," she added, brightening, "I didn't make that vow!"

We laughed.

And so I became class scribe. I didn't copy transcripts verbatim but nipped and tucked, inserting subtitles and footnotes, which I managed due to weekly contact with the master. Usually we spoke over the phone, but sometimes we met at the cottage or in town, and I felt my friendship with both Lonsdales growing alongside our professional relationship.

Each week before class I handed out the previous week's transcripts, and later sent copies off through the mail. Chapter by chapter the transcripts grew and my apprenticeship deepened.

As the project evolved, the material seeped into my pores from the threefold experience of hearing each class live, then on tape, then editing. With added insight from private talks with the mage, I advanced rapidly through my post-graduate course in metaphysics.

I began to notice something others remarked upon as well—the peculiar synchronicity of how things we discussed in class foreshadowed specific events of the following week. It was uncanny. Truly, some inexplicable magic seemed woven into this work. William was a genius—on that almost everyone agreed—and Sara was a quiet phenomenon in her own right, but the work itself seemed to be in a league beyond any of us. I realized we were learning many things besides what we were learning.

Even though we weren't studying basic astrology, early sessions included enough technical data for me to finally grasp the mechanics of how William breaks down a chart. From those sessions as well as follow-up interviews with the wizard, I learned a system for identifying which planets in a given chart weigh in stronger than others, and how they all blend. This is huge in the study of astrology, because when you first learn planets, houses and signs it's difficult to sort out who influences what, and how much. Many novices find themselves staring at a birth chart that has Mercury in Gemini in the Twelfth House, for example, wondering if Mercury affects the twelfth house, or the twelfth house affects Mercury, or

Gemini affects both. It can be very disconcerting to wend one's way through the thousands of astrology books out there trying to find a clear course of chart interpretation.

Now that I applied the criteria of identifying key planets and the Four Directions of Star Genesis to my former studies, I gained a strong feel for how to blend planets, houses, signs and aspects into a coherent whole.

Questions on basic technique I hadn't even known I had in the back of my mind now found answers that spawned notebooks of their own. I evolved a step-by-step method to measure the complex factors of each chart that had previously eluded me, and to distinguish themes and counter-themes. My childhood passions of astronomy and mythology now paid off because these are the twin classical roots of astrology. Lessons I'd absorbed from Homer, Virgil, Joseph Campbell and fourth-grade science had equipped me to decipher the complex code of a single human being. I felt like a jazz musician who grew up on classical and later burst out of that tight cocoon into full-blown structured improv.

I perceived how some grand design seemed to have been guiding my life from the start. How else could my teacher and I have made the same six moves across the U.S.? What are the odds of that? At Harmonic Convergence our paths merged, a fact that seemed instrumental to wherever both of us were headed in the future.

As the weeks went by I resumed my former role of devil's advocate because I became conscious of the way certain things we discussed would read on the printed page. I often found myself asking questions I already knew answers for, challenging William to clarify concepts for readers with little experience of astrology or metaphysics.

"The future," William taught one night, "belongs to everyone or it belongs to no one. The whole point of the Aquarian Age is that enlightenment spills from the ancient jurisdiction of the few to the many. In earlier, more authoritarian times the mystery wisdoms we're going to study were reserved for high initiates. Things were much more segregated. There were rigorous initiations one had to accomplish before being admitted through the hierarchy to the inner sanctum. In our day that has to change because we've become a global village, and what affects one affects all. The mysteries must be released to everyone."

True to these words, the Lonsdales ran a mystery school completely open to the public. There were no criteria to get in, no rites of initiation, no one kept outside the gates. Anybody could come and go as they pleased. They didn't even charge money! We got catapulted from Bonny Doon to Cosmos three hours a week scot-free. Over the weeks dozens of satellite members wove in and out of a fairly stable core group of about twenty of us.

Each class began with William reading from the recent chapter he and Sara tapped into. As he read he paused to edify and illuminate. Sara spoke occasionally, elucidating or challenging some bold statement of her husband's. At times they seemed like a cosmic George Burns and Gracie Allen, except she was the straight man.

In the second half of the evening, our cosmic George and Gracie encouraged discussion, and things often became animated and intense. Unlike the earlier group, the new larger classes revealed not just one facet but the whole sweeping cosmorama of Star Genesis, which embroiled us in many rigorous debates. Bit by bit, through dialogue and lecture, like the ancient Greeks we carved a path through nebulous regions of time and space, always coming back to Crown, Root, Inbreath and Outbreath.

When an evening's theme pertained more to certain individuals, they entered the spotlight where they were challenged to reveal their biographies. With increasing self-inquiry the new class gained depth of intimacy. At the same time I grew closer to the Lonsdales I formed other friendships. Val and I grew closer, too, from absorbing the four directions: "Hm, I think this carrot-beet soup is Root-Inbreath," one of us would proclaim at a restaurant. Or, "Santa Cruz is all Outbreath-Crown with no Root...." "I spent most of my childhood on the Inbreath...."

I grew to see the chart as a multidimensional theatre containing *everything*. This radical revision of astrology was hatching a system of thought big enough to boggle the mind, yet simple enough to provide a handy tool for understanding the twists and turns of human nature. The leap I went through when I first learned astrology seven years earlier, I now had to go through again, because Star Genesis was as far ahead of normal astrology as normal astrology was from everyday thought. This was *astrology-plus*, and each week it stretched my mind and exploded my notions of the twelve signs.

Gradually classmates began calling me for readings, and it was both scary and titillating the day I first heard my work compared favorably to the master's. *You can't remain an apprentice forever.*

Bolstered with chapters of the growing book, encouraged by my radio broadcasts, talks and classes, my client base expanded until I was doing more than a hundred readings a year. The beast of self-doubt and financial panic backed a few steps away from my door, and I began to hold my head higher as I made my crazy improvisational way through the wacky west-coast world of the early nineties.

—7

Engagement with Everything

"Everybody talks about the world changes of 2012," said Mike, a blond San Jose cop who'd recently joined the group. "I want to know what each of us can do to make change happen *now*. What does all this mean to me, to my life at present, my wife and kids? What can *we* do?"

It was early November, and scattered bursts of rain pelted the skylight. William thought for a moment. "You have to become a kind of cosmic martial artist. All the pressure of what's most wrong must become something that *starts* rather than stops you. We need to be drawn toward passionate *engagement with,* rather than detachment from, everything." He let these words sink down through the ranks gathered in the warming cottage, most of whose faces were now familiar to me.

"Our political channels have become compromised," our teacher declared. "Our media's been hijacked. Our instincts have been damaged. Our psychic faculties are shut. If you change outer reality without changing yourself it'll revert back. But if you dissolve the barriers that prevent you from aligning with your core nature, reality tends to follow suit. If you heal your inner split, in other words, your world will heal, too. But this has to happen on a very deep level, which is bound to raise your demons, before it's strong enough to work.

"We're talking nothing less than revolution! But, unlike political revolution, which depends on drastic reformation of outward existence, the current revolution hinges on inner transformation.

"When we inhabit our center, when we drop out of surface into core,

113

we gain power to pry our most severe obstacles loose, which we formerly couldn't budge because up there on the surface we were wobbly and had no true leverage to apply. The things we were up against seemed to take on a substance we ourselves lacked.

"But when you drop down and inhabit your depth nature, few things in the world can sway you. You gain an inner resolve that holds you true to yourself and gives you leverage to move mountains.

"Admittedly, this transformation is much easier to discuss than to actually pull off. In fact, it's the most difficult thing anyone can ask of you. I've been working at it for years. Sara and I have been working quite diligently at this, with help from various sources, and are gaining headway.

"For a long time it'll seem like it can't be done. You have to keep valiantly at it forever. You have to keep vigilant. Because there are layers and layers, and each *layer* has layers. You can't ever become smugly convinced of your enlightenment. *Woo boy.* Patting yourself on the back for spiritual awakening is the surest way to plummet to a nest of scorpions. Just when you think you've got it, the gods have a disarming habit of pulling the rug out from under you. Things you swore you got through years ago return with a vengeance on some unexpected new level. But the reward that awaits you for doing this work far outweighs whatever it takes to get there."

"Why does that happen?" I asked. "Why is it that I've already learned so many lessons in love that kick my ass all over again each time I fall in love with someone new?"

William smiled. "You mean the experience where you're alienated from your lover, and you swear that when you see her again, this time you're not gonna fall for the trap? You're going to stay in your clearer, higher state, no matter what gets thrown at you?"

I nodded.

"Then you walk into that room—and what happens?" William scanned the class. *"Wham!"*

People laughed, but I gasped.

Amidst groans and cackles William said, "It's love's job to introduce you to yourself on a level you can't ignore. Until you deal with your own negativity, relationship will mirror it back to you. It's easy to blame your lover until you've been through a sufficient amount of relationships to realize the larger pattern."

Ah. I took this in as deeply as I could, feeling my stomach churn.

Jade raised his hand and William nodded. "I hear and agree with everything you're saying about the need to clear layer after layer and get down to the core. With the support of everyone here it's easy for me to feel the truth of this. But I know from experience that when I leave this room I'm gonna sink back into the mirage. What can I do to stay out of jail for good?"

"If we can just clear a space around us," replied William, "cosmic forces will rush in to show us life's so much more than we imagined. Clearing a space means breathing in, going within yourself, becoming involved with your own magical world, allowing each day to be fresh and new and something different than it's ever been. Wonderful things happen when you approach life this way.

"When you clear this kind of space, then the pressure of not being enough, or not having enough, or not getting enough—enough *whatever* (it doesn't really matter enough what)—gives way to the fact the universe itself is good and true, and life can work right on the most profound levels.

"If you clear this space, despite the crazy tangle of difficulties most of us are caught up in, it becomes evident Earth is positively awash in spirit, and nothing is cut off from anything! This approach taps a way of life that makes complete sense to the inner mind. This is what the soul craves more than anything. If we do this we'll break the paralysis of the species and get on with something infinitely more satisfying.

"Until we clear that psychic space we're yanked by every strong force that comes our way. We lack a center. We get jerked around by rampant collective thought forms."

"I've been applying some of what you're saying for at least a year," stated Kayla, a gardener who'd recently joined us. "But things don't seem to be getting easier." She pondered for a moment. "In fact, my life's more hectic than ever. Right now it's all coming at me at once. I have no luxury to take this higher view you're advocating when daily circumstances force me to respond and respond and respond, just to keep my head above water."

"*Phew.* Thanks for bringing this up." William bowed slightly in her direction. "There's an important principle I forgot to mention. This is key: Once you commit to the work of awakening, you'll catalyze everything in the way of it!

"That's a very crucial spiritual principle which they left out of the *Human-Being Incarnating Manual.*" People laughed. "Nobody tells you this, and it's a crime. 'If I'm doing things right,' says the naive mind, 'if I'm awakening to an enlightened way to be—then why is everything falling apart instead of coming together?'

"*Because when you awaken, the first thing you awaken to is the extent of everything that prevented your awakening!* It's how the gods keep us on our toes. When you de-numb, you're immediately bombarded by every impression you've kept out.

"If your awakening is founded on the deepest levels of your being— if it's a genuine awakening, in other words—it's bound to shake you to the root. In fact, the sign of everything breaking down is the surest sign your awakening is real. It's a test. It's only a test, brought to you by the Galactic Broadcasting System to see if you're paying attention." People chuckled.

William peered around the room. "The False World ain't givin' up without a fight, though. Each forward stride you make will be countered by many seductions backward. Each time you chop the monster's head off three more sprout. Spiritualization of an authentic kind—not the quick-fix variety going around New Age circles these days, but the genuine article—is designed to expose each of your hiding places. Spirit packs a catalytic force that will absolutely shake the hell out of everything. It would have to, wouldn't it? Of what value would a revelation be that kept things in place?

"The spirit path is the flight from the alone to the alone. If you take that road you'll never return. Spiritualization destroys everything in its way, forcing you to grasp something deeper. Sustaining this awakening will ransack you to the gills because spirit is deeper than matter. Matter is temporary. Earth is passing. The sun will die. Everything here will die. All security systems based in physicality must ultimately fail.

"So when truth dawns in a world culture that clings desperately to appearances, it'll shatter everything straight up the middle, to free us from bondage to illusion. Of course! How could it not? How else can deeper reality penetrate? How else can the gods get it through our thick heads that we're here for something more than paying bills and feeding the Machine? How else can the world change?"

William paused as gusts lashed through the orchard, kicking up debris. In the autumn darkness I imagined spirits dancing and howling a couple hundred feet up atop the redwoods.

"The current Cosmic Weather Report," said the mage, "is that we've entered dangerous squalls of long-term high-pressure crisis that can be creatively understood as a major planetary death and rebirth. In your own way, whoever you are, wherever you live, the coming world pressure is asking you to midwife this process."

"How?" I asked.

William turned to me. "By renouncing the deadly dualistic mind of modern man that pits each thing against the other. We have to *negate negation* and claim a fiercely alive creative path through the end-time of a false civilization."

"*Hoo-hah,*" said Blythe, the redheaded Texan who'd been my sweetheart for a short time between Alison and Val.

"Why's this happening now?" pleaded Kayla. "Why are we the ones who have to break the mold?"

"Every five hundred years since five hundred years before Christ," replied William, "a new mystery wisdom entered the world: Buddha. Christ himself. The Grail mysteries. The Knights Templar. The Rosicrucians. We're due for another—*The Post-Atlantean Aquarian-Age Nouveau Arts &*

Sciences (doesn't matter what you call it)—it's here, summoning us to take the truth of the ages into a sufficiently deep enough part of ourselves that it becomes renewed for the living moment.

"We're at the greatest blind spot or greatest pivot point of the ages. Depends on how you look at it. It's either. It's both. It's both-*and* rather than either-or. Our task is to burst forth the soul in an authentic way that sustains the living future. The need of our time is to turn Earth into the place we re-member ourselves. I mean *remember* in the root sense, to bring back into our bodies. If we re-member ourselves we'll seed a new world even as the old one crumbles."

Outside the cottage the rain turned to mist that shrouded the gnarled apple trees. William opened his hands to the room. "Have you ever heard coffee-house discussions bemoaning how the greatest geniuses lived in the past? Where's the current Michelangelo? Where's Leonardo? Where's Rafael and Dante? One time they were alive simultaneously. Where's even one today?

"The answer is: *everywhere.*

"You know the secret hiding place today's avant-garde lurks? The most hidden place of all—plain sight. You know the most cutting-edge modern art? *Life.* Until we find a way to refashion normalcy, we're screwed.

"We need Monday-morning Michelangelos, Leonardos of daily existence. We must become each other's Muse. We must seize the vast creative potential in simply being alive, and push that and push that and push that till the stuck world loosens. We have to get as obsessed with ordinary life as the greatest artist was ever enamored with her creation."

"That's hard to do," said a doe-eyed girl sitting cross-legged on the floor in front of the couch, "when our culture's gotten bogged down by addiction to material things."

William looked at her for a long moment. "The biggest problem with modern human beings," he said point-blank, "isn't that we're too material, but that we *haven't become material enough.* We have to first *become* who we are before transcending who we are. We have to get *in* before we get out. We've never been who we are! We're not physicalized. Humanity hasn't arrived! Our full force of human soul is still eluding us. We started to do this at earlier times in history but got sidetracked.

"Incarnation only begins at birth—to make good on it we have to become twice-born, have to die to all we used to be and engage existence with the full force of an awakening soul. Or else we lead a diminished life accessing a mere fraction of our cosmic inheritance.

"Physicality holds a great secret we need to uncover. The truth is we don't yet truly know Earth or love or sex or cosmos, because we've been looking at all these things from the viewpoint of a half-manifested, half-alive species.

"Earth at this point is the most scarcely inhabited planet. We're hardly material at all! There's no population problem. In fact—nobody's here! We lead an impoverished existence. We float like disembodied spirits. Nobody meets. Nobody engages. Nobody has intercourse. The barest surface of us brushes the surface of life, and as soon as things get heavy we head for the hills. The gods threw a paradise and nobody came!

"The only reason Earth turned into a place anyone would ever want to get out of, though, is because humanity has never fully arrived. Things look much different when you do, because life becomes different when we enter it this way, and because we become different. We change life and life changes us when we have deep intercourse with it.

"Arrival is a long-term process bound to raise everything in you that thinks it can't be done. Arrival means wrestling existence into something that actually works rather than pretending to. It means busting your ego, catching yourself at the sly ways you evade, negating your negation, escaping your escapism, calling each particle of yourself to meet everything rushing to meet you without flinching, without making excuses, without reducing, without limiting, without turning away.

"We don't need to transcend life, get past life, get outta life, but *experience the full-force, broad spectrum of life from a position of wholeness and integration.* Each time a person does this the world changes. Each time anyone claims their full multidimensional presence, they midwife the

Living Green Earth fighting to emerge from the corpse of the past, and usher in the future.

"If you persist and persist and persist beyond all reasonable expectation, with naive determination, to arrive through everything that arises, you'll crack the mass trance state and meet the new life force regenerating at the center of this absolutely sparkling blue-green planet, and the world will change."

"Easy for you to say," protested Kayla. "You're an astrologer. You found a way to live your dream. You spend your days dealing with people already halfway there. What about the rest of us who have to work each day in the *real* world?"

"It's even more crucial for you to pull this off, because you're further embedded in the Machine than I'll ever be. Everyone who works in the system has an incredible opportunity now to become a double-agent of the soul, an infiltrator with the capacity of looking normal while secretly going about the work of Change. Find the secret creative tunnel through the midst of what's boring."

Kayla stared at William, unconvinced.

Our teacher raised an eyebrow. "It's true that when we look at everything in the way of change, love, and peace, things are an unholy mess. If we believe what we see, there's a lot of evidence to support the theory we'll never learn. We keep making the same asinine mistakes through history. Truly, it's beyond belief! What devil keeps humanity smashing its head into the same brick wall over and over, when we know better? What dark double has taken over mankind? Who put the aliens in the White House?"

People laughed.

"But, we have to realize, that very mindset of us never being able to learn itself keeps the whole thing in place. Something's gotta give. To change the world you have to believe the world can be changed."

"But how can mass consciousness ever become enlightened," Kayla pleaded, "when so many of us are caught up in survival from day one?"

"That's a myth," replied William. "Survival, I mean. I don't think there is such a thing. I don't think it exists. I think survival is one of the biggest current fallacies. I don't think anything survives. I think everything *evolves*. I don't think anything is interested in maintaining, but in growing, groping, challenging, changing.

"Change is the biggest constant in the universe, which means even when you seem to be the same person day in, day out, year after year, you never are. Never! Your body isn't the same. Your thoughts aren't the same. Your cells are constantly changing. The whole galaxy revolves, and there are millions of galaxies. Not a single thing in the universe is in the same position it was in when I began this sentence. Earth never returns to the same point in space. *It's only the human mind that gets caught in a rut and then views everything from that position, which makes life seem like a rut.*"

Seeing he wasn't getting through to everyone, William changed tack. "Granted, there's a lot of obstacles to Change. 'There's always been war, there'll always be war,' say the experts. From that flat, bleak, jaded viewpoint of experts I agree—we may as well croak." He said this in such a Ralph Kramden-y voice that it got a sardonic laugh.

"But you know what? Earth herself has a different point of view. Oddly enough, She seems to resent the notion our planet would be better off without us. That notion is a dangerous delusion hatched in a dark corner of the human mind that gets no support from Earth or cosmos.

"The truth is that without humanity Earth would be barren, forsaken. Far from wishing us gone, She yearns for us to enter more fully into Her. Like an outrageously beautiful woman sick to death of having men flirt with her without consummating, Earth longs for humanity to end its endless courtship and come in, come in, come all the way in, and stick around this time, so the two species can finally have deep intercourse, cross-fertilize each other, and give birth to the future. And we long for the same thing.

"When one of us conquers his resistance to fully showing up, fully meeting everything here to meet him, Earth rejoices. Spirit surges to our aid. And the reward we get is what mystics call The Pearl of Great Price—

the magical potency life becomes whenever a human soul awakens. Like a precious gem formed by a grain of sand irritating the digestive tract of an oyster, when we allow the things that most torment us to bring us *into* life rather than pushing us out, we gain richness and value that can't be taken away.

"The greatest longing of the human race is not to *ascend* but *incarnate*. We want to go *down* more than up. We can't be free of this world till we give heart and soul to it. We can't transcend materiality till we become material. We can't get *out* till we get *in*.

"This is the great riddle of our time, which modern spiritualists tend to get backwards. New Age doctrine is fixated on white light, transcendence and ascension. If I had a hundred bucks for everyone I've given readings to who comes to me hoping I'll tell them their real home is on the Pleiades, and this is the last human reincarnation they'll ever have to deal with, I'd be sittin' pretty."

People laughed—me loudest of all, because I knew firsthand exactly what he was talking about.

William went on. "We've screwed up pretty badly along the way, I admit. Anyone who studies history has to despair at the odds of us ever learning. I mean, *sheeesh*, boy, we have blown it, haven't we? We have really really blown it. . . . " He shook his head dolefully, and the spirits of the room dropped a few notches.

"And yet, Earth still holds a place for each of us to claim our full-spectrum presence in the midst of her fertile fields. Don't take my word for it. Try it. Try one ounce more of showing up each day and see what happens. See how life responds. See if life says, *'I see you, brother. I see you and I raise you.'*"

From that night on our classes took off, rocketing the mind to other dimensions, places and times, which our mad professor fleshed out with such verisimilitude that I could believe he'd been there. When he talked of ancient days he described them like a gnarled old man might describe the distant city of his youth. He spoke not only of what historical peoples did, but of how it felt, how it smelled, how they thought, how they got to be the way they were, how each stage of civilization flows into a great progression which the Lonsdales said is being assisted by spirit forces whom they referred to as Destiny Architects. Once again I wondered how William came by such knowledge.

As weeks went by, we were guided through the ins and outs of a cosmology that permeated every part of our lives. We discovered planets, houses and signs in a way that brought them to life for everyone, whether they knew astrology or not. We launched an ongoing Socratic dialogue that flashed a search beam through many dark corridors of history and culture.

Sometimes William seemed to be under pressure to convey the import of the material he and Sara had tapped into on previous days, and it took noticeable effort on his part to launch the class. Other times he seemed to be laboring under some other vague strain.

I began to see that many of the things the Lonsdales were bringing forth were being given to them only one step ahead of us. They were midwives and we were doulas. They plunged their hands into the thick of a newborn cosmology, which we got to wrap blankets around and coddle on the winding road home. I barely had time to acquaint myself with each new phase, even with my additional exposure editing tapes and doing readings and meeting privately with the master, when Monday came and I was called to attend another delivery.

The key element of this new cosmology was its inclusiveness. Each of us, with our glaring imperfections, stubborn ego and thick-headed resistance to change, nonetheless came to feel we had a special place reserved for us in the grand design, a role to play, a task to fulfill, a destiny to follow.

I got the impression all our lives were converging at a rich junction of ages that might never happen again. Maybe it was ego; maybe it was only *my* world rather than *the* world that was changing; after all, I was getting the mysteries handed to me for free in a way that provided classical apprenticeship to my craft. But I don't think I was the only one who felt this way.

As word spread that something unique was going on in Bonny Doon, more and more people were drawn to the cottage. From San Rafael in the north down to Big Sur in the south, and east across Silicon Valley, students arrived on the wizard's doorstep.

We came, most of us, to learn cosmos but ended up learning *life*. We tackled the toughest questions of all, mind-numbing riddles that plagued mystics and philosophers through the ages: the paradox of predestination and free will; the nature of life after death; the meaning of good and evil; why humanity doesn't learn from its mistakes; how atrocious things can happen in a world watched over by higher powers.

When we bumped into each other around town we lit with the recognition that we were on a shared cosmic pilgrimage. Even though we came from different backgrounds and had different lives that required different solutions, we were also bound together as a band of souls seeking to crack the code of human transformation. Through it all I absorbed as much as I could, corralling the mage with questions, poring over each new chapter late at night, reading class transcripts aloud with Val and others, probing deeper and deeper into the mystery.

2012

—8

Dancing with Death

By early December, a couple months into the Destiny classes, a few of us realized something was up with the Lonsdales. Lately they seemed to be struggling with a burden.

One Monday evening William handed the reins to Sara. After spending a moment gathering herself, she took in the full scope of the class gathered in her living room, then drew a deep breath. "I'll start by saying that if I weren't in front of this group tonight I'd be in bed," she began. "It's amazing I'm even sitting up in this room. I don't know whether to start at this end," she mused, "or ten years ago, at thirty-six, when I discovered the *Course in Miracles*.

"I sat in the closet of my home in Auburn, California, with the door closed: 'I don't know anything.' 'Everything I see is not what I'm seeing.' 'I know nothing.' Erase everything. Open to a completely new world. Over and over I did that.

"I had created for myself a family and community. I was even kind of a pillar in the community, a Waldorf teacher. I had a child and a husband—not William—whom I'd known for years. We'd grown up in the same town. Things were real tight and tangled. I'd created a fully functioning life, which people looked up to me for, that had nothing to do with me. So I latched onto *Course in Miracles* and began to clear away and clear away in order to get to something real.

"Okay. Then, a couple weeks ago I went to a surgeon and had a biopsy because I had some problems with my breasts. He said, 'Well, yes, you have cancer. I'd like to see you Monday morning and on Wednesday we'll get rid of all this. We'll give you a double mastectomy.'"

The group gasped like one gaping organism. Val clutched my hand with a look of horror and clung to it painfully. The intensity of her clutching made it difficult for me to gauge my own feelings. I had a hard time digesting Sara's words. After swallowing dryly I pried my fingers away from Val's, feeling the shot of Novocaine spread through my chest.

Sara went on. "That's the quick-and-dirty method of Western medicine: *We'll cut it off*, ya know?" She shook her head in disgust. "That day I found out for sure I was dealing with this so-called life-threatening disease and was gonna have to do something about it right away, thorough and complete. So I related back to that time at thirty-six when I was clearing everything away. Because in that time, too, I had to immediately take stock of everything, take my life into my hands at the exact moment of completely surrendering it. Now the same thing's being asked of me on a much more intense level, where I haven't yet connected with my own strength of will.

"I've learned that with cancer, the spirit isn't completely aligned with the body. They're needing to come into alignment. So I've been engaging myself on a very deep level these last few weeks, deeper than ever, to get to the bottom of my chronic self-division and root it out. It's the most difficult thing I've taken on. Just last night I became fully aware of what's actually being asked of me—and it boggles my mind.

"I have a profound choice to make now: Am I gonna let my attachment to the False Earth completely burden me with all the difficulties of this snarled-up world? Am I gonna get further snarled inside myself? Am I gonna let everything going wrong now completely pull me apart?

"Or am I gonna strengthen that spirit side of me that's been coming on and coming on since thirty-six, so that it finally comes all the way into the rightful place it's been striving to get to?

"Because I'm dancing with Death. Now. Here, tonight, in this room. I'm doing a mamba with Death right beside me. And so you see I have tremendous motivation to take up the spirit side. Everything William and I have been doing for years, all this information we've been bringing through from spirit since the Harmonic Convergence, has suddenly become very *real*. Even if I never got there before, I have to get there now, even if I don't know what 'there' is."

When Sara coughed then paused to clear her throat, the class hung on every move. "So,'" she continued, "the doctor said, 'we'll take care of that for you—we'll cut it off.' And I said, 'No, thank you. I don't want surgery.' He said, 'I hope you know you have your life in your hands.' I said, 'Yeah, I do. I have my life in *my* hands.'

"But, I can tell you—I *don't* have my life in my hands. My life is entirely woven in with spirit, with greater cosmic beings, with karmic patterns, incidents that go back to earlier lives where I first gained propensity for this disease. I'm taking full responsibility for myself now, to break out of this half-realized state I've been trapped in for so long."

When group ended that night I walked across the porch with Val, recalling my visit to Bonny Doon two weeks earlier. I'd asked Sara if she wanted to drum with me in the redwood grove, and she lit up like I was offering the key to the universe. *She already knew. She's already changing.*

The following Monday, haggard and hoarse, William told us he'd undertaken his most comprehensive chart work ever, an exhaustive study of Sara's complete nature and past lives. He'd spent sleepless days and nights penetrating deeper and deeper into her psyche.

That evening Sara introduced us to past dead selves she was getting in touch with—unintegrated parts of herself she'd unearthed in the ongoing depth excursion her life had become. She considered these subselves to be karmic characters left over from past lives. She viewed each as if it were an independent being with an agenda all its own, linked to its own time and place in history, which Sara had managed to unearth through years of diligent exploration along the spirit trail. She said these recalcitrant characters had been haunting her from the sidelines, often sabotaging her greater intentions, and she was now ready to take them on directly.

Her attitude galvanized me. I didn't know what I'd done in past lives to create the strange brew of love and dislocation that chased me through the world, but I knew something down there ate at my wholeness. *Stranger in a strange land,* the mage had said in Ross, ... *never the home team ... never on your own turf.* Silently I prayed for Sara to win this fight, not just for her, but because if she prevailed that meant I too might claim my own true place in the world.

She told us she wanted to bring these subselves to light in front of our collective witness. They each had a name. One was Rocky—an armored muscle-bound oaf who rushed to protect her from some threat or injury that might or might not be real.

After Rocky had his say, two more subselves took over one at a time, declaring in their own words what they thought of this whole thing. This performance was arresting and convoluted and eerie, and left me in awe of Sara. Along with using extreme methods of alternative medicine to confront the symptoms of her disease, she was tracking dysfunction to its lair, excavating her entire root structure and staring straight into the bloody jaws of all she disinterred.

"If we come back life after life," asked Ken after witnessing Sara unravel, "what's the purpose of death?"

"The biggest thing we need to know about death," said William, "isn't really about death itself. The reason we fear and resist death is because we haven't yet learned to *live*. We sleepwalk through life as the Unborn Species. From this half-alive state, death's job is to awaken us suddenly, irreversibly to the fact we're not yet alive. The most crucial thing happening inside Sara right now is the same thing rumbling in the core of our species. We're being asked to die so we can finally live.

"Due to various factors she's uncovered and owned traumatically-miraculously in the last few weeks, Sara has failed to show up in life after life. This does not make her unusual. What makes her unusual is she's stripping that resistance now, layer by layer. The result is ... I have to tell you"—he peered into the room—"I'm witnessing the most powerful transformation of a human being. Sara's process is to find something lodged deeper inside her than all that's rushing to meet her now, and

despite the odds, she's doing it. She's really doing it. It's quite something."
Husband and wife regarded each other with a long, poignant look.

"As for death itself," William turned back to the class, "that's a whole
other thing which we're not going to fully understand till we begin to
fathom life. Death itself, originally, was not a bad idea. Death isn't something bad. In fact, it was one of the greatest ideas of the universe!

"Death is a system of digestion that eliminates layers of karma which
accrue during the course of each incarnation, easing the amount we then
have to tackle in our next life. Death gives the soul a break from the rig-
ors of the world. It sends us back to commune with source before once
again picking up the threads of our greater reincarnational purpose."

He thought for a moment. "The main thing that dies at death, actually, is the necessary fiction we maintain that we're these limited beings.
We kind of have it backwards. In order to be born, the soul goes through
a tremendous death. We die to the *all* to be born to the *this*.

"While we're alive we maintain a necessary fiction that that's who we
are—you know, that person looking back from the mirror? We really
think we're Joe from San Jose or Sally from Santa Rosa. Lost in our mundane awareness, we forget the cosmic side of the picture. We forget we're
Everything pretending to be Joe. We forget that our soul spirals down
from infinity to assume Joe like an actor assumes a character.

"Do you remember? Do you remember the time before time when
you chose yourself? Do you know this nature you possess is a borrowed
vehicle, a temporary construct your soul acquires to make its presence
felt in the world?

"This guise of personhood is necessary," continued William, "to enable
us to do the job we took on when we agreed to reincarnate. We all have
reasons, even if we don't recall them, why we come back. We each make
prenatal vows, two or three key projects to accomplish in accordance
with the needs of Earth and spirit.

"Even though most of us forget these vows, they're the most binding
force linking us to the physical plane. These prenatal intentions remain
at work beneath everything we do. They're our prime mover, our oper-

ative force, our very reason for being, which the deeper part of us *doesn't* forget and constantly seeks ways of holding us to.

"At death, this construct of personhood falls away, freeing the soul to return to essence, to resume our cosmic journey unhindered by physical constraints. We get a past-life review, learning how our previous Earth existence fits into the greater scheme of our larger reincarnational journey. We merge with spirit.

"So death is a greater birth to our fuller solar-cosmic nature, really, just as birth is a death to our fuller nature. Death releases us from a vehicle too constricting to accompany the next stage of our journey.

"My view of reincarnation differs substantially from traditional views, and differs as well from the neo-hippie view, which is a kind of generic rehashing of Hindu-Buddhist cosmology. Some views of reincarnation believe we do it to work off karma from previous lives and perfect ourselves, so we can end up in nirvana and never have to come back. In other words, *we come in to get out.* That idea never made sense to me. The idea that resonates deeper in me is that we don't come in to get out, we come in to get in!

"In between each life, our soul slips out of the body back to the etheric anyway, so why the rush? Why would repeated life on Earth be a device to get us to higher planes, when we come from higher planes and will ultimately return there anyway?

"Instead of viewing Earth as the booby-prize souls get relegated to when they can't access heaven, I see life as an arena for the full awakening of spirit in matter. This is the monumental task Sara's taken on, and it's astounding to see what she's doing with it. She's not just doing it for herself, though. Full-spectrum incarnation isn't a selfish act. Existence needs Sara. Earth needs all of us. Earth needs each of you to show up, now more than ever, because we've run out of other options. Earth wants *you.* You know, like those old recruiting posters with Uncle Sam?

"But here's the catch: Earth doesn't need you to just show up generically—Earth needs you to show up fully, personally, idiosyncratically, entirely in your own way, authentically, genuinely, constantly, which is something you can't know beforehand but have to find each moment all over again, especially in the hardest place of all. That's what Sara's taken on and I am simply in awe.

"Who would ever attempt this if they didn't have to? Who would even begin to risk this much unless they had absolutely no other choice? In this way crisis is our greatest ally. What Sara's doing now, many layers down, even as she sits there with that beguiling Virgo look on her face, is fighting to arrive fully in the physical plane. And, let me tell you, it's absolutely contagious. When one person breaks through they can't help but haul others along with them.

"As you can imagine"—William glanced at his wife—"the state we've been in lately in this house is indescribable. Things have turned inside-out. Semblances are falling away. Spirit leaks through everywhere. A reversal is taking place. Cosmos is funneling into Earth. Everything is being formed of spirit, till there's very little *us* left. It makes it hard to do things like talk to landlords or teach a class." There was a sympathetic chuckle.

"We're inviting each of you to join us in a radical process of mutual discovery of what it means to be fully alive here and now. Not just tonight but always. Not just in class but everywhere. Things are coming to a head and we must quicken to meet them.

"Granted, it's not easy. This is no longer a normal astrology class by any stretch of the imagination. But, if you wish to engage this depth process we would like to help you with it, because that's what we've just dedicated our lives to—the ineffable journey of essence."

"This is my first time here," said Lee, a mountain of a woman with poofed-up flaming red hair. "And my initial impulse is to say, 'Yes!' But I want to know what I'm getting myself into. What's the object of this journey?"

"The benefit of journeying with us," William replied, "is that you'll jerk yourself out of the Trance of Normalcy and engage your deeper nature. You'll strip away layers of conditioning and get to who you really are inside. This journey is bound to push your limits."

"I believe in homework," Val interjected. "Is there something specific you're asking us to do that we can work on after we leave here?"

William turned to her. "That's an excellent question." He stroked his beard. "The path from detachment to engagement is via inspiration and enthusiasm. You have to shift the dead weight of a culture that crushes our sheer exultation at being alive in a hopeful, ever-changing universe. Give yourself the benefit of the doubt something extraordinary is happening. Pay attention to subtle cues that life is so much more than it seems."

"The key piece," added Sara, "is trusting yourself. Beyond all voices of self-negation. Learn to intuitively trust the deep affirmative voice within you that's there even when you don't listen to it. And stay with that always."

William nodded. "And, it turns out, trusting yourself does not mean imposing your way on everyone. It does not mean falling for your own glamour. Trusting oneself does not mean believing one's trip. It doesn't have anything to do with imagining one is omnipotent, omniscient and omni-wonderful. It doesn't mean any of that.

"It's rather a state in which you trust your free becoming, your right to claim a vital creative existence in this world, and to offer it up the moment you find it." He snapped his fingers. "You trust your right to fully become who you are, and you trust everybody else's right too.

"You enter this volatile state, and open to it and open to it and keep opening even as you offer it to the world. Enlightenment isn't yours to keep—it's only yours to share. Like the old song—*Love is nothing till you give it away.* Regardless of who you are, this process will engage you the instant you engage it."

Val said, "When we speak about 2012, are we talking about this kind of awakening for all humanity or for small sub-groups?"

William considered. "There's a ripple effect. The momentum builds if a certain wave of souls awakens. If they go through these doorways, then everybody else is suddenly not very supported in their assumption that it's impossible. If the awakening is fast enough and clear enough and strong enough, then everybody can't regroup immediately and forget the whole thing, like they did after the sixties.

"Remember? Remember how in the seventies we came down with a massive case of amnesia that love and peace actually happened?

"If small pockets of society catch this wave, it frees the whole thing for everyone. Eventually the world can't help but notice."

William rose to put a log on the fire. When he came back he flipped the cassette in his recorder then sat back in the rocker. "In this room right now we're seeding the future. From small outposts scattered on the fringe of mass consciousness, we will infiltrate the mainstream. Consciousness is pooling together. There's strong spiritual support massing up. The soul of humanity's crying out for something *real*. You can feel this building all over the world. We just have to stop stopping ourselves a little and get on with it.

"Understand—I'm actually advocating something simple rather than complex. So simple it's hidden in front of your nose. We don't need to concoct some elaborate program of learning a whole new skill; we simply need to *stop stopping* ourselves. When we stop stopping ourselves, a deeper beingness automatically engages. When we strip cultural conditioning away, life fills with force. When we fail to keep cosmos constantly at bay, it surges right in."

Val asked, "Can you say more about how we stop ourselves?"

"What's the stopping?" William glanced around the cottage. "It's actually an evasive maneuver. We hide from our higher awareness because it seems to ask too much of us. We hide from our greater nature, our future self.

"The hiding is a reflex action coming from the part of you that knows a terrifying secret, which is that you're being constantly pursued by a being who has greater love and wisdom than you do, *who is you*. You're being relentlessly hunted by your future self, who is honing in on you like a Tiger of the Spirit. Like an absolute Tiger.

"And, as this greater being leaps out of the grass straight at you, it says, 'You, who you think you are, *ain't*, and you're gonna have to allow space for who you really are to come through.'

"Which is not gonna be easy, because you're gonna have to humble yourself fantastically to be able to receive someone who's a little more in touch with eternity than you are. Enlightenment is always much more terrifying to the little self than ignorance, because ego knows it'll get obliterated when your greater self takes over.

"And so we hide. You dodge your destiny. You hide from your greater self inside a kind of astral envelope, or soul-coating, made of stories you tell yourself. And all of those stories are about to amount to nothing because they're not true. *Do you know the stories you tell yourself are not true?* See, the one who hides also *lies.*

"Oh, we don't lie blatantly in some extravagant style. That wouldn't be too cool. That would become obvious. We lie subtly, constantly, pervasively, with the idea that all we're doing is being realistic. We tell ourselves a constant litany of stories that boil down to: 'I'm this limited being who can't do much of anything in this impossible world and it's all getting worse and *blih!* and *blah!* and *bother!* and *humbug!*'

"But it's a lie. The Scrooge in us is the biggest imposter of all. He's about to get busted, though. The jig is up. But it takes a great turnaround, a great reversal to awaken to these stories, because we think it's some other force doing it to us. It's them, you know—the famous *THEY?* The jerks next door, my idiot neighbor, the cancer, the boss, the billionaires who run the world, the moron who cut me off on Highway 1 this morning. . . ." People laughed.

"As we approach 2012 we'll have less support for prolonging these constant stories we tell ourselves, in which we're the victim of all these insidious conditions, and if only they'd stop we'd be *ollie ollie um-free.*

"It turns out that in this whole scenario, you're actually making up the story. Clients bring me stories all the time, and few are as intriguing as the ones I tell myself. Sometimes, in fact, it's a beautiful story! It's a wonderful, compelling, fascinating story you're making up to avoid facing the deeper part of yourself."

"So, coming out of hiding," I conjectured, "means climbing out of your stories. If you want to change a world, change its story."

"Exactly," said William, raising his index finger.

"Then we're in need of a new story," I thought aloud. "The whole world needs a new story that can get into us deeper than the old story, the story of us never learning, the story of us never loving, the story of there always being war and rape and something wrong somewhere. We need a modern mythopoetic tale of magical realism, a Creation Story that transcends the broken old pieces of our race, drawing the human soul back to the Campfire of the Ages. We need a new story to empower us to change this world into the place we know it really is."

"And to create that," William snatched the baton, "you have to deal with one insidious opponent of evolution—the human mind. *Ooh boy* . . . You see, you have a lot of evidence to back up your stories. A lot of factual experience. A lot of historical layers of story you inherited from people who inherited stories from whoever raised them. By this point here in the muck of the ages it's real thick. There's a thick, gummy karmic goo swirling with negative assumptions, hard to dislodge, because they seem like common sense. Because it will look so reasonable, you know.

"On the surface, you see, *your stories don't sound like stories.* They don't appear to be flimsy concoctions of the little self that keep the whole thing in place. On the surface your stories look like life. They play rationally and realistically rather than as the deadly obsolete thought forms they really are.

"Everyone around you *loves* to support your Tales of Limitation because that supports theirs. Your stories have so much evidence supporting them, in fact, that you may almost be excused for not recognizing that they're draining the wonder from life.

"Compared to the stories you tell yourself, in fact, this idea that there's a whole other existence waiting for you, a whole other luminous being inside you, that idea itself will seem like a crazy story. I mean, what I'm saying is crazy! Isn't it? Isn't it just gonzo to think there's a star-being at your deepest core who can remake the world?! Isn't it bizarre to contemplate love and peace? What kind of trip is that?"

"So how *do* we climb out of our stories?" said Lee.

William acknowledged her. "Awakening from your hiding places entails a great transition from mind to heart. It's not enough to find a new story to supplant the old. You have to effect a huge paradigm shift away from the self-canceling mindset to a very open state that can crack the doorway to something entirely different.

"This kind of awakening is the wave of the future, not limited to special-interest groups, but available to all. It's contagious. Dropping into the heart, you contact a power that's positively infectious because the soul craves it and the world body is ready for something new. Across the planet the urge for change is rising and may eventually do the impossible and uproot the dead weight of the past. Until that happens we have to give ourselves the great benefit of the doubt.

"And, let me tell you, being that open is the scariest thing of all. It's much less threatening to remain closed. It's far more prudent, says racial wisdom, to not hope. What I'm saying will scare the bejeezus out of your little self, who'll interpret what's being asked as *Structures Threatened!* ... *Structures Threatened!* ... *Structures Threatened!*

"To climb out of obsolete stories, you have to de-numb yourself, which feels harsh when the state of everything already being far too much to deal with has caused you to numb out in the first place. That's what Sara's cancer is doing for her."

Lee perked up. "Forgive me for saying this, but does it take the prospect of death to awaken us, or is there some other way?"

"The best methods," replied William, "are inspiration and enthusiasm, because the peculiar brand of shutdown we've fallen for in recent time is the stuff-your-soul-to-make-a-buck version. People rush to punch the clock of a life nobody in their right mind would wish on anyone. You have to stand up for true nature in a world where that's not prized, recognized or acknowledged. You've got to follow gut instinct instead of buying into society's rules of engagement.

"Enthusiasm is the main instrument the gods use to bring us back to ourselves when we've gotten lost. And inspiration is the gift when it's gotten a little further along its path. But enthusiasm has to be real rather than hyped."

Hands shot up across the room and William nodded to me. "If humanity has always been presided over by greater guiding beings," I postulated, "then what was the purpose of us needing to get so lost? What higher spiritual need has it served for us to forget who we are and build a world around *that?*"

"The short answer," replied William, "is that we got a bit too full of ourselves in a certain way, in Atlantis. We lost Earth and have been trying to come back ever since. But even that was not totally off-track. We had to get lost in matter, had to forget how cosmic we are, in order to learn Earth. We had to step out of heaven into physicality. The whole point of our Current Eternity System is to see if the higher essence of the gods could be stepped down into a form conveyable into the low regions of dense material existence. Can Love come down that far and still awaken?

"It's just that by this point we've taken it a little too far, gotten *so* stuck in Earth that we've lost cosmos and now have to remember who we are on levels many layers thick.

"This drama of separation is maxing-out at this time in history to launch something beyond the drama. We've got to get past the endless posturing of a culture that *sort of* works, a love that *almost* satisfies, a job that *ain't half-bad*. When we talk about 2012, we're talking about a new start for the human race. We're talking about opening the stuck gates of the future, the first of all possible futures for the world, not the last. We're talking about achieving a *beginning*. We need a good beginning now more than we need anything.

"After 2012 there's a lot more to come. This is the great task of our time—opening the stuck gates of the human mind to the immense possibility of life on Earth actually happening. If we do this then everything else can come to pass. The whole point of our time is to seed an appropriate future for our species, with enough momentum to counteract the dead weight of the past."

When class ended it spawned a further round of discussion with people standing around in clusters, gravitating about Sara, though I could tell she didn't want to speak of her cancer in any kind of poor-me way, so I waited for the clusters to dissolve.

"Hey," I said, as she was about to walk out of the room.

When she turned to me I opened my mouth to say something significant but found myself tongue-tied, so I hugged her, resisting my urge to clench. *If you squeeze hard enough you think she'll never leave?*

—9

Wheel of Colors

"You talk a lot of Atlantis," said Nancy at the next class. "How do you know so much about it?"

It was mid-December 1991, a chilly evening in the Santa Cruz Mountains, four years to the day since I'd met William. The woodstove doors were open, the fire roaring toward full strength in its cast-iron box. I registered the new tone of sobriety in the room out of concern for Sara, who was sitting on a cushion in front of the couch with her back to me. Impulsively I reached down and rubbed her shoulders before realizing I'd never touched her like that. When she uttered a little moan and leaned into the touch, I continued.

"Okay. I can't put this off," William confessed. "I've got to tell the story behind the story." He and Sara glanced at each other, and I felt a jolt pass between them.

"Seventeen years ago, in the White Mountains of New England, I had a dream," he said softly. "At that point I'd spent years searching for a deep astrology that spoke to my heart and soul. In one way or other I'd worked through every major astrology the world had to offer. I learned method after method while crisscrossing the U.S. to see if anyone had a vision worth sustaining.

"I lived in communes in the northeast and southwest. I dropped in on Charles Manson's group, before they did the things they became infamous for. I saw the Grateful Dead play the Fillmore. I attended the first Human Be-In in Golden Gate Park. I dropped acid. I befriended the top

Western astrologer of the twentieth century, Marc Edmund Jones, and his co-genius, Dane Rudhyar. Jones took me on as his apprentice and taught me esoteric astrology methods that never made it into his books.

"Jones's great innovation, which he achieved in the first half of the twentieth century, was to free up the medieval context of the birth chart as *fate,* and view it instead as *potential.* This fit with the times. Jones revolutionized astrology for the psychological age, priming it to later usher in the sixties. Jones's big revelation, along with Rudhyar, liberated the chart to be an indicator of what *might be* rather than what *is,* because what *is* is a product of many things besides the chart. Suddenly astrology was revitalized, as it has been periodically through the ages, and back in vogue.

"Even with all my searching, and with these two intellectual giants in my corner, though, astrology failed to give me what I sought—a living, breathing, vital, supercharged link to cosmos. All the star work in the world amounted to far-out concepts that pointed me toward something that I just couldn't get to. I sensed there was something more out there calling me but I couldn't find it. I couldn't shake my gut feeling that astrology was a dead dinosaur. It kept promising something it never delivered. I had no clues of anything else to go on but my gut.

"Then, in the autumn of 1975, in Franconia, New Hampshire, I had a dream. I found myself inside a great gold room. A kind of gold that doesn't exist anymore, pure light of gold. Golden essence we were bathed in. I dreamed my way back to our first civilization. I found myself in the Temple of the Sun, in the high court of Atlantis. I was the Star Seer, the wise one, counselor to the king. The king brought me in to read the souls of two women.

"Here's where the dream gets interesting: I take from my cloak a timepiece, which I put in the palm of my left hand, a small disc. This etheric timepiece is the heart of the dream. It's a multidimensional disc I hold up to each woman to read her inner nature.

"To use the device I have to steer clear of bias and let the inner nature of each woman speak to me. As I do, the timepiece streams with twelve etheric colors that swirl into a living pattern. The moment I saw these lifestreams, worlds shattered. The person living in northern New England in 1975, who had exhausted his study of the world's outer astrology and was busy plunging into mundane consciousness, shattered.

"When I held the disc in my hand I knew it like I've never known anything. And more: I suddenly knew who I was and what I was doing, on so many levels. I saw past lives. I saw what got me from there to here. I saw worlds rise up and give way to other worlds." William leaned forward and held the rocker in place. "And I saw something else—I saw that my dream was not a dream."

After a moment, he released the chair and sighed a deep sigh. "In the actual progression of events, what I had to do was to read the timepiece. If you were to just look at the disc you'd see streams of extraordinary, protoplasmic swirling colors—as though the instrument were alive. To read it I had to dive right through the swirls to the center of this cosmic clock.

"I put the timepiece to each woman, I pierced through the center of the swirls, and I read them." He closed his eyes for a long time and the house was silent.

"In order to grasp the meaning of this dream," he continued, "and what it did for my life, you have to understand one thing. The best way I can describe it is how I felt when I awoke.

"Now, I have magical dreams, astounding dreams. I've probably had a hundred life-changing dreams. But I've never woken up in that state. When I came back from this dream I was changed as we rarely are by our dreams. I'd gone back in time and merged with an ancient self to such an extent that I could not fit myself back into the tight clothes of my customary being, *ever again.*" As he said these words our teacher searched out our faces.

"I was compelled to seek the source of my dream, to follow where it led. And where it led was through the heart of the colored swirls to the Twelve Lifestreams of Atlantean Astrology, the original mystery wisdoms that later became the twelve signs of the zodiac as we know them today.

"I was taken on an inner journey through the twelve colors, which drew me deeper and deeper into so many worlds that had been forgotten. Words cannot describe this journey. In fact," he said, raising a bushy eyebrow, "I'm still on it. I've never quite returned.

"That journey led eventually to total recall of my past lives. I now know who I was in each. Sometimes I wish I could forget," he added, glancing at Sara, who held his gaze until he turned back to the class. "Before tonight I haven't mentioned a word of this in public. I couldn't, until I'd spent decades testing it." Sara nodded.

"The real reason I'd searched the world's astrologies so assiduously," he continued, "was because all along I'd unknowingly carried a body of wisdom that was the genesis of all subsequent systems of human knowledge. I'd carried star wisdom from the dawn of the world."

After a long moment he added, "The power of the Atlantean Zodiac streamed from the Temple of the Sun through the ages to the me I was in New Hampshire, a kind of intellectually bloated/life-force-weak me, a pale William who, you have to understand, had had no connection whatsoever with *beings*, with *Atlantis*, with past lives, other than a vague understanding of these things." He paused, then looked to the orchard where the yellow porch light illumined eerie silhouettes of fruit trees in the gloom.

"I'm having the oddest experience," he confided. "It's a funny reverse echo, where each thing I say echoes *before* I say it. Hmm. Oh, that's it." He snapped his fingers. "I'm experiencing a pre-echo, because when I emerged from my dream I found myself with the bizarre ability to remember the future from the past. It's a very strange sensation, which some of you have had without knowing it.

"You see, in the high court we were clear enough to gaze through the future to today's world, not in a hazy way, as with modern clairvoyance, but concretely, with no blurriness or question. In fact, we saw this present time back then more clearly than we do *now*. Because in those days we saw everything very intimately, unlike how we do now, living at a great distance from things."

Seeing that some of us were having trouble following his train of thought, William switched track. "Atlantis wasn't just Atlantis, you see— that's another way to put it. Atlantis was all times, one of two main instances, along with the ancient Mayan period, where we rose above history and saw straight through the ages. It's hard to imagine such lucid clear-seeing these days, even for me, and I'm fairly clairvoyant. We've come to doubt our inner eye and place all emphasis on outer vision. It wasn't like that then," he mused wistfully. "And so, after many lifetimes of forgetting, I *remembered.*

"I remembered my initiation. I remembered the hidden meanings of the stars. I remembered being taught to read souls. And I saw that the full force of these ancient lifestreams was still completely encoded within me, and could revitalize my whole approach to astrology and to life itself.

"When I awoke in Franconia I felt as though the golden touch from Atlantis was back with me after many centuries—and do you know how that made me feel?

"Scared to death! Because it meant I was going to have to work very, very hard for a long, long time in ways I could scarcely begin to imagine, to become worthy of even talking about these things. The glaring impurities in my character immediately became painfully obvious. I mean, compared to that gold, I was seriously flawed. I was about as ready to inherit this mantle as I was to fly to the moon! I knew what was being asked of me but couldn't do it. I was young, that's the point. Saturn Return.

"So, I had to spend from that autumn day in 1975 to this day in an intensive process. I had to spend almost twenty years living deeper and deeper into the wheel of colors to find out how to use it.

"This dream is what led to Sara and me communicating with star beings at the time of Harmonic Convergence. It's what gave me the peculiar way I look at charts. It's what the whole system of Star Genesis is based on, along with the astrology of Rudolf Steiner." William's gaze locked with his wife's, and they seemed to acknowledge the ritual significance of the moment.

At last, the magician reveals his tricks. So many riddles I'd had for years about how my teacher was able to see what he saw now fell into place. *He sees through a wheel of colors. He penetrated the mysteries of Time.*

"So," said William, "you may be asking yourself, so what about this? What *is* this? What about this timepiece? What does it mean? What value does it have to the world?"

"One thing it means," he continued after a moment, "is there's a twist we must go through to put things right.

"When Atlantis fell, the original mystery wisdoms got twisted. The psychic arts that arose in the post-Atlantean world are watered down. The astrology practiced today is a thin distillation of the original. We worked the mysteries much differently then. They were absolutely primal, closer to a starving man's need for food than an intellectual concept, which is today's approach. We couldn't exist without higher truth and we knew it. We had no ego about this—this was before the development of ego, which came much later and has now taken over everything. The mysteries were just plain fact, like food or water. We couldn't live without them.

"The twist we must go through is this: all other astrologies I've ever come upon are consistent with each other, but the Atlantean zodiac disagrees with them all in one simple respect—the sequential order of the signs. This is why it's taken so long for me to talk about it. I never knew how to present the twist. All other zodiacs go Aries, Taurus, Gemini, Cancer, Leo, Virgo, Libra, Scorpio, Sagittarius, Capricorn, Aquarius and Pisces. And this one goes Taurus, Virgo, Sagittarius, Pisces, Leo, Aquarius, Aries, Libra, Capricorn, Cancer, Gemini and Scorpio.

"Yeah, I know," said William, looking into blank faces and raising his hands to fend off protest before it occurred, "it blew my mind too. I was an astrologer for years at that point and had studied very hard all that the world of astrology had to offer, and had no notions there was anything wrong with the customary order. None at all. But that's the way the lifestreams lined up on the Atlantean disc, and there's no way I was gonna forget the power of that. It took me years to fathom the reason for this sequence.

"Meanwhile, I had another problem. I mean, *why me?* Why was I picked to stand up and say the emperor has no clothes? What were they thinking?"

I laughed.

"Understand, I spent the large part of those years conceiving of myself as a major screw-up and, with hindsight, I have to say I was largely correct. I can hardly tie my shoes, even now. And I'm the guy who's supposed to remake existence?

"But, I realized, in the final analysis it didn't matter. The fact I barely had my head screwed on just meant that I, like everybody else, was a flawed vessel, but a vessel nonetheless. I had to learn to use myself, regardless of my obvious shortcomings, regardless of all my neuroses, as a conduit for something greater than me. So I tried this new zodiac on for size.

"And what I learned, over the years, is that the Atlantean zodiac describes an *inner spiritual progression* more than a literal astronomical one. It encodes the lost path from Earth to cosmos and cosmos to Earth. It follows the precise journey each soul goes through to get and depart from here, the spiral journey of incarnation, death and rebirth. Because this was the high Atlantean art—mapping the path from spirit to matter, and maintaining a link with those realms while being present in this one.

"And as I studied this new zodiac I learned that something funny happens when the soul hits the Earth field, shortly after conception. The cosmic contents within us become swirled, like a photo-negative image of a galaxy, a spiral-vortex action. The soul is turned upside-down and inside-out. Everything we've retrieved out of cosmos is scattered to a different pattern. Just about everything becomes what it wasn't. Earth *is* exactly what cosmos *ain't.* We're on the other side!

"This wasn't a problem in days when we understood there was an inner sequence, a spiritual dimension underscoring all life, a direct link between the tangible and intangible. Since then modern thought, including astrology, has gotten stuck on the outmost semblance of things rather than their inner core.

"Our culture has abandoned its link between spirit and matter, and based itself on semblances, which is delusional. We suffer from a peculiar modern delusion known as the Idolatry of Appearances. We worship idols. We think things actually are the way they look!"

A slew of hands shot into the air, but William quelled the mutiny. "Before you get all worked up over the two zodiacs, let me first acknowledge something. I understand the normal astronomical sequence of the constellations. I recognize the planets still revolve through that seasonal zodiac in their orbital progressions. That still continues. Sara and I are not denying any of that. That traditional zodiac exists. It's valid. It has its meaning and value. But it's not the way things *are*. It's the way things look."

I shook my head at the twists and turns.

William went on. "The Atlantean zodiac has immense power but one very staggering implication, which is: if you're upside-down and inside-out, if you're in that kind of strange conundrum, it means most things we experience in this Earth are extremely *other* than they are elsewhere.

"Not just some things are a little screwy, but *everything* here is Alice-In-Wonderland- or Through-the-Looking-Glass-oriented. Like a fantasy novel. We've gotten marooned in a book. We see things in a mirror. We're scrambled. Reality has become so twisted that we have to *twist the twist* to get back to something normal. We have to hold a mirror to the mirror to get accurate reflection. That's what the Atlantean Zodiac does."

The faces of my fellow students revealed a mixture of enthrallment and confusion.

Sara leaned forward. "I used to teach Waldorf kindergarten, Steiner-based, and we'd play the game 'Sally Go Round the Sun, Sally Go Round the Moon, Sally Go Round the Chimney Pot on a Saturday Afternoon'— *Boom!* And everybody splatters. We were playing getting born!—mimicking the incarnational journey of the soul. Ring-around-a-rosy. Or 'all fall down': London Bridge, all those nursery rhymes about spinning—'All around the mulberry bush'—are really reenactments of what kids go through to get here."

I shook my head—leave it to Sara to find some childlike explanation for advanced metaphysics.

"Yes," said William, "in fact, on this level there are stories and stories. There are a lot of stories about this. Not even *about* this—some are perfect incarnations of it. Some are in a science-fiction vein. Most are in a fantasy vein. Some are in a fairly straight vein but then they go crooked. You know, they seem to be just thrillers or romances or regular things and then they flip on you?

"Why is there a convention in fantasy stories that you have to go through a wardrobe? Or have to have your consciousness suddenly twisted around, or some tornado has to hit? Is that just a fancy device to make you lose your bearings, or is there some remembrance? Do stories have real remembrance in them? I mean magical stories, not all stories—ones that touch the heart.

"I grew up on *The Twilight Zone,* the mass market TV-ized version of this, which indicated to a lot of kids in the sixties that everything around here's a little screwy. We're the corkscrew people. The twisted ones. In fact, we're so turned around that the main reason cosmic beings have difficulty manifesting to us is because they have to go through the most incredible trouble to not blow our circuits!

"Because when you're used to shadows, light is pretty intense. It's the most intense thing of all. Light blinds you. They're not permitted—the highest beings—to blind you, so they have to shrink down to almost nothing, like we do, to get here. *Ha!* But when we shrivel down to almost nothing to arrive, did we just do that? Can it be that we live off our rocker, inside-out, without ever knowing it?"

Rob asked, "Are there other worlds on the same sort of twisted journey as our world?"

William scowled. "You gotta pay your penalty here. This is the prison world where they put the convicts—no, that was a *joke!*" He scrunched down in his seat and raised his palms to fend off the backlash. "I only said that in order to bring this stuff up from where it's hiding in our subconscious, but I don't really mean it. My joke was to reflect our fears and doubts, in order to clear them.

"The truth is you have to be a *very ready soul* to volunteer to be alive in the body at this time. Everyone here in the flesh now needs to be. Every soul is being summoned toward awakening as we approach 2012, because we're on the verge of something the whole universe is rooting for: *The Long Overdue But Fully On-Time, Much-Disputed Arrival of the Human Race.*

"The process is quickening," our teacher explained. "Ages ago people used to spend far more time in the etheric and less in the physical. It used to take anywhere from five hundred to fifteen hundred years between lives for souls to reincarnate. In recent centuries it dropped to three to five hundred. By the late nineteenth century, one hundred fifty. Nowadays, the period between lives can be as brief as thirty to fifty years, in rare cases even less.

"This means the tremendous amount of evolution souls used to handle in the interim between lives has shifted to material existence! Instead of tackling our growth in astral planes we're doing it all here on Earth, which is wild to consider.

"This is a key signature of our times with profound ramifications. As magical as Atlantis was, and ancient Mayan times, and Celtic days, in some ways we're living in the most magical age of all, because everything is pointing toward *us* now. Earth is the new hot spot where everything gets worked out rather than spirit. That's why everything's become so gritty. We simply don't have enough time to work things out in the etheric anymore. We gotta do it here and now with each other, moment by moment, in real time. That's what's behind the accelerated feel of our era.

"This isn't all positive news, mind you. It used to take ages to get at the entrenched karmic stuff that now comes up on the spot. Everybody in this room has a lot to deal with simply to be alive, much more than our parents had to, and incredibly more than our grandparents. And it's going to get more so, because that world our parents were born into is *gone*. We can salute it or mourn it; retrogressive elements of society can yank hard in a futile attempt to bring it back; but that world's gone and we have to push on toward something new.

"You can see evidence of this in children coming in now more than you can see it anywhere. These kids have no patience to wade through karmic gunk their parents used to take forever to get at. Life's accelerating. Evolution's quickening. Metamorphosis of the species. The strangeness of the brew is just right to seed mutation. The balance of forces is raw and volatile. We have a good edge to work with. It's the best and worst of times.

"The bright side is we have tremendous karma to burn and can get through things faster than ever. The down side is there are very few rest periods anymore! Humanity has now become the greatest schooling this cosmos has ever known. Pure unadulterated absolute School of Experience. Hard knocks. *Everything* here is lessons.

"This isn't the only game in town, mind you. All those other worlds are far more sublime and fulfilling. At this point, in fact, Earth's the draggiest world ever. That's about to change, though, because something's about to happen that's never happened anywhere in the whole Eternity System: *the heights of spirit are about to awaken in the depths of matter.* The soul of humanity is about to recognize itself in the least likely place of all—the dregs of history."

"I've been studying spirituality for thirty-five years," said Barbara, one of the elders of our group. "What you're saying about freeing ourselves from illusion is no different, really, than what saints told us throughout history. What makes you think people are going to start listening now?"

"Because," said William, "when saints and avatars gave us their higher wisdom, we hadn't bottomed-out yet. We were still plummeting through the fall of the ages.

"After the cosmic heights of Atlantis we had to sink through every layer of Earth we'd transgressed, deeper into history, deeper into the animal, plant and mineral kingdoms, deeper into reincarnation, deeper into genealogy, deeper into all the thick stuff of ego and matter we're so bound up in now. The karmic plunge of our species had to ground out before we could gain traction to resurrect. Sara and I were shown in a recent tap-in that the actual bottoming-out occurs within one turn of Uranus around the sun (the planet of revolution) from 1930—discovery of atomic power—to 2012, Age of Aquarius.

"We're at bottom now. Visionaries and prophets offered us higher truth many times, but they told us while we were still on the way down. We couldn't act on their wisdom till we'd completed the fall.

"Their attempts weren't useless, though. Bits and pieces got through. But mass consciousness itself had far too much inertia to be turned around until it landed. We're in as deep as you can get, which paves the way for resurrection. Resurrection is primarily an internal job and secondarily external. We have to awaken *ourselves* to awaken our world. We have to grasp the fact that life is so much more than we've been told. Even in a time of great deceit, deep force lies buried in the soul of the species, aching to come out.

"We have one great obstacle to overcome: fear of our power. We're terrified of the light more than the darkness. Because the light holds you to it. The light demands you live up to the new view of you it reveals, which can be blinding when your eyes are used to shadows. After centuries of living a lie, we now fear our power more than anything because it won't let us off the hook.

"Also, we carry an unconscious memory of what happened when we abused our power the first time, in Atlantis. But we've run as far as we can from ourselves till there's nowhere left to run.

"The purpose of our current social system is to reflect the extent we've gotten marooned outside ourselves. But if we release the vast soul force within us, we'll get back to something we started way back at the beginning, and follow it through this time.

"That's what Christ came to show—that regardless of how torturously devastating it is to become achingly, totally, ravishingly present and potent and alive and real—that we can and we must and we will. And until we pull this off in the most impossible place of all—the bottom of our long fall through the ages—we'll never be at peace."

"Can you say more about Christ?" Helena asked. "I grew up Catholic and would love to have another way to think of him." Murmurs of commiseration spread through the room.

"If you were around when Christ walked," William said, warming to the subject, "unless you tuned in you saw *nothing*. He didn't walk around beaming cosmic rays. You saw a street person on the sidewalk in San Francisco. You didn't notice a thing. You kept going.

"But, if you tuned in, you may have noticed a tiny spark arc up and out of his chest into your chest—an offering, which, if you took it, began like a homeopathic drop to change your entire nature and the nature of every one of your lives for all time.

"It was a spark of *Thou art*. It was a spark of *Be. Be the you that you are. Just be*. Everything's a disaster. You're being nailed. Nothing is what it's supposed to and *be*. Just be. *Just be who you are. Just release every particle of resistance to being fully alive and present right here and now. Just be.*

"We need this spark now more than ever, which is sleeping in the heart of even the most tuned-out human being. Christ was one of a dozen or so people who walked Earth free and clear. He didn't start that way—he earned it. He carved a way to be which proves that no matter how excruciating the pressures of incarnating become, we can draw a force of soul right up the middle to meet and match every obstacle, and then some.

"The reason the Christ story lingers so keenly in mass consciousness after two thousand years, when there were a hundred other marketplace messiahs in those days who have long since been forgotten, is because we haven't gotten the lesson yet. We haven't imitated him, haven't followed his lead.

"Outer Christianity thinks Christ came to uplift mankind, but his real achievement was opposite—to bring God down in one impossible consecrated deed that resounds through the ages, which makes Christ more significant as a carpenter than a teacher. He nailed spirit into matter. He performed a pure embodied outrageous act of love, which blazed the most direct path of incarnation from heaven to Earth. Since the time of Christ, the path to enlightenment has been downward into full engagement with matter, rather than up and out into the blue, like many New Age teachings dangerously advise.

"To self-embody we need to honor the highest law of manifestation, which states:

You must not do anything to extinguish the creative spark in self or other, and you must do everything in your rightful power to preserve and enhance the creative spark in self and other.

"See, our normal way to deal with the heaviness of the world is to get lighter. But there's another way, the shamanic path down, which is to *get heavier than the heaviness,* crack through the ground you stand on, and thrust your burden off by sheer force of presence. That's the depth journey, the Christ path, the Cosmic Christ. Notice—I'm not talking about *Christianity.* I'm not talking about what's been *done* with him; I'm talking about the man himself, as described by Steiner, who was a time traveler.

"That's the power of Leo, the sign I ascribe to Christ—the power of true selfhood, the power of a fully awakened 'I'. And since Leo is the opposite of Aquarius—the shadow of the coming Age—we have to get Leo in order to get Aquarius. *We need to individuate before we can merge.* We need to humanize before we transcend. We can't get past ego till we fulfill it. This is a very Western viewpoint, I admit, very non-Eastern, but then I come purely out of Western mystery tradition."

"I'm sorry," said Ken, "but I tried the self-glorified approach in my younger years and you know where it got me? It created such chaos that I'm still trying to pull my life together from then."

"Let me clarify something," William said. "When you fully enter selfhood, you become the opposite of egotistical. When you claim selfhood on the level I'm describing, you free it. I'm not advocating the self-filled self but the *selfless* self. We're not being asked to dominate the world with separative ego. That's already being done. That's not selfhood. *We're being asked to so become who we are that it's no longer an issue.* We're being asked to develop a transparent form of selfhood. We're being asked to show up in such a way that we become vessels for a greater force of destiny to act through us.

"Self-mastery doesn't necessarily explode across the sky in blazing colors. It doesn't have to. That's not its deeper nature. Its deeper nature is inward clarity. Its power is in receptivity. What it does is *to offer.* It offers others to partake of the same thing within themselves. As soon as you do this, the world begins to change."

Margie, one of the few students who'd been to both sets of classes, asked, "Why has it taken so long for the Atlantean mystery wisdoms to return to mass consciousness?"

"Because we're in emergency," said William. "We're in crisis. The future's at stake. For a long time the world's been poisoned by false consciousness that's reached epidemic proportions. Human beings have become distorted caricatures of themselves. Politics is farce. Education is blackmail. Food has become poison. Media is distorted. America is drowning. Down deep we all know this but have become numb to it. When you live in a censored state, when you live a shutdown, distorted, numbed-out version of yourself, the most telling feature is *how much you don't know it.* We're so shutdown we don't even know we're shutdown!

"This dark delusion that passes for normalcy is actually a heavy mass trance state that persists until something—usually crisis—yanks us through, as with Sara's process. It's one reason people turn to drugs— an attempt to detrance the trance by finding yet another trance. But when crisis passes or drugs wear off, we revert to the main trance.

"At our current stage of evolution," William continued, "you don't get to freedom by always being free, always being infused with cosmic joy-juice, always flitting around the galaxy radiating bliss. No matter how seductive that hypnotic New Age picture is, that's not the way to freedom. When you twist yourself around to fit into this twisted world, then get *untwisted,* you become free like no other being anywhere."

Our teacher turned to his wife. "I've been witnessing the most amazing miracle—Sara's regeneration-healing-restoration process. In the last few days there's been a quantum leap. The only part of one's nature that can do this is the absolute core force of one's innermost being.

"When you harness the resistance of everything massing against you to incarnate the full presence of the Radiant One inside you, you conjure a force of love stronger than all the hate of the world. You Christ. You resurrect. You become twice-born. Sara's calling upon this force now, to resurrect out of her trapped state into her unlimited nature.

"We've been told in a recent tap-in that, like Sara, humanity has to virtually self-destruct to resurrect from a deep enough place. You have to be forced to this point where you have no more margin left, individually and collectively, before the pressure's great enough to force the change—which is where we are now. *Between 1987 and 2012 the destructive impact of humanity peaks out so it can resurrect.* The world's getting worse in order to get better."

2012

—10

Where Is Love?

Val and I sank into a quagmire. We couldn't meet sexually and didn't know what to do. We'd tried everything from abstinence to gentle touching, to sensual massage, to Taoist sex practices, to counseling, to invoking the full force of my desire, and none of it brought us one step closer physically. It was as if there were a skin around her I couldn't penetrate—an invisible hymen. I found myself in the unenviable position of being emotionally bonded with an alluring woman whom I couldn't get sexually intimate with. Our mutual passion for Star Genesis highlighted the awkward truth that we met on astral planes more than physical.

"I know our relationship can handle cosmos," Val declared, "but what about *toast?*"

We decided to go to Harbin Hot Springs, where I'd been getting away to since the mid-eighties and found myself vibrantly renewed every time. Harbin's land and water contain a healing power nothing short of miraculous. Many times through the years I've seen cuts and bruises heal within a fraction of their normal time from soaking in the mineral-rich waters.

I longed to immerse myself in the spring-fed pools, especially because Santa Cruz was closing in on us more than ever. Val worked two part-time jobs besides her career teaching singing, and I had to content myself with dribs and drabs of contact that felt dissatisfying and left me hungry for more. Each time my deeper passion arose it had nowhere to go.

So we packed our things and drove over the Golden Gate Bridge, north through the wine country, past Calistoga. Cruising by the vineyards I felt a surge of anticipation. Harbin is a "clothing-optional" resort open three-hundred-sixty-five days a year, twenty-four hours a day, the way churches used to be: *sanctuary.* Any hour with no reservation you can enter the Garden. In my mind I was already sinking into the geothermal waters even as I drove the winding country road up and around the mountain.

We pulled to the front gate, paid and parked. We unpacked in our room, showered, and walked up the hill to poolside. Lake County's air—the cleanest in California—was so sweet that it felt euphoric simply to breathe.

I was here to see if I could make Star Genesis real. Could I incarnate a version of myself so inwardly alive it would burst the barrier? Not just remove the barrier between me and my lover, but also the veil obscuring the face of this lifelong goddess who taunted and teased and tormented me by dangling luscious fruit in front of me that I could not sink my teeth into and swallow?

"Have you ever had *watsu?*" Val asked, referring to the water massage that originated in the warm pool at Harbin in the seventies and spread through the world.

"Many times. From getting so much of it, I learned to give it. I can work on you if you want. . . ."

"That'd be divine."

We disrobed and walked down the flowing steps to the large contemplative warm pool. A handful of nude bathers were sprinkled between our end and the smooth gray branches of the graceful fig tree overhanging the far side. Some were talking quietly while others stretched, or stood meditating.

Holding onto the steel bar that runs across the length of the pool, I floated in the enervating currents. *Two days of bliss.* "Ahh." I took a deep breath, then, wrapping my hands around my knees, closed my eyes and sank into warm bubbly silence.

After a while I made my way to the far end and walked up the short fanned staircase to the enclosed hot pool. The warm pool, like a large swimming pool, guards this much smaller echoing chamber. I entered with a sense of reverence, observing the "Silence" sign above the altar.

Whispering was tolerated (within reason) in the warm pool, but the hot pool was more like a chapel.

Below the sign, the stone bust of the Harbin goddess with long thick wavy hair was adorned with seed necklaces. Someone had pressed a yellow rose petal in each of her eyes. Like bright flames, the petals flickered eerily behind steam vapors rising from the pool, as candles on the altar uplit her enigmatic smile. Over the years the goddess's expression changed, depending on how eroded she became from the mineral waters, or perhaps on where I stood in my love life. Today she looked so much like Sara that I couldn't imagine why I'd never noticed it before. All serene on the outside, with a deeper fire blazing within, her face shone translucently in the steam as I paused to pay my respects.

In the late afternoon, muted southern light slanted down through the stained-glass windows high on the terra cotta wall. I walked down the stairs into the hot pool, steadying my exhale in a long even release as I sank into the immense heat and my feet finally found the bottom. *You've done this before; you're not gonna die,* I told myself, willing my body to draw its attention from the point of contact where the heat seemed unbearable, in to my organs.

In the depths of this dank sanctuary my muscles relaxed, then my organs, then my mind, and then my breath. *Ah, heaven.* Steam rose off me and a couple bodies on the other side that blurred into misty silhouettes.

I turned from the others and pressed my chest into the shoulder-high wall where I leaned my head on my arms, closed my eyes and released a deep sigh. Amidst the damp heat and scent of ozone I became entranced by the flow of water echoing all around me. The spring pouring into the hot pool mingled with gentle splashes from the warm pool and the steady gurgling of the cold plunge above.

When the heat grew too much I latched onto the horizontal bar, swung out, and walked around the corner, up the cement steps and then down the short immersed stairway into the frigid little cold plunge where every molecule in me snapped to life. Gasping, I sank to my knees on the pool floor in the frothy water and leaned my elbows on the cement, letting the chill currents invigorate me. I gazed over the stone bench to the milky statue of Quan Yin nestled against the base of the spreading fig tree.

Bond me to the heart of Earth, I prayed. *Release my illusion. Dissolve this lifelong barrier between me and the Goddess. Open my heart. Deliver my Love. Let me in let me in let me in. . . .*

As my body relaxed, the cold began feeling hot, and I climbed out and walked back into the warm pool, where I found Val.

"Want me to float you?" I asked.

She nodded then whispered in my ear, "What should I do?"

"Surrender. I'll catch you."

She closed her eyes and went slack, and I caught her under the shoulders and waist until she was floating. With flowing strokes I danced her horizontally in sinuous motions, starting small, slow and subtle and working my way toward larger, more emphatic wave motions. I used the water as an active force. Together we teamed up on Val's body as I grasped the back of her head, holding her hair, and weaving her body back and forth through the currents.

As Val surrendered to the dance she moaned, dark hair spreading along the surface of the pool like an enchanted mermaid.

I worked for a long time, feeling trapped energies shudder through her as they released. Then I sat on the pool ledge and lowered her onto my lap. During the watsu I'd gotten aroused at her undulations but had repressed my desire because we were in public, and because I wanted her to sink into the womblike state water massage produces. She sat on my lap swaying lightly in the cross currents.

When she opened her eyes minutes later silent tears were falling. My heart swelled, and I felt the urge to make love to her.

She leaned over and whispered, "Can we go back to the room?"

"Yes," I said, throat hoarse with desire.

Languidly, we climbed out of the pool and donned our robes. We walked downhill to our room and lay on the bed dripping. We kissed and began touching, until I hit the barrier. My immediate sensation was anger. I'd been through this so many times—when would it end?

I swallowed my irritability and put my hand on her heart, hoping to use the force of my lust—or even my anger—to burn through. We ended up having intercourse, but it was only partially satisfying for me. Afterward I felt I'd lost the bliss attained in the waters.

This pattern continued the whole time we were at Harbin. We'd already talked about this so much that I was talked out. Once again, I couldn't get in or out of a love I'd created. On the drive south I felt physically replenished but emotionally drained.

Back home I pulled the transcript of my reading in Ross to find which way to turn when love was stuck: *You're basically at odds with yourself,* the master had said. I wondered how much of this had been cleared in the four years since. *Fighting to emerge from a sea of unbelonging onto solid ground.* Was Val the former or the latter? *You carry a shadow from the past that poisons your well.* How could I get to the root of this and weed it out? *Get down to an authentic way to be and stay there no matter what.* I wondered if that was possible in this love.

If every outer reality reflects an inner, what inner need did I have to manifest such torture?

I leafed through the manuscript: *Stop running. You can't let yourself get sidetracked.* Maybe this wasn't about Val. Maybe it was me. When is it appropriate to drop love's problems and walk away, versus digging in for another round? In which direction lay my optimal destiny?

Relationship is your "Keep-You-Honest" arena. Everything you'd rather not deal with and would rather get away from keeps coming up and coming up and coming up to meet you there. Until you resolve your underlying split, every love will turn out the same. I remembered how pissed I was when William said this, but now saw how prophetic it had been.

Had I gotten anywhere at all in four years? Was I evolving or running around in circles? What was love trying to show me? That there was still some kind of barrier between me and myself? Was I going to have to let go of Val to find my power? Was I going to have to let go of yet another love?

The truth, bubbling just below my conscious awareness, was that I felt miserably trapped in this relationship. Val was beautiful, funny, and creative. She had a marvelous open mind. We shared radical politics, spirit, astrology. She played music and sang and we talked and joked and studied the stars and laughed. But on some deeper level I couldn't find her, which prevented me from finding a part of myself. Stymied by this riddle, I thrust the pages aside.

The only remedy I could think of was Ecstasy. At our most stuck point Alison and I had taken Ecstasy, invented by Marin therapists to help couples dissolve emotional blocks. It had worked, even though we eventually broke up.

So I suggested Val and I go on a day trip with the intention of conducting a private visionquest. She agreed. A week later we drove to Big Sur and found a sheltered spot in a small cove on the beach. It was unseasonably warm. We spread a green army blanket next to a tall stand of beach grass and sat facing each other while the sea wind blew.

I held a milky green-and-white chunk of rainbow fluorite which a Puerto Rican shaman had given me for my birthday. "I want to get clear about what we're doing with each other," I said. "I want to break through this passion block. I want to make love with abandon and meet you in the flame."

I passed the stone to Val, who said, "I want to inhabit my core and align with what's being asked of me in this relationship. I want to get out of my way and open to love."

We swallowed the capsules and went exploring, my ceramic doumbek hanging on a woven strap over my shoulder. I was feeling good, opening to life, recognizing that existence is so much more than I make it. Once more I'd gotten crumpled; *didn't you learn that on the mountain?* Instead of remembering I was Everything pretending to be Mark, I'd gotten lost in another unrequited-love story.

Have you learned anything? What good are these teachings if you can't use them? Why do you keep doing this to yourself over and over?

Shaking my head to clear this debate and come back to the present, I paused and waited for Val to catch up as we walked a trail to the beach. I lowered the doumbek into position and began drumming a zydeco beat that she hummed to.

"There—" she said in a way that made me start. I thought she was pointing out a snake or something, but it turned out she was trying to get me to change the rhythm. At first I was annoyed—one more thing I didn't seem to be doing right for her, one more place I felt controlled by the feminine rather than met by it. But as the Ecstasy took hold my irritability dissolved, and I saw she wanted to compose a song to my rhythm and needed only a slight alteration to make it fit what she heard in her head. I switched the accent of the beat and she sang:

God is playing marbles with the planets in the sky
We're all kinds of marbles, everyone. . . .

As she sang and I drummed we danced around each other, snaking across the sandy sinuous path all the way to a large radiant madrone tree, which we circled flirtatiously. The tree took on the aspect of a red-tinged goddess, beckoning.

With a mischievous look Val threw her shirt off and hopped onto a taut wine-colored branch effortlessly as a bird, and I laughed, seeing her move that fast. As she nestled into the trunk I saw a new version of my lover: Years fell away and her face shone with dazzling light, nubile and erotic, as if all the lust stored up since adolescence unveiled itself to me beside the pounding surf. Topless, Val became a sea-nymph luring me toward her breasts. Instead of giving in to the hot charge between us, though, I kept singing and playing and letting it build, gazing at her as unabashedly as if she were an erotic dancer.

By the time we played the song out we were fully into our trip, sweaty and aroused. I put the drum down, reached around Val's waist and drew her out of the tree. We kissed during a sweet embrace, but then I bumped into the barrier: As long as I kissed tenderly we had a full circuit going, a mutual sizzle. But as soon as my animal instinct arose, she'd pull away. I knew it. I could feel it. I hated it. This time I didn't get angry, though, only philosophically detached.

I stopped kissing.

"What?" she said.

"I'm sorry. I can't do this. Something's in the way and I don't know if it's you or me."

"But I'm right here!"

"I know. I feel that. But I sense that if I really let myself go, you're gonna bolt."

"Try me."

I pulled her in and kissed her hard, until she broke away.

"You're right," she said. "I can't."

"Hm."

We spent the rest of the evening watching colors flash on each other's faces, huddling against the wind as the sun set in the sea. We talked of childhood, love, sex and desire, Sara and William, music and astrology, and what we were doing with ourselves and each other. We talked about the future. We laughed and cried and lay down and sucked the sweetness from each other's bodies.

Underneath it all, though, throbbed the old wound. *When will I be loved? Where the hell is my life? How can I get to the heart of the heart of the goddess? What's it take to make love work?*

What was spirit trying to show me? That something was so flawed in me that I just could not make love work no matter how I tried? What kind of karma was I working off? The more I thought about these things, the less clear they became. *It doesn't have to be this hard,* something told me. *Love is much simpler than this.*

I sensed so strongly, in the wake of Ecstasy, that there was a core in me I still hadn't gotten to. There was a division in me that was getting exacerbated by endless divisions between me and my lovers.

Perhaps each love was a mirror reflecting my own lack of embodiment. The pain I felt about Val was really about not getting to myself. But did I need to release her to get there, or did I need to release myself? Where was the path?

The more I thought about this, the more I realized this wasn't about Val at all. This wasn't about the passion block. This wasn't about sex. This was about getting to the core nature William and Sara were driving toward. It was about becoming so alive inwardly that no external force could keep me out of the heart of the Heart of the World.

The state of being self-aware enough to recognize your flaws without being able to do anything about it should be a special rung of hell in Dante's *Inferno*.

After Big Sur things felt freer between Val and me, but privately I wondered about our deeper connection. Could I really go through life without making love the way I wanted?

—11
Return of the Light

At the next class Val said, "This is a much different astrology than anything else out there. How does it fit with normal astrology?"

"That's the question I asked myself for decades," replied William. He thought for a moment. "During the last few centuries we've depopulated the world of all beings. We like to believe now, in scientific parlance, that humans are the only beings worth dealing with, and so-called 'lesser' beings—trees, animals, plants, rocks—are rudimentary creatures. And beings beyond us are pure supposition, very much a sign of something wrong with you to have imaginary friends beyond a certain age.

"We've depopulated the world. We've isolated ourselves. When you take that to the current extreme it becomes essentially a barren and lifeless thing. I'm busy reversing progress, going right back to magical-realism, back to animism, back to the world view in which we knew we belonged to a universe where everything cohered, in which everything was *living beings interacting.*

"It was never the case, until modern times, that when you talked about an angel, when you talked about an ancestor, when you talked about someone who was dead, when you talked about a god or guide or greater being or elemental, or animal spirit, or a being from another dimension, it was never the case that you talked about them as though they existed for certain people in certain times and places, but didn't just *be there.*

"They were never considered specialized, narrow-band beings that have little if anything to do with us. That's a modern fabrication—that you can take or leave beings. When a native of this planet used to talk thousands of years ago about communing with a guardian spirit, so far as they were concerned that was at least *as* real as contact with any fellow human being.

"In astrology when people talk about the abstract cosmic forces of the planets and signs, at best they usually conceive of them in a mutated form of modern physics—with some kind of energy forces impinging on us in some way, and *isn't that fascinating!*

"I'm not interested in that model. I'm an unapologetic neo-animist. I'm totally involved with a living world in which beings are interacting with me."

A whiney meow stole our attention as a ragged gray tiger cat stretched up on hind legs and clawed the wooden arm of the rocker. William mugged for the class, and Sara removed the cat with a haste that made me think her husband had allergies.

"When I started in astrology," the mage flashed a sidelong glance at the limp hanging feline, "I really did think planets and signs were the way modern astrology describes them—integers in an equation, mathematically precise containers of neat little categories of behavior.

"As if something profound as love, for instance, could ever completely be the province of one sign (Libra), as if Cancer had a market on apron strings, as if all Virgos are neat, all Capricorns leaders, and all Taureans charge like bulls.

"Bulls don't spend much of their lives charging, I can honestly report. Speaking as a Taurus, I can say a bull will go an awful long way to avoid charging. Charging is a last-ditch resort. My Taurus spends a lot of its time ruminating. The Taurus in me is very content to be left alone to ponder, like a cow, on a rainy day, in a field, chewing its cud, minding my own business, thank you. . . .

"I bought into the traditional limited version of astrology until my inner life exploded in Franconia and I started to realize there's far more to the universe than I'd imagined in my wildest dreams.

"What I've learned since is every form of astrological influence comes to us from *beings*. (This is pure Steiner.) Not abstract forces, not equations, not correspondences and synchronicities—although all those things can be used in their own way—but actual *living entities* unpredictable as other beings, rather than neatly pigeon-holed categories of fate.

"The universe is made of beings. Planets are beings. Earth is alive. Stars are beings. Signs are angels that presided over your birth. During your birth angelic beings stood over you and allowed your karmas to stream through their bodies, softening the imprint of these karmas on the way to you. We call these beings Aries, Pisces, Sagittarius. As they interceded, they lent some variant of their hue and tone to your nature. Libra blue. Taurus cinnamon. Aquarian cherry-vanilla. . . .

"Each sign is a being inviting you on a journey. Librans don't know everything there is to know about love—they're *finding out* everything they can about love, which, let me tell you, is more than a lifelong ride. Expect any Virgo's house or car to be immaculate and they'll howl with laughter.

"Very few astrological clichés hold up under scrutiny, because *beings are more unwieldy than neat little clichés.*

"Existence is a neighborhood of beings. The dead speak to the living. Trees and roots have their own consciousness. Animals speak. The universe is teeming with visible and invisible life.

"If what I'm saying is true, then if I want to know what's really going on here, I have to open myself to communion or conversation or interplay with another *being*. And if you're gonna interact with another being, especially one from a higher dimension—not necessarily *better* or *more*, but from a greater dimension—you're gonna have to become responsive and receptive and open and really there, right?

"Because if you don't, *they can't come through to you.*

"Don't get me wrong—it's not that spirit beings are moralistic or religious or punitive; they're not—it's just they can only come through where you're willing to have them come through in terms that are meaningful to you, when you make yourself an open vessel.

"I see spirit beings as *artist* beings. They don't care how long it takes you to get it right, they just want you to bring your all to it. They just want you to soul-wrestle with existence until you carve out a place for yourself, so you can fully engage with this multidimensional community.

"Throughout life, greater beings come into this realm and bring what they have to bring. We bring what we have to bring, and each gives something to the other. It's a potlatch. That's the terms. *The main principle of this universe is mutual co-creation.* We co-create reality each day with many different levels of beings, dead, alive or otherwise. The chief difference between us and them is most of them know it!

"The piece the gods hold is the memory of your prenatal intentions. After your last life and before the current one, you made prenatal vows which the gods hold you to, setting up roadblocks or opening up routes and synchronicities in accordance with those intentions. Existence is a conspiracy designed to force you to come to yourself.

"Even though most of us forget why we're here, the gods don't. They hold the piece of how each individual life fits into the main blueprint in the Akashic Records.

"Spirit beings hold your intentions in a special karmic sphere dedicated to you, a personal zone of influence, within which you're intended to work out your life task.

"One person's karmic domain may be an urban neighborhood or trout stream, another's—like John Lennon or Mother Teresa—may be the whole world. This domain is where you have your greatest influence. Outside that sphere you can work like crazy without getting anywhere. Inside, you have a marvelous opportunity to engage in the Dance.

"Life is an opportunity to allow the influence of various beings to assist you in coming to the self which you agreed to come to, before you came to this world. Reminders.

"It's not that these spirit beings form you and create you. They don't. We're dealing with freedom here, not enslavement. We're not turning the clock back to worshiping gods—that was the Age of Pisces.

"In the Age of Aquarius we're dealing with co-creative evolution. The great message of the universe to man at this point is: 'Wake up to the living community of forces you are so much a part of. Get on with it. Get on with who you really are! Come home from the Long Masquerade Ball of the Ages.'"

Rob said, "Where do these greater beings come from?"

"They are together with your greater self, which lives in another world, of a little finer vibration than this, that intersects with this world and comes directly into it in a certain way. These beings stand in for our greater self and try to help that self to speak and live in this planet. That's the point. Spirit beings are mediators, agents, not beings one looks to as the very purpose of existence.

"*Your job is to come to yourself.* The reason your soul took a body is to experience creation fully from the unique individuality that is you in this lifetime. Your soul has been here many times—but this life you've taken is unique and non-repeatable. You're here to manifest the fullest version of that. *But these beings are much closer to who you really are than is the person you think you are!* You need their help to remember. You can't pull this off in a vacuum. You have to train yourself to recognize others who recognize you.

"Notice—it's a peculiar edge I'm invoking between a religious, worshipful attitude and a very independent, modern, 'I can do it myself, thank you!' attitude. We're not going for either of those, but we're also not denying either. We're right between. You need a lot of *yin* and a lot of *yang* to make this world. We're not going all yang—ME—or all yin—THOU. We're at the squiggly border between yin and yang, trying to encompass both, because all of us live in both. We're not just receptive and not just active."

William sat back in his chair. "Okay. On a slightly different track, I have something Sara and I feel is important to say.

"These Destiny-in-Action meetings are changing," he declared. "We've gone far enough that we need to address what we're doing as a group. We've established something that has transformed from what it first was.

"We need to expand the work now, bring it out to others. It's reaching critical mass and is ripe to be given. We need to take what's coming through and plow it, fertilize it, use it. You don't have to use it my way, you don't have to use it Sara's way, but you have to use it your own way. That's what Star Genesis is all about: not imitating Sara and me, but activating the *you* inside you and following it out through the world.

"Until now the class has been leading up to, on its way toward, but we're entering the depths and must start to work the material rigorously on every level. Everyone who gets the deeper aspect of this work will be required to go forth and give it away, for which you'll find various methods.

"Let me be clear—you don't have to be an astrologer to do that. Most people in this room aren't astrologers and never will be. You can do it through the lens of astrology; you can do it otherwise. Star Genesis is a convenient language. I recommend you find your own path into working the material. How?

"Of all paths that are good for applying this, the very best is to use your imagination. Your imagination is the one part of you that can do this because it doesn't have that many 'shoulds.' Imagination doesn't really know what it's supposed to do, so it does what it does. Particularly for everyone who has a vivid imagination, it will be helpful to develop creative ways to make this your own."

After this evening, class morphed. People dropped out, new ones came in, old ones came back, people moved away or got divorced, little pods separated out from the main school, then swam back in, as we pushed on. In the rainy autumn chill of green Bonny Doon, William and Sara led us into territory that eclipsed my former studies of spirituality and metaphysics. Despite Sara's disease—or maybe because of it—there was no holding the Lonsdales back. They booked workshops from Marin to Carmel.

When William gave public talks I often introduced him. A few times he repaid the favor and introduced my talks. When he spoke to large audiences he was just as provocative as he was in mystery school, though he adjusted tone and content to fit each occasion, and I saw the world begin to catch fire with the conflagration of our class.

Along the west coast my own work became recognized as something beyond traditional astrology. Readings started to veer off the chart. I developed a way to do ninety-minute sessions without mentioning a single sign, planet or house—these were my favorites. I didn't care about the chart other than as a window to the soul. The more I got to the soul, the less I bothered with the window.

I gave talks and readings in bookshops, churches, radio stations and community centers in Monterey, Half Moon Bay, Palo Alto, San Francisco, Petaluma, Willits, Garberville, Ashland, Eugene and Corvallis. True to my Russian blood I entered a radical state where I ate and drank astrology like a mad poet. I remained mindful of William's original advice to never think I know what each sign is but to let them become something new every time.

While reading Rudolf Steiner I learned of his belief there's one time each year when the most direct ray of cosmic force streams to Earth—Winter Solstice. In keeping with the request to dig in and really work the material, I asked William if he and Sara would be interested in conducting a private retreat with Val and me at the cottage on Solstice weekend.

"What would the intention be?" my teacher asked.

"I've been frustrated," I replied, "because there's so much more than we're ever able to get to in class. Everything you teach could be the basis of *years* of study, and we get three hours. I want three *days,* at least, to deepen my grasp. I'd like to delve into a four-way communion of birth charts, and get to know each other better."

William said he'd think on it and get back to me. A few days later he phoned to say Sara was enthusiastic about the idea and they'd like to do it.

"Oh, *boy*—" said Val in rising intonation, flashing her mischievous Muppet face.

When the weekend arrived we drove to Bonny Doon and were greeted by Sara, beaming. "I want you to know," she said, executing a little pirouette as she took my arm, "the moment William told me your idea I got such a big Yes!" Leaning close she added, "I'm very glad we're doing this."

Friday evening we passed the talking stone and expressed our intentions of what we'd like to achieve from the weekend. Afterward, William pointed out areas of our charts "lit" by current planetary cycles. We spent around an hour discussing this before calling it a night.

In the morning I awoke with the idea to cast a giant chart by laying Sara's thick rope of golden yarn over the round floor of the yurt, so we could experience our planets kinetically. The others agreed. One by one we entered this giant ring, which provided a much different perspective of a birth chart than glancing at a piece of paper.

William read us information on the degrees of pertinent planets. Someone might have Mars opposite Venus in his or her birth chart. Whoever played Mars would stand in the house Mars belonged in and confront Venus, who stood opposite. The two would improvise a scene based on each holding their ground, trying to get something important across to the other, coached by William from the sidelines.

This lent a new dimension to my understanding of astrology, and resonated with my theatre training. Instead of *talking* about the stars I entered into them. This first performance of Planet Theatre sprang to life as half-improvisational theatre, half-shamanic healing. It was exhilarating and scary to see my psyche on display like that. (Years later I founded a troupe of actors and trained them in the same approach—*Planet Theatre*, which toured northern California in 1996 dramatizing audience birth charts for consciousness and healing.)

After the performance we ate lunch, then painted watercolors based on our insights. We clothespinned the results across the latticed walls of the yurt and referenced the pictures through the weekend, spotting themes in each other's images that dovetailed with the planetary themes.

Then Sara guided us into inhabiting our bodies—her field of expertise. She led us through a series of physical exercises she'd learned from a Mayan shaman to clear stuck energies and tune into the sun. After this William disappeared.

He didn't say anything, just dropped out for a few hours. Val and I were thrown. I asked Sara if she thought I should talk with him. She said we should probably give him space and continue on our own. So the three of us grabbed apples from the kitchen and walked through the redwood grove and the woods beyond to the sunset grounds of the neighboring Bosch Baha'i school, where we could see the sea. The forest seemed to be holding its breath, and Sara, who stood between Val and me and the sun, disappeared into the mist for a moment.

When we gathered for dinner William told us the physical exercises had triggered unresolved feelings left over from high school gym class, and he'd rebelled against group structure without knowing why, until he'd gotten the chance to sit with it. He didn't apologize, just explained, which made me wonder if he was avoiding apology more out of recalcitrance or enlightenment.

Even though we'd grown close professionally, I felt a gap in our personal relationship, which was part of why I suggested the workshop. I noted instances over the years that made me wonder how good William was at taking his own advice, but I hadn't gotten close enough to tell. Like a ruminating bull he kept the world at a distance I was unsure how to cross, or even if I should, or could.

That evening we played music in the grove. By candlelight, like ancient bards we improvised on guitars and drums and vocals, and the redwood amphitheatre funneled our sound like a medieval offering to the spirits of the trees. Sara and William played percussion. It was the only time I jammed with him.

Later in bed Val and I were buzzing and couldn't stop talking deep into the night. We felt we were on the verge of some big breakthrough.

Sunday afternoon William called us to the massage room where he said he had something important to share. "For a while now I've known of a chart inside the chart," he explained. "A prenatal, or Cosmic Conception chart."

This was the first I'd heard of it.

"We each have an inner sign, different than our birth sign. Lately I've begun to use this inner sign as the main source of a person's nature. I got the formula from ancient Egyptian astrology, brought back through a Steiner astrologer.

"We're completely caught in threads of past-life necessity by the time we're born, even before we're born, while still in the womb, but especially by birth."

"What's the purpose of karma?" Val asked. "Why do we need it?"

"Without karma we'd be lost souls," replied William, "drifting through physical existence with no set-up. Karma is the bass and drums of existence. It provides a groove, a tempo, a track laid out ahead of time for us to work into. The more karma you have, the more fuel to burn, the more capability for growth. The less karma, the less driven, the more free to choose what you *want* rather than what you need. Either way, you get exactly the right amount.

"Unlike what people think, there's nothing intrinsically 'good' or 'bad' about karma. Karma is simple celestial physics, pure cosmic cause and effect. Forces set in motion in one lifetime continue in another (though sometimes they skip a life or two). Calling karma bad or good is like calling physics bad or good. Is gravity good or bad? Is the twenty-four-hour rotation cycle *good?*

"Therefore, karma is not your burden, oppression, punishment or damnation. It's your rhythm, your path, your underlying track to help make it through what would otherwise be a hopelessly neutral maze of dizzying possibilities. Without karma you'd float through life rather than ground into anything substantial.

"The Sun in your birth chart, like everything else there, is karmic. But there's a deeper Sun, cast for the moment your soul slips into the physical plane, before the karmic imprint begins in the womb. The Sun in this chart is karma-free. It's the clearest, brightest part of you, the true light you were born to bear into the world. Your prenatal Sun, more than anything else, is the essential *you* inside you.

"At this moment of Solstice, Sara and I thought it would be a nice touch to end our workshop and welcome back the light by invoking the power of our inner Suns. What I'm about to read each of you is a snapshot of your core nature, based on the degree of your prenatal Sun. It should provide the clearest picture possible of who you are beneath everything else you are. It should invoke your essence."

I suggested that after William read each description, the rest of us could take turns round-robin style reflecting how we saw that manifesting in the person.

I was the last to go. When my turn came William leafed through his degree binder until he found what he was looking for. "Mark, your inner sign is Capricorn. By birth you're Libra, looking outward toward expression and connection. Libra is your karmic journey through the world, the journey for balance amidst love and relationship. The Scales in you are constantly weighing a wide array of factors that life sends rushing toward you, so that you can define and express your ideas.

"On the innermost level, though, you're not air but earth, not Libra but Capricorn, not ephemeral but solid, not mind but *body*. On that deeper level, you're strong and substantial, self-contained, capable of great self-mastery.

"Because your Destiny Point is also in Capricorn, you're seeking yourself! You already *are* the earth you're after."

I laughed a big belly laugh: *Cosmic egoist!*

The wizard glanced at the binder opened in front of him. "Your inner Sun is at Twelve Capricorn: *A student of nature lecturing.*"

I quipped, "No wonder I asked us here!" Now it was the others' turn to laugh.

Then we closed our eyes and contemplated. *A student of nature. Lecturing.*

I reflected how my journey through the world paralleled William's, how my first astrology talk coincided with the earthquake. I saw myself under covers in Stratford, reading myths by flashlight. *Wheels within wheels. . . .*

"A student of nature lecturing," repeated the mage.

"This degree phase is about demonstrating the laws of karma, the cosmic forces of cause and effect, and the power of intention. Mark, your

2012

life is a walking demonstration project to fathom how all existence reflects higher principles."

After taking this in I asked the group, "How do you see this image at work?"

Sara turned to me. "You're a young student of life as well as a wise old hermit, looking into the core of things to fathom true nature in many different areas."

Val took my hand. "You bring gifts you learn from animals to people. You're a translator. You speak poetry as a matter of course. You bring the voice of the river to people through words. You have a natural ability to surround someone with words that produce a sensual experience of the direct event."

William added, "Twelve Capricorn is the degree Saturn is at in the chart of Beat poet Gary Snyder, and the Mars of Zen philosopher Alan Watts. Like them, you delight in learning from nature that which makes perfect sense and dwarfs mankind. You shine when illustrating to people how right and good and true life can be. It's all there already and anyone can share in it if they just show up a certain way."

Val added, "You have bold bravado others learn from. You give away in the moment that which you find. Like Gandalf, you're a wanderer studying each phase hard to a culmination, then needing to move on."

Sara grasped my hands and looked into me for a long moment. "Mark," she told me, "I have to say that sometimes your intentions are so strong and capable that they help create things that then don't always go the optimal way but lead you to something else, which ends up being optimal, and results from your arduous preparation in other true ways."

After that, nobody spoke.

The air in the room turned golden as the first rays of winter sunset slanted over the garden through the west window. We sat on the rug, eyes closed. We sat in silence while the Solstice light waned, and I heard a squirrel chittering through leaves.

Learning of my inner Sun—that regardless of how crazy my life gets, there's this force-of-being burning bright within me—and that my core essence is a student of nature lecturing was heavy medicine. Hearing these dual revelations at the powerful turning point of the year, in such intimate surroundings, freed something deep in me, producing a silent flow of tears.

The group's comments revealed something I hadn't consciously known: While I peregrinated from state to state and home to home and woman to woman, all along I'd been pushing hard into life to see what it and I were made of. There *was* a method to the madness! In my erratic bohemian way I'd been bending the laws of the world to find something that couldn't be bent. *Cosmic Fool*, William said that first day in Ross, suggesting my blunders served some higher purpose.

As the four of us sat in deepening silence I felt extracted to a homeopathic drop of *me*-ness. Like Sara's hand had done in this same room the previous year, I was anchored by a deep peace that rooted me to the floor. The silence was so strong it seemed to radiate off us in waves.

As we sat on the braided rug by the fire I felt the depths of companionship we'd shared, as well as a tinge of sadness it would soon be over. Meeting this way with the others, in mystery, in the open air, under the trees, in the yurt, here in the massage room, on this ancient Holy Day, felt so deeply real that I never wanted it to end.

I wondered if anybody else felt the longing to create a whole life based on spirit and camaraderie, rather than keep it tucked into a three-hour-a-week class.

"Evolutionary soul work," William said a moment later, concluding the retreat, "works best in twos and threes and small groups. We can't get to the future singly anymore. The future is multiplex. Evolutionary gates open when small groups knock. Others can often see our true nature better than we can."

The part of me revealed in Sara's massage room that day hasn't changed; I haven't somehow managed to get *more* core than core. The student of nature is still grappling with existence, still wondering what it's all about, still lecturing.

There's an irreducible part of us, a soul nugget that stays that way throughout life because it's beyond karma, beyond dilemma, beyond each rise and fall of the wheel.

William and Sara taught that each of our souls came from eternity a fully developed being with a life purpose all its own. Even when we don't know what in the world we're doing, some part of us does. Some part of us dwells beyond the need for transformation and improvement, beyond any need to be changed. All things change but *essence*. Since that day I've been aware of myself in a much more powerful way.

After Solstice our teachers inaugurated a twelve-week series-within-a-series that took each sign of the zodiac and journeyed to its core. Every Monday for the next three months, the Lonsdales plunged us into the molten process of reforging the zodiac into an instrument for releasing deep cosmic force buried in human beings.

Each sign was linked with a historical epoch that stretched back to the origins of the world, as I watched the wheel of the zodiac turning spoke by spoke through the ages.

When we talked of Aries I saw the Ram gamboling through the streets of ancient Greece, when the pioneering spirit of human consciousness first thrust so boldly into its empirical environment. When we spoke of Gemini I heard the tale of the Cosmic Twin we each possess in another realm. Week by week each sign became filled with forces and fleshed out with Deep Tales of Creation that stirred something primal in me.

Group never gained so much passion, astrology never came so alive, as in those twelve weeks. One night William was our field guide to the airy domain of Libra, which he said contained the secret formula of how to turn life into an ongoing workshop in wonder. The next week we trudged up the austere, rugged hill country of Capricorn, wrestling with gnarly questions of good and evil. The following week the mage led us into the watery land of Cancer, and we were streaming fluidly through blue-green seascapes, learning of psychic bonds made in the womb between mother and child, exposing humanity's cry for belongingness.

Step by step, we midwifed a new zodiac hidden in the old. Each time we ended an evening's journey through one sign, the others became clearer by relief. With every class the wizard's demeanor changed. His vocal delivery and body language shifted, displaying a subtle mastery of theatrics I scarcely believed he could possess. He didn't just talk about the signs; he *became* them, shapeshifting like an Islamic *soukh* merchant selling flying carpets in the marketplace of Time. *Something rare and wondrous is happening here that the world needs to know about. . . .*

The Lonsdales fired me up and I was burning. Life became fused with cosmos, cosmos inseparable from daily existence. Sometimes I felt guilty because I got so juiced up by my readings and still got paid. Sometimes I fell so deep into a person during our session that I feared I would never come out again.

Times when I'd practice my craft days on end I was swept into heightened states of awareness that were volatile and seething with spirit. I saw past lives. I saw my soul streaming along telephone wires in New York City on its way to the womb. In a deep watsu session I received at Harbin, I saw pinkish-yellow hospital lights glimmering through the translucent skin of my mother's vagina as I was born out of her.

Along with Star Genesis, one of the most valuable things I learned from William and Sara was how to hold space, the gift of Taurus, William's sign, and of Virgo, Sara's. I discovered an exquisite value in simply sitting with someone and holding space a certain way.

Many of my clients took their seat and burst out crying before I said a word. Some magical force became evident that, like a grow light, engendered a communion of souls which informed the new basis of my practice. Sometimes the air became as golden as it had that Solstice day in Sara's massage room. I've come to relish this communion as more rewarding than the actual reading itself. The *soul* in Soul Level Astrology took over, freeing me to improvise further off the chart and do star jazz.

As William had taught, I learned to pay more attention to things people don't say. Over and over I saw how we shrink to inhabit a fraction of ourselves, and how we can break through that. Just as my teacher championed my inner nature the day we met, so I learned to champion the nature of others as I grew toward mastery of my craft.

All the places I'd gotten twisted in love, sex, art, money and friendship began to untwist, equipping me to help others untwist. As a student of nature, *everything* now became life lessons.

—12

Between Utopia and
Apocalypse

"Sara's in crisis," William announced one Monday in May. "She can't be with us tonight." The group tensed. "She doesn't need our pity but our support, because she's using crisis as an opportunity rather than a curse." He said this with such calm authority that it was hard to doubt.

"During crisis," he continued, "we're trained by society to turn everywhere but within. Who ever tells a person who's shattering in tiny pieces that something within *her* may know, more than anybody, exactly what she needs at that moment?

"What if massive breakdown provides the greatest opportunity to break down everything in the way of truth? What if, instead of people being drugged back to so-called normalcy, crisis gives them their only chance to get down to the core of their inner nature?"

William thought for a moment. "When I was in my late twenties I had a perplexing realization that I want to share with you: almost anybody who ever gets anywhere at all in this world seems to go through a total identity crisis of a radical and extended kind, somewhere between their late twenties and mid-forties, and probably constantly.

"I felt, 'Hey, wait a minute, if that's true, what is it that *I* at twenty-six—how much do *I* have to overcome if everybody has to go through this kind of initiation? Why is it *that* tough, why is it *that* involved, why is it *that* extended that it could take twenty years?'

"What I didn't know then, and now know, is it's like this because that person at twenty-six has no ability to feel, experience, see or know themselves anymore. Their instincts have been tremendously damaged. They think up is down and in is out and are a complete wreck and don't know it because they're propped up by a culture even more wrecked. They don't have anything going for them.

"The thing they *do* have going for them is something they left back in the pre-nine-year-old state. Somewhere between four and eight a massive soul force awakens and floods the body, transforming the child into a supercharged, erotically alive being of infinite hunger and thirst, constant curiosity, magical affinity for life.

"And, just at that point, society says *Gotcha!* Your guardians begin to warp you into something manageable. Because they got warped and think it's their duty. Of all human betrayals, this is the saddest: how your caretakers break you to fit into a broken world.

"To be fair, they rarely have a clue there's any other way to do it. They rarely grasp the simple fact their child is closer to things than they are, and may actually be offering *them* a way out of prison.

"So, the late-twenties person, in the midst of crisis and breakdown, turns out to really have no choice. You really *do* have to break down, but boy, you're gonna have to go through something around here no matter who you are. You're really gonna have to go through something. Unless you're brought up in a traditional culture—not in which you're coveted and adored but where you're given a *place to be,* given a life that makes sense to your insides, that resonates with your core nature and there's no question about it. Unless you're in that kind of situation—and which of us is?—you're gonna have to go through extended relentless self-deconditioning for anywhere from ten to twenty years, from that mid- to late-twenties space, to get back to something real.

"Why?

"Because that False-Earth person at twenty-eight or thirty-four has no roots in cosmos or Earth. They live a substitute version of themselves that passes for the real thing. They've been rewarded by society to the extent they've proven false.

"There are various degrees of this, of course—not everyone is infected with the Virus of Normalcy to the same extent—but at this point violent self-betrayal is what runs the World."

Val sat across from me in a kitchen chair, engrossed. I envied her single-minded ability to get lost in things. Even when I was captivated by William's words I rarely stopped tracking with everything else going on, like Jade over there, inwardly wrestling with some personal dilemma, and Rob, hanging aloof with a bemused smile, back by the kitchen, or Texas Blythe, angelic Virgo face with long red hair, bucking up for another wild ride through the galloping cosmos.

It was spring in the mountains, and I now knew almost everyone in the room. The only unfamiliar thing about this evening, which made me sad, was the absence of Sara. Until now she hadn't missed a class. I knew, because I'd only missed one.

My La Honda friend Nancy raised her hand from the futon. "So, if we all get what we ask for, as you've told us, if we each get the life we need, you set up a situation where you need twenty years of crisis and breakdown to get in touch with yourself? *Why?* What's the point? Are we just the greatest masochistic culture in the history of the world?"

People chortled but our teacher took her seriously. "I used to wonder about that. I used to really puzzle over it," he said. "I spent years obsessing on this one, and it's finally become clear: The basic principle of evolution is that if you wish to get through something in this world, if you wish to really, really get through something, *then you have to gain the lesson in such graphic, immediate, unmistakable form that you can't help but get it.* If you could keep it more moderate you wouldn't pay attention. You wouldn't get it on a deep enough level."

I raised my hand. "You'd think by now we'd have gotten it. Didn't we expose the hypocrisy of the system back in the sixties? Didn't we figure out all you need is love? Didn't we awaken to the fact we're here for some higher purpose? Didn't Lao-Tzu and Christ and Buddha and Rumi and Mother Teresa and Martin Luther King, Jr. and Malcolm X tell us these things over and over through the ages?"

William considered my words. "Evolution moves in cycles," he said.

"You don't get the world to change by telling it to. Or even by teaching people how. *You get the world to change by changing yourself, and holding that position until underground force building in collective consciousness gains critical mass to catalyze world change.*

"We have now totally cut ourselves off from every higher force striving to get through to us. Ordinary existence has become an extreme state of denial.

"That's the melodrama of alienation we're playing out—*The Species Without a Home,* Drama of the Exiled Species, which kicked in during the fall of Atlantis. As we awaken from the trance, and the destructive extent of this obsolete folly gets through to us, we'll move on to something more interesting.

"Until the old drama fully plays out, though, we rarely break through to something different. Which is why that youngish person, caught in extended identity crisis through their twenties and thirties, is the only one who stands a ghost of a chance. Until crisis, you see, the modern 'personality coating' is slathered on too thick for something genuinely transformative to get through.

"So identity breakdown isn't something to be avoided at all costs, but a wake-up call from the soul. Crisis has the power to break the mass trance and open you to something resurrective being seeded in the midst of loss and despair. Crisis undrugs the drugged state that passes for normalcy. It cracks you into a raw enough state to pry loose and repattern."

"Isn't there any other way to do it," said Kayla, "a little less brutal?"

"Yeah," said William, after a moment's thought. "Avalanche control. You generate an ongoing state of mini-crises, little landslides that keep you on your toes so that one day the whole mountain doesn't fall on you. Anything that jerks you awake can work. Art. Love. Drugs. Sex. Madness. Of course those things can also put you into an even deeper trance. Depends on how you use them."

I recognized this as the method William used in Ross. On the day we met I'd come to him in the midst of my biggest meltdown. Instead of steering me back toward sanity he'd pushed me further over the edge.

He'd used every trick to get me to see that the crisis was the best shot I had at freeing the real me. *Instead of running to safety, go the opposite way,* he'd said. *Get some place you can midwife your own death....* Advice like this often rang true for me at first blush but took forever to actually apply. "What if somebody doesn't make use of the crisis?" I asked.

"You do exactly what society's currently busy doing," he replied. "You play the game till it gets played out. You play out the full fate of what it is to make yourself think you want what you don't want, and don't want what you do. You exhaust every version of *not being you* until something else happens. You push the pendulum so far in that direction that it swings back to something authentic."

Is that what I've been doing all my life? Exhausting everything that isn't me? Everything that's not *love,* not *desire,* not *sex,* not *writing!?*

Hands shot up across the room. "When did this all start?" "What's the origin of the modern trance state?" "How did life get this way in the first place?" "How can we turn this around for good?"

"It began in Atlantis," said William, stilling the barrage of questions with a wave of his hand. "But even that was not without higher purpose. Even great evil serves to illustrate good, by pushing the pendulum so far in the opposite direction that it has to swing back. If there's one thing I've learned from astrology, it's that no cycle freezes, all waves swell up and die down. At the very moment something peaks it also begins to die, like a blossoming rose or a full moon.

"Even the most massively corrupt state is not somehow outside the jurisdiction of cosmic law. Regardless of how it looks, this world is still presided over by Destiny Architects."

"I find that hard to believe," said Daniel, a young tortured intellectual who'd recently joined us, "when the world looks like it does."

"Yes," William replied, "it *is* often hard to believe. But it makes sense once you realize higher beings have rightful limits within which they're allowed to work, as do we—as do all things. Just as we each have a Karmic Domain—a rightful sphere of influence within which we're intended to release our fullest potential—they do too."

"And there's the matter of free will," I added.

William nodded. "Yes, human beings are an obstinate race that has to find out everything for itself."

There was muted laughter.

"Understand something," William continued, "our first civilization was incomparable in its magical affinity for existence. Atlantis before the fall still had traces of Garden consciousness, of Lemuria—the previous stage of Oneness with all things. That age lives on even deeper than the Atlantean period in species memory, as glimmerings of unfallen paradise, before the division of the sexes, before the rise of gender and polarity and ego and all that was to come.

"But as wondrous as these first stages were, there was still something lacking. What we lacked then and have gained since is experiential knowledge of self and world.

"When we were newborn of the gods we lacked selfhood. As cosmic infants we lacked ego, we lacked a full separate identity. We were blurry.

"When you're in Oneness you fail to recognize everything because you *are* everything. We were much more in the etheric, in spiritual planes—even in the latter days of Atlantis—than we are now. But we didn't know world. We didn't know self. We needed to physicalize, to pit ourselves against physical matter during the fall of ages and rise of history and karma, to learn what we were made of. We needed to come down from the heights, and boy did we!

"As impossible as today's world situation appears, though, it's nowhere near as bleak as it looks to outer mind, which sees the view from exile and fragmentation. A whole other story is being written from within. The inner tale is that each of us has enough cosmic force packed into us to power a small city.

"The inner nature of humankind hasn't been damaged one whit by the ravaging of the ages. We haven't really lost anything on the inside. Inwardly, the soul of humanity remains intact, in a special Venusian sphere, a chamber of sanctuary the Goddess maintains in the deepest core of human beings, where the promise of love abides, mankind is still innocent, and the Garden still flourishes."

Suddenly I found myself back in the healing waters at Harbin where time stands still and souls open. I recalled the lurch it always took to break away from that and head back to the "real" world. Lately I'd begun to see Harbin *was* the real world, and that place that looks like life most of the time *isn't*.

"Here at the cusp of ages," William said after a moment, "humanity is caught in its most severe crisis and therefore has its greatest chance to get down to something real. What I'm busy trying to do now, and what Sara's off on retreat even more busy with, is recovering a sufficient amount of inward soul force to regenerate our lives.

"We don't need to turn back the clock. We're not interested in redoing Atlantis or Lemuria. As much as those periods were extraordinary, so is our time. We're now so earthbound that lead can become gold. We've burrowed so far into the material plane that we've become lightning rods of the gods. If we wake up here at the Bottom of the Ages we'll draw the highest spirit force from elder days all the way down into the depths of matter at the End of the Lost Days."

He glanced at me and I nodded. *Underneath each tale he's weaving something in another dimension. He's reading souls and adjusting his words to unlock destiny from karma.*

"We don't look to ancient days nostalgically," the wizard said as he turned back to the class, "only to recapture enough original spark to remind us there's another way to be."

William leaned forward. "At this moment Sara's waging the fight of her life. She's struggling to uncover a root-level belongingness in the teeth of the whirlwind. She doesn't need pity, though prayers are helpful. She needs to break out of isolation. She needs community. After class, those of you interested in helping can stay to discuss it." There were many nods throughout the room.

William grasped the arms of the rocker and leaned forward. "Sara's mustering every ounce of determination to meet each curve being thrown at her, and she's barely able to handle one before the next one comes, and the next and the next. Though most of us don't have a life-threatening disease, we're all being asked to do the same thing: to clear away every particle of resistance we have to being alive."

In the following weeks Val and I attempted to break through our own barriers. I studied the cosmic weather and got William's help to design a public talk for me: *From Atlantis to Aquarius: Jump-starting the Millennium Shift,* my attempt to spread the gospel from Bonny Doon over the hill to Silicon Valley. I felt a bit guilty receiving the charity of my teacher's insight, but over the years he's never withheld free advice, and I continue to call on him every so often.

Armed with this information, I tackled my studies with renewed fervor and set a date to go back on the radio. Val infused new passion into her teaching and music, writing songs of the soul, pouring her heart into performance, taking emotional risks on stage.

But sexually we were a mess. We couldn't get past the passion block, which maybe frustrated her even more than me. Nothing seemed to work. We went to couples counseling, but I didn't get much out of it. Few therapists seemed to think outside the box enough to meet me where I lived. I felt I'd already journeyed deeper through love than most of them had, so how could they lead me?

I began to wonder about the role Santa Cruz played in the karmic theatre piece of our difficulties. I fantasized what might happen if we moved to a simpler place. Also, we yearned for a more affordable existence. Even though my reputation as Soul Level Astrologer was spreading, my career never seemed to smooth out. It lurched. I found myself praying that my Volvo wouldn't break down on the way to readings. Val's finances seemed similarly afflicted. *Maybe that's our shared karma,* I reflected, *amplifying each other's lack of self-belief till we bust through it.*

I kept wavering over whether my frustration had more to do with my nature or circumstances. Had I gotten so screwed-up in an earlier life that I kept sabotaging myself in this one? I couldn't shake the nagging sense that the answer was staring me in the face, that some whole other path through love and money was available.

If I could unite fully with my life force as Sara was fighting to do in the fight of her life, would external reality follow suit? Were Val and I meant to stay together? How much of my search for happiness was based on internal rather than external components?

Earlier in the year we eased financial stress by deciding to stop paying rent, and embarked on a series of house-sitting jobs, the longest of which lasted six weeks, the shortest a day or two. This traded rent pressure for the new set of challenges of how to juggle two careers while playing musical homes. Life became a jerky dance of voice-mail and date books, with little constancy except that provided by Monday night group. But by June the class was winding to a close.

We'd grown weary of house-sitting by the time of our final session, when the magician rolled up his sleeve and pulled another rabbit out of the hat. It was a balmy evening in Bonny Doon, as northern California days lengthened toward Summer Solstice. The windows were open, the wood-stove empty and silent. An arid pine-scented breeze fluttered through the living room. William sat in the leather-backed rocker, Sara on the futon. She hadn't missed any classes since the previous month.

The living room was brimming—stalwart regulars mixed in with people I hadn't seen in months: Chellema, brow furrowed as she wrestled with the scientific implications of our metaphysical forays; Nancy, my music partner; Hina and Bhasa, the Brooklyn-born lesbian career consultants I called my fairy godmothers; Blythe, Jade, Rob, Val, Margie, Barbara and many others were squeezed onto the living room couch, futon, floor and chairs.

"Most information I've read about 2012," said Ken as the boisterous group settled down, "seems either to be pie-in-the-sky visions of paradise or bleak predictions of doom and gloom. What do you think's going to happen, William?"

The mage planted his foot on the hassock and went into his thinking pose. "I see 2012 as a gateway to a future we're being invited to co-create with spirit," he said after a moment, "a future which has been trying to emerge for a long long time, a crucial probability, a distinct scenario which hangs in the balance of the choice now facing us: Will humanity awaken and claim its greater awareness, or make the same mistake all over again?

"That's the edge we have to work with," he added, "the great burden of our moment in history.

"Let me be clear. There's an actual living future forming beyond the gate of 2012. It's been shown to me. I've seen it. But that doesn't mean it will happen. It needs our help to usher it in.

"I don't think this future's gonna sweep over us in a surfing wave of *WOO-WOOO*. I don't think by 2012 the world will be one and we'll dance into the sunset with unicorns and rainbows. I think it will stream in rather as *an ongoing inward leaning toward a fuller experience of life on Earth.*"

"We're not going to all become One?" Blythe said innocently. *"Darn."*

"At this stage of evolution," William replied, grinning, "oneness is reserved for spirit. In the etheric all things are one. Before we incarnate we're One. After we die we go back to oneness. But around here we have to deal with multiplicity. Spirit is One. Earth is many. For a world civilization as multiplex as ours to suddenly fuse into cosmic oneness is unlikely."

A moment later William smiled. "I was remembering that period in the sixties when we really thought that if enough people smoked pot and dropped acid, the world would change."

People chuckled.

"How do we deal with the fact so many different ingredients are thrown together here in the crucible?" he pondered aloud. "How do we tackle multiplicity as *invitation* rather than *curse*? How do we overcome polarity karmas that pit one thing against another throughout history? How do we claim the living future?"

Our teacher swept a lock of hair out of his eyes, and I noted that his hair and beard were the longest I'd seen. This was a wilder spiritual outlaw than the one I'd met in Marin four and a half years earlier.

"Let's see if we can leap across the impasse of this stalled choice point, and see what kind of future we find," he decided.

"The first sign, as the future approaches, is that we experience a crisis in consciousness, a maximum meltdown as the necessary prelude to a collective journey of re-gathering. Unweaving the world in order to reweave it. The closer we get to 2012 the more acting out will occur. Of course, there's no guarantee we'll make it through this initial meltdown stage all the way to the reweaving.

"There's a bright future forming over there on the other side of the bridge, wanting to come through, but we've each got a lot of work to do to pull it in. Especially those of us with a bit more awareness than others, a bit more savvy to these things. We're going to be pressed into service by Galactic Central. Because polarity karmas are going to act out like crazy."

"I wasn't here for polarity karmas," said Lee. "What's that?"

"Us versus them," someone replied.

"Jews and Arabs, men and women, Irish and English, Democrat and Republicans," I added. "The maddening illusion of duality."

"Oh, that."

William scanned the ranks, hunching like a hunter stalking big game. "If we use world pressure to crack through the Trance of Normalcy and awaken to the greater truth of who we are," he said, "we'll find not utopia so much as actual life on Earth for the first time, stripped of illusion, a wholly new prospect of what it means to be alive in the physical plane.

"Which is euphoric in its own way, because it comes as a huge relief to the alienated part of the human soul marooned outside itself. Actual life in the here-and-now is a much more exquisite premise than any far-flung fantasy I can think of. Wouldn't it be great if we could just be who we are, from birth to death, dawn to dusk, each day of our lives? Wouldn't it be amazing if we could just be who we are? What would that be like. . . ?

"In order to cross the bridge to the future, then, I want to advance to one final level, which we've been building up to all along. The mystery we've been leading up to in so many ways this year is the mystery of Time. What is time?"

The question hung in the air.

"I've been puzzling over this since I entered astrology twenty-one years ago, and it's slowly dawning on me that time is our way of trying to unite with this world in life and in form. Time is the mind's attempt to come deeper into existence. Time is rhythm. Time is synchronization. Therefore, there's something exquisitely rightful and beautiful to time if you can find your way inside it, but something incredibly off-putting and destructive when you're *outside*.

"When you're out of time, time seems like a terrible injustice to eternity. There's never enough and where did it go? You can't stop the clock, and you can't catch up with yourself, and life is passing you by, and each moment is ticking you closer and closer to oblivion.

"But when you're *inside* time you find your own way of going, which will lead you exactly where you need to go if you keep right on time. You tap an internal rhythm, which is a means to synchronize with the Mother of the world. Time brings us into matter."

"For a number of years," interjected Sara, "I've had long chunks of time that seem timeless, where I'm not aware of the clock ticking. Life forms itself organically, things fit together and are synchronistic. When I'm out of harmony it seems to be when I can't get inside one of these flow currents, and things become jerky and a-rhythmical. It has to do with rhythm. It has to do with pacing, at a very small and subtle level.

"Lately," Sara continued, "I'm striving to enter the timeless state and stay there. I'm striving toward new time. Because we're totally alive in that time! No parts of us are gone or trying to pull in another direction. We're right in the flow.

"The best way to set up this timeless time," she cleared her throat, "is to give myself maybe three hours a day which I allow with no constraints. Then, if something comes up after that, it's okay. But if I don't give myself those hours I feel I'm not holding my part of the bargain to develop in this new way."

William turned to the class. "Now there are many ways to interpret what Sara's saying, but please pay attention because we're entering a field of paradox. We're about to go down the rabbit hole.

"You've probably had the experience of being inside an effortless flow that carries you through an hour or a day, or maybe a few days. You slip through a sweet spot in time where a little goes a long way. A greater wave of things weaves itself into the lesser; you stream along an inclusive life current that leads you to the most exquisite timeless place, where existence is charged with a strong force of essence.

"And, you've probably even more had the counter-experience, that whatever you do is *out of time*, working against the grain, swimming against the current. Things require three times as much effort. You spin through a revolving door that exhausts you when you've hardly begun. You're at odds with everything. You can't find the flow.

"What's the difference? What makes one experience radically different from the other? Is it pure subjective perception or is there some larger force at work?"

William opened his hands to the class. "And so, the highest mystery of all, then, is Time. Where does time come from? Who thought of it? What are we being asked to do with it? How does time affect consciousness? Will the nature of time change after 2012? Is it already changing? Is there another way to envision it, another way to use it?"

In the long pause that followed I felt a lump in my throat as I scanned faces in the room. *This is really happening. We've made it. In days to come how will I ever describe what went on here in a way that does it justice?*

"The normal way to handle time is to limit it," said William. "Limited time is the sense there's so little time and so much to do—the archetype of the White Rabbit from *Alice in Wonderland:* '*I'm late! I'm late! For a very important date!*' Regimented time. Obedience to external pattern. But there are signs that time is evolving now to something new.

"Lately, as Sara descended deep into her healing process, I've watched a time-regeneration at work: the return of an inner time she inhabited in childhood. It's been one of the most remarkable aspects of the whole healing process. Right when outer time is falling apart, a regenerative force is surging into her. It's as if she's had to count herself out in order to tap this frequency. Where's the regenerative force coming from?

"*From the dead into the living.* Sara's proximity to death is regenerating her life—an irony that's become very apparent to both of us.

"Because as things accelerate on our side they also accelerate on the other. Barriers are thinning, worlds grope toward each other dissolving our fierce Illusion of Duality.

"A new time frequency is streaming to us now from across the veil. The dead are offering a vast regenerative force to the living.

"In order to cross the bridge to the future, then, we must do one thing above all—and this is on the level of grand sorcery—*we must unbind time.* This is key because our normal way of doing time is paralyzing us more than we know. We've got to get this before disbanding the class.

"The chief problem with clock-time is it banishes cosmic forces of renewal from coming to our assistance, and locks our planet into a purely localized timestream, cut off from the main flow of the galaxy. Current Earth Time is more of a universal snag than asset. Like a black hole it swallows cosmic frequencies seeking to assist our planet. It casts a barrier around us that repels higher thought.

"But outside the barrier the galaxy is super-alive right now. If we get out of our way and open a blowhole in time, we'll link Earth with vaster realms that can renew the scope and magnitude of what we're doing, and bring our planet into the greater Galactic flow."

"How can I do that in my own life?" Val said. "Because I think I know what you're talking about. But when I'm not in the flow, like today for example, when I just couldn't find my groove, what you're saying sounds like a lot of hooey." People laughed. "I know there's a greater reality out there, because I've been there enough in the past to vaguely remember what it feels like, but I can't find it."

Our teacher regarded her. "The basic principle I work from, which is my Jupiter-in-Scorpio personified, is that *wherever lies the greatest confusion, immediately comes the greatest opportunity for breakthrough.*"

William raised his hand like a boy scout. "Now, I know not every-body would agree with this method, but that's the way I see things. There-fore, in most sessions of this group (I can finally let the cat out of the bag), I intentionally created a formative chaos, purposefully whipped ingredients to a boiling point sufficient to catalyze some force of your own greater awareness.

"That may sound like a strange way to do things, but from a Scorpionic perspective it's the only way likely to work. I teach like this because mod-ern life is a thick trance state. Just to participate in civilization from child-hood on is to put us all far under a hypnosis we're not aware of. Those of us with strong Scorpio have been insufficiently drugged." I laughed. "It's hard to go along with the program when you're writhing inside!

"This hypnosis is so acute, reinforced each day by television, radio, false education and false diet, that to bring people out of trance you have to get them further *under* before their awareness turns. I admit this method has its risks. I don't recommend trying it at home, boys and girls. But for awakening this group it's been my main approach."

Nancy raised her hand and William acknowledged her. "I want to say something about the timeless experience in the midst of time."

"Let's hand the microphone to Nancy," William announced, "since she's a Gemini and is gonna take it anyway—." When Nancy's jaw dropped he quipped, "Just kidding. Actually, I want to defer to Nancy because Gemini holds the key to time. Gemini is the sign of the future. Despite Gemini's fabled fickleness, the most evolved version of Gemini is here to show the world an effortless way to transform. Watch a really tuned-in Gemini get out of their own way and you'll see effortless transformation."

Nancy nodded. "I think I know the part of me you're talking about. There are times when I inhabit that. But most of the time the world as it is doesn't allow my highest experience to come through the door. So I, as a human being in *this* world, in this culture at this time, with all my responsibilities, am usually functioning day to day, trying desperately to keep it all together, while my real being is knocking on the door and nobody even hears the knocking. . . ."

She paused to collect her thoughts. "When I'm in that timeless state that I often enter in this class, everything is self-evident, clear, free, expansive. And when I go back to my regular life, I often can't even remember there was anything else out there. It's like two completely separate worlds I bounce between, with little reference from one to the other.

"The difference lately, though," she continued, "is I'm learning there's a way of bouncing from time to timelessness often enough that you build some timelessness into time." People murmured.

"There's a way to cross back and forth," Nancy added, "which gradually enables the greater reality to weave into the lesser. There's a way to get stuck that isn't so stuck, because some part of you watches the whole thing even as you fall."

William nodded. "Well said." He turned to the group. "Now we're onto something. We're right on the verge of something that I want to follow up with open dialogue.

"Can what Nancy's saying be true? Is there a way to be *in* the world but not *of* it? A way to weave timelessness into time?

"Or, to put it another way, could the limited self somehow be the *most vital part of the equation?* Can all of modern civilization, in other words, actually be the most appropriate precursor to something yet to come?"

Kayla raised her hand. "I have a lot of empathy toward the dualistic process Nancy's describing, but lately I don't feel I have a choice, because I've been thrust into the unlimited state almost relentlessly. The sheer energy I'm running is scary, though, because it seems to have no limit. It's almost orgasmic. I can't stop timelessness from taking over my life!"

People laughed.

"I'm serious! I've always had a lot of energy, but not like this. It goes day and night and just keeps pushing and pushing and I never seem to fatigue behind it. It makes no sense. There are no drugs, sex or rock 'n' roll on the planet that would give you anywhere near what I'm experiencing stone-cold sober. It's like I'm standing in the ocean and the waves are so gorgeous I can't stand it. I'll see wildflowers, or just beautiful green grass growing, and want to share it so badly with somebody, but who can you explain this to who won't think you're crazy? It's outrageous. But it can't continue forever, can it?" Kayla looked to William and Sara until it became evident they weren't going to reply.

Rochelle, a spirited young redhead who recently joined the group, turned to Kayla. "I so associate with what you're saying. It happened for me on a dawn morning in August 1987. I didn't know anything about astrology and had never heard of the Harmonic Convergence. When I walked up the hill that morning and looked back at the sunrise, the entire world was different. I don't know how I knew, but I *knew*. The trees were different, everything had changed and has been changing ever since. It's reached the stage now where when I come smack-dab up against a concrete wall of material something, I just don't understand that anymore. Because—nothing's solid! There's a constant liquid state as far as my senses are concerned—it's all liquid now—that's what changed. There's this constant bleed-through state. Nothing seems solid anymore."

Rob spoke up. "I wonder if I'm missing something. I'm hearing what all of you are saying. But there's a conundrum I have. I too have had experiences of timelessness where things blend and shift. And I love that! But during the midst of it I feel compelled to honor the substance and solidity down below more than the energy blasts and timeless merging from above. Because when I sail into the blended state I feel no longer of the Earth, and like I'd better get back to something solid, or I'm not gonna be able to do what I need to do around here. Am I missing something?"

After a moment William nodded toward Chellema, who'd been holding her hand up for the longest time. "I've been pondering what's been said tonight about time from an astronomical point of view," she reported, "and I'm trying to relate physics to the metaphysics. It seems to me it's not so much the substance of time that's the issue here as the *direction* of time.

"See, there's an outmoded Ozzie-and-Harriet view that Monday follows Sunday, that we're in a direct line of linear time like an arrow, that things progress. This version of time is the scaffolding upon which we look at the pictures of the past and try to form a cohesive sequence.

"But there's another theory, that matter would be fluid if not for the static-ness of time. That time affects matter. That if you opened time you could walk through matter like water. The crystallization of molecules would no longer be as it is."

She thought for a moment. "There's a strange anomaly in space where nobody knows what's going on, where you have a red shift and a blue shift, which means it's coming toward us and going away from us at the same time! This has got astronomers bent backwards and befuddled, because it doesn't match our conception of time going from one place to another. Perhaps what we're coming to with 2012 is a new definition of time, and how that affects matter."

William grew very animated. "Bingo! You hit the nail on the head! You got it. I'd like to amplify, exaggerate and take off from what Chellema just said.

"Our current perception of time is based upon eighteenth-century classical order and sequence. Everyone goes about their business unaware of how rigidly this perception controls things. We have no idea how insidiously this handicap lames us at the threshold.

"To grasp the extent of what I'm talking about, we must understand time didn't always work this way. The modern Western concept of time is a megalithic historical construct massive as the pyramids, which required just as much effort. We take it for granted without realizing how much of a dinosaur it is. We're slaves to the clock. Time is the tyrant that terrorizes us. Time is a Pharaoh. What we think of as normalcy is actually a violently shutdown state, which is a frequency of strictly limited time.

"We take it for granted that time moves from past to present to future. Nobody questions this. *Why?* Why do we accept this view as the be-all and end-all of existence? Just like we take it for granted that there are five senses. *Why?* Steiner found twelve senses.

"There's another way of looking at time, another time movement, which is that time isn't developmental at all, but instantaneous. Time moves instantaneously. You know Krishnamurti's idea that we don't come to awakening in incremental stages, but all at once?

"It's this awareness of lightning striking. Awareness that the infinite reality doesn't operate in time. It does operate in time, but it undoes our usual sense of time. I don't know if you want to call that time or not. But it undoes what we think of as time. Everything becomes kind of *here-and-now-ish*.

"This is the sense of time as instantaneous cosmic event, which takes you where you're going if you're ready to go. You're beamed up to the Infinity Field. It's about voyages and adventures, about infinite reality in its many different manifestations. It's not about inching along the ruler from Point A to B to C.

"Pay close attention now.

"If we have past selves, then aren't we the future selves of them?

"Might we then have future selves already in existence, which we're the past selves of?

"Can we possibly retrieve information from somebody not born yet, who knows better than we do how to get through our dilemmas because they've already done it?

"*Stay with me.* Can something you do today change yesterday? Can the 'you' you are now get a crucial piece across to that junior high kid sitting in that room all by herself, that she doesn't have to get quite so distraught, because she's already made it through that hurdle, and many others, and you're the living proof? Can you reach through time to take advice from your future self and avoid duplicating its mistakes?"

Chellema interjected, "And when we talk about the Mayans being the main ones to clue into 2012, well, their thing is totally about time."

"Absolutely," said the mage. "The Mayans are more into time than anybody. They use time in a much more complex and sophisticated way than we do, with all our advanced technology."

William leaned back in the rocker. "Okay. Let's get our bearings for a moment before diving further in. The first thing to understand is that standard time equals limited mind. Linear time sequence is a frame of reference concocted to get you through normalcy. It's a convenient way to look at things. I mean, I recommend linear time if you're driving or walking or living in this planet at this time. You have to keep the fiction going. However, it's merely convenience. It's not true.

"As we approach 2012 we're entering a state which Jean Gebser, the most prophetic of all modern prophets about time, called *aperspectival* perception, where you don't come from a single side or place or aspect. You come from *all* places but not one place that you fix, not one perspective, not one limited identification stream. Hence your red shift/blue shift." William glanced at Chellema.

"Gebser was more obsessed with time than any individual I've come upon. He kept trying to get it through to us that this massive chronology, which we built up painstakingly through the ages, locks us into a state of fear and agitation that's devouring everything.

"Time is a monstrous pyramid hanging over us. We dwell each day in its megalithic shadow. We have listened to Pharaoh, and he's a rapt storyteller, and we've been a rapt audience, and we've gotten a basic picture that renders this world of ours meaningless. You see, if everything's really in linear time, forget it! Because it means you can't possibly be who you are.

"Because our being does *not* exist in time. The whole point of non-time, or timeless time, or trans-time, or meta-time, is we have to learn that this being who I am, inside here, isn't corded-in with time. This being is corded-in with eternity, with simultaneity, with free-becoming.

"To cross the bridge to the future, then, we need to unbind time, because time is the highest mystery, and space follows time. If you're fluent with time, you're fluent with space. And then space can be anything it wants—including even as *solid* as it likes—for just a moment. Only it won't stay that way. That's the point. Time, space, things, beings, you and I won't stay *any which way* for long, because outside the barrier of limited thinking, everything's always changing.

"And since we normally think of solid as that which stays the same, we're not gonna get static, rigid, mass-consciousness types of worlds anymore, where 'he said,' 'she said,' then 'they did,' right? It's gonna be more like beingness spoke and speaks."

Jade shifted on the other end of the couch. "So, if time is changing as we approach 2012, then we need to reconsider our entire worldview," he reasoned aloud. "Because as long as we're trapped in linear time, visions of paradise are always relegated to some *other* time. They're never present. Happiness is always *there* rather than *here*. We're never in the now.

"But if we begin to experience that things actually happen in the now-moment," he conjectured, "that all times are present to some extent in this time, then our dreams and nightmares both manifest. All sorts of things materialize that previously didn't seem possible. Therefore, we need some new kind of capacity as human beings to be able to go with that."

"But if everything's always changing," said Val with a look of befuddlement, "if everything's morphing, and all times are suddenly here and now, what's solid and stable anymore? Where can I hang my coat?" People laughed, but she waited for William to answer.

"Okay," said our teacher, raising his hand like a traffic cop. "Okay! Hold on. I think we've stirred things up sufficiently to have something to work with. Now we can take this to another level.

"Oddly enough, Val, the one hook where you can hang your coat is *karma.* The extent to which we're captured by past karmas is the extent to which we remain solid. Nowadays, most of us remain solid karmic beings trying to navigate free space. The world itself has become freed up, but we *haven't* so we don't notice."

I asked, "Why is karma so solid?"

"Because the karmas we have specifically prohibit something. They prohibit us from passing them over. And you would have to pass them over if you were to leap full-power into this futuristic new world I'm describing. You'd have to become a meta-karmic being.

"But—and let me tell you this real clearly—when that's in the offing for the human race, when the actual possibility is at hand to transcend karma, then *all the karmas of the world sweep in fast and furious to be resolved.* All times become present in this time.

"Everything you've gone through in any life recapitulates in time-lapse photography in order to speed you through it. Because if a whole way of doing human karma is about to change, it's not like the karmas suddenly say, 'Well, we're gonna be gone in 2012, we might as well go now.'

"No. If a whole karmic shift is actually at hand, the karmas say: 'Oh, so you wanna resolve me, do ya? Okay—HERE I AM! HERE I AM! HERE I AM!'" William collapsed in his chair amidst laughter, and I caught a glimpse in his face of the price he was paying inwardly to be able to teach this way. Rounding his lips, he blew his breath out then pried himself back up on the arms of the rocker. "The main principle we need to master at this stage of evolution is *we can only get to freedom once everything in the way of it comes up for clearing.* This is ultra-crucial. I can't stress this enough.

"Let's face it—we all want to be free—especially here in Santa Craze, you can feel this as a palpable longing. It's the whole purpose of California, right?"

People chuckled.

"I'm well-acquainted with this longing because I've spent my life chasing it in various absurd ways. But true freedom, I now know, does not result from getting *out* of anything. No matter what story you're running in your head, no matter what New Age vision of utopia you may be seduced by, freedom will not happen via escape of any kind.

"I'm saying if you win the lottery, if you get a divorce, if you move away from your obnoxious neighbors, if you dump your screwy relatives, if you impeach the president, if you finally get the girl of your dreams— you will never never become free. If you change any of these outer things without changing yourself, it'll revert back again.

"Freedom comes not from getting *out* but getting *in*. Freedom comes when you show up with all twelve senses intact and meet everything here to meet you. Freedom comes when you live each moment as the conscious, awake, hopeful, half-blind/half-divine, quirky, magically alive, flawed, perfect, transformative, erotic being that you are. That's what we long for—not the freedom of *escape* but the freedom of *arrival*. And the only way to arrive is by dealing with every crazy thing in the way of arrival, which is why the world's acting out like crazy now.

"In order to clear karma, karma has to come up to be cleared. It's the basic operating system for Planet Earth.

"When karma creeps in, though, we don't tend to keep cool and say: 'Hey, man—that's just karma.'" William said this in a slack-mouthed jazz player lingo that cracked up the room.

"No. When karma comes we contract into a fear state, we wipe out because of what happened every other time we got hit by the same thing. But—and this is the glaring error in most New Age teachings—we can't get out of the pattern till we get further *in*. We can't just wish the shadow out of existence. This is the great moment facing the human species— how do we spring ourselves in the place we can't be sprung?

"The old polarity karmas of humanity are acting out like crazy in order to be released now. In the thick of that, it's hard to believe in a bright future. I admit, there's more evidence for considering 2012 a gateway to apocalypse than to that brilliant Aquarian vision of love and peace.

"Nonetheless we're at the dawn of a whole new way to be. Underground momentum for this has been building for centuries. The world is changing. Time is shifting. Karma is quickening. The veil between worlds is thinning. The dead are coming closer to the living. Spirit forces are flocking to our planet.

"If this freaks you out, you're not alone. But to get to the future all you have to do is turn left-right. Head north-south and you'll be there in no time."

People laughed.

"To most appearances," resumed William, "the change is hard to notice. Things still look the same. Life seems as it was. But, as I learned from my dream of Atlantis, things are *not* the way they look.

"As Rochelle learned that morning of Harmonic Convergence, the real story is the world changed one summer day in 1987 and is continuing to change within us and all around us. Some of you tuned into this when it first happened. Others tune in at their own discretion. Some don't tune in at all—but that only obscures the transformation rather than stops it.

"The cosmic weather report approaching 2012 is: *Liquid states streaming straight from galactic intelligence across the Great Plains of our consciousness designed to flip us off our rocker.*

"As polarity karmas heat up and the Trance of Normalcy ratchets to breaking point, we're going to have to reimagine our whole purpose. We're going to have to redefine our basic relationships. We're going to have to summon great presence at the gates of breakdown. We're going to need to drop into our authentic selves more than ever.

"Of all things most crucial for us to imagine now," added William, "it's that the future exists, with great power. I don't know why this should be so difficult—I mean, we spend so much time imagining the past exists, don't we? If it's true the past really does exist, then we're the future of it—and *we* exist, don't we? So there's got to be a future which we're the past of! Even on a pure linear track it makes sense. We're being bombarded by future, now more than ever, because we need it so badly. *We need to believe in a bright future for the human race more than we need anything.* This raw aching need is what underlies the stuck state of the world. We need to *believe* again.

"Beneath business as usual we're getting bombarded by futures that we're always busy forgetting. We're sort of all busy forgetting. We could put under our shingle, 'Busy forgetting.'"

People laughed.

"In this busy-forgetting state, what we're mainly busy forgetting is the *future.* You have to forget the future constantly, you see, because it keeps coming at you and coming at you and coming at you. The Destiny Architects are whipping up future like crazy these days."

Jade said, "What happens if we cease forgetting?"

William regarded him. "Unlimited time takes its rightful place at the center of existence. What would that be like? What would it be to not have present time as the center of our existence, but to have ancient/future time converging as the center of our existence, and present time almost get crowded out?

"From a fully-awake perspective of time, the first thing you see are your past selves and future selves, and you see yourself in the middle between them. And you see that all of your selves are indeed here now together, but in a very different sense of here-now than we usually think of as here-and-now.

"I want to give you a sense of *now* that's peculiar: Now is really a razor-thin here-now, rather than a broad-sweeping-plaza here-now. The true here-now from a cosmic-spiritual perspective is the moment you're in, each moment, perfectly balanced between your past and future.

"You walk a tightrope in time. The only moments you're perfectly balanced between past and future are when you're out of ego. Because ego-mind is past-fixated. The ego experiences itself as an accumulation of experiences it tries hard to control.

"The reason it's so challenging to dwell in timeless space rightfully, Rob—what you were alluding to when you said you feel the need to honor solidity over timeless merging—is due to one simple fact: *we don't yet have enough future built up at this point in history to counter-balance the past.*

"At this stage of civilization, we've got a lot of past built up and a teensy bit of future. Past-fixation is what keeps the world in check. Newspapers, radios, schools, jobs, marriages—the whole thing is saturated with past. We don't have enough future in the mix to balance our past, which is why we fail to get to the present. These days the present moment only really happens when the past doesn't outweigh the future."

From the futon Sara said, "Future vision?"

"Yes," replied her husband. "We're being asked to gain future vision, to see beyond the tremendous ring of past bound around us like a noose. When the past closes in on us so tight, it's impossible to breathe into the actual possibility of something new happening.

"You see, for most people this present moment is past." William snapped his fingers.

"Almost everybody experiences the present as the past. You don't know you're doing that, of course. It would be absurd. But that's what you're doing, because the present moment recedes into the past very very fast unless your future lights up inside you."

I said, "Like Neal Cassady, whom Kerouac lionized in *On The Road*, and who drove the bus in *The Electric Kool-Aid Acid Test*, who seems to have seen the present as the present."

"Yes," replied William. "I've been around a few people like Cassady. Suddenly the present becomes multi-dimensional instead of uni-dimensional. All directions open instantaneously."

Jade said, "Whereas typically there's a lid on the present."

"And the lid," prompted our teacher. "What's the lid?"

"Everything we're taught to believe?" said Blythe.

"Past lives?" ventured Nancy.

"Fear?" said Kayla. "Karma?"

"I want to describe to you how the limited self looks to spiritual beings," William replied after a moment. "One thing we haven't talked about yet in this class is the way higher beings see *us*.

"Now this may sound ridiculously hopeful, you may think I've swallowed optimism pills since our last class, but the fact is that spiritual beings are in love with us. Passionately. The gods are crazy about us. Simply nuts. I know this contradicts religious programming and the whole thrust of Western history but is nevertheless true. We're the absolute darlings of the gods.

"What does that imply from *their* perspective?

"As beings who are passionately, obsessively, constantly in love with us, the gods forgive us everything. Instantly. Much better than we forgive ourselves, boy, do they ever forgive us! They forgive even this crazy choice we continue to make to spend so much time in limitation. They forgive us that, but they're baffled by it. Spiritual beings are baffled by this limited self of ours. It's the one thing they can't understand about us—the part least like them, right?

"How do I know this? Because they can't even give you—and I work with spiritual beings all the time—they can't even give me a clear image of the limited self. They never come up with that in a full full *full* way. It's the one thing they can't ever describe.

"Because *I'm* the one that has to understand limitation. That's my thing. That's not their thing—that's the one part of us they *aren't!* They can equip me to *deal* with limitation, true. But they can't quite ever get it into central focus, because they can't believe in it. They can't sustain the fiction we're busy sustaining that this limited self down here on Earth is actually who we are.

"How does the limited self appear to greater beings?

"We—most of us—have these bubbles strangling us around the neck. The way spirit beings see us is with our head in a bubble. This gets our heart in trouble. The bubble is where I'm going around just being me, and you're going around just being you, and everything's going around just being everything. You know that state? *Normalcy.*"

People laughed.

"How does time work in that bubble?" continued William. "The bubble is composed of time. It gobbles time. It subsists on time, feeds on time. Why? Because time is the validation of it. Limited time validates limited self constantly.

"If there's such a thing as linear time, then I exist completely unto myself in my separate bubble. You exist in your bubble. Everything exists in its own bubble. Then we don't have to worry about anything. I'm here, you're there, this is this and that's that.

"This is why I dream about cars and boats and vehicles all the time, vehicles that never do what they're supposed to and never remain what they appear to be. In my dream life I can never get my vehicle to do what all the others do!"

The class chuckled.

"Dreams are one method galactic intelligence selects to inform us of what's happening on the meta-level beyond the bubble. Dream, art, creativity, intuition, imagination—these are free channels through which each of us can tune into the meta-level of what all of us are going through. Those channels have not yet been co-opted by the Thought Police.

"I tend to dream of cars because they're just like this limited bubble of selfhood, passenger cars. We bubble down the highway of life from birth to death in our own 'cars.' We're bubbling over with ourselves in linear time all the time and then we die.

"Our future self, which has no boundaries, no boundaries at all—taps on the windowpane of the bubble and says, 'Er, um, excuse me—are you done yet? Or do you need to go around that block a few thousand more times?'"

As people laughed I spoke up. "Okay, I grasp what you're saying about unbinding time—at least the present-self me thinks he does—I read a lot of science fiction and fantasy growing up. And when I go to Harbin or the Oregon Country Fair I enter the timeless state, and for years I've been trying to sustain that in my day-to-day life. But I don't get what's the big challenge here. What's the practical side? I don't yet get what I'm supposed to do. I mean, what are we supposed to *do* with the knowledge that we can unbind time?"

"That's a good question, actually." William tipped his head to me. "What we do with this knowledge is we learn to pay attention to subtle cues. Because the part of ourselves that's not in the bubble is trying very hard to get through to the part that is.

"The part of ourselves not caught in the bubble is our higher nature, the part of us that's in contact with spirit beings. This greater self stands above and behind the bubble and is constantly bursting the bubble, even while the bubble constantly reconstitutes itself.

"This is how spirit beings see us.

"We perceive messages coming from our greater self as subtle, if we perceive them at all. Most of us, when we receive these messages—which we receive all the time—perceive them as super-subtle, super out-there

things we don't pay much attention to, don't really notice, except the
fringe of our awareness."

Sara said, "You might put them in the category of weird things."

"Right," said William, "that category has been used a lot in our era. Our
age is famous for storing a huge amount of stuff in the Weird Box."

"So," I said, "the knowledge that we can unbind time can be used for
us to pay attention to subtle cues. All the time, as you say, our greater
self, in league with higher beings, sends us messages."

"Yes," said William.

"Okay," I replied. "But if karma's the thing that gives us substance
and solidity, when you unbind time what do you do with karma?"

"You don't do much with karma when you unbind time," the mage
replied, "because from the highest perspective of all you must know that
spiritual beings see karmic beings as truly blessed. A karmic being *is* truly
blessed.

"We usually think of karma as a terrible burden," William went on.
"When I speak in Vancouver, BC, and mention the word 'karma,' the whole
room falls through the floor. That British-based world has got such a heavy
dose of history, such an oppressive sense of past stuff trailing around the
globe that you can't get rid of. But from a free perspective, here in California, looking from outside the bubble, karma's a tremendous gift, the greatest the gods could give us, because then we have a clear trail."

"Breadcrumbs," said Sara.

"Ariadne's Thread," I put in.

"That's the best image," William concurred. "Karma is Ariadne's
Thread, from the myth of Theseus and the Minotaur. When our soul
takes a body it stumbles back into the labyrinth of physical-material
existence, back into ancestry and past lives and whatever patterns it
agreed to be part of, and needs a thread to follow through every twist and
turn and tangle that arises here, to get to the center of the maze.

"So karma's not your retribution, it's your trail following you around
so you won't lose the way. It's the set-up mandatory to do our work
around here."

I asked, "Is there anything in our lives that *isn't* karmic?"

William thought on this. "Moments of grace have nothing to do with karma. They're just downpourings from out of nowhere for no reason at all, that we don't deserve, and of course *bloody well perfectly deserve.*"

Blythe said, "So what happens after 2012 when we're no longer karmic beings?"

"We'll still be karmic beings after 2012," said William, "but we're gonna enter the next level of karma. What does that look like? Well, even though karma is our ally, that's only the view from on high. That's how spirit beings see us. The subjective human experience, though, is more often that karma's a bitch, because we can't beat it, we can't beat it, we can't beat the rap, can't get out of it, can't get off the hook, and we very much want to get off the hook.

"The kind of karma we're working with currently is like we're convicted prisoners on death row awaiting execution, perhaps getting a stay of execution, perhaps not. We're living back through all our days that led to this plight. You can imagine if you were in prison in that situation—everything you've ever been through would be haunting you, right? 'All the mistakes I made, and all the things I could've done differently. And how did I get to this point?' Naturally you'd be internally self-scouring.

"After 2012, this phase of self-scouring death-row karma is intended to give way to a more released version. My sense is that physical matter is going to become infused with inner light. The sun's going to permeate our bodies. Right now these are more earthbound bodies." William looked down at himself. "They're going to become solar bodies. I've met a few people with solar bodies. They look and act like they're not of the world as we perceive it right now. Those kind of golden, radiant people. They have a different kind of body. They're very unusual, very rare folks. 'The sun-eyed children of a marvelous dawn' is how it was put in a fascinating prophetic poem by Sri Aurobindo."

"I like that inner light thing," Lee said. "But can't we transform without having to wait for 2012?"

"To do that, we have to get through the Idolatry of Appearances," replied William. "The Idolatry of Appearances states that if something's in space or time, then it's in another space or time from something else. Our vision is very, very literal these days.

"If these two iris flowers here, for example," he said, pointing to the vase, "are a few inches apart, then according to limited mind they're in different worlds. They in fact happen to be linked with the same life force, happen to be absolutely *inside* one another, but I'm gonna see them as separate if I'm obsessed with a certain surface phenomenon that makes their separate space seem all-powerful, and their inner link somehow subliminal and not the point.

"When we renounce this overly literal vision of the modern mind, the underlying unity of all things becomes apparent. Nothing is disconnected. We're in community. Not just a global but a Galactic Village. Earth always intersects with higher worlds. Vast realms stream into here through certain nodal points, junctures in time and space.

"The universe is a cyclical flow of beings in motion. The possibility of us tuning into this is mostly a matter of our readiness and willingness to show up at these occasions.

"Certainly, if the stars are in a particular place, or if we're in the right situation, with the right combination of ingredients, it helps. But essentially it's a free open matter. It's just that we're usually preoccupied. We miss this because we're generally caught in various other things. But if we're not, cosmos is right here," he snapped his fingers, "which is important because that means it's an unconditional event.

"Instantaneous time comes to us in free unconditional events. Which means cosmos is always on tap. The cosmos is freely available. I mean, in our modern consciousness, we often need various rituals and preparations and things to bring ourselves to meet cosmos. I'm not saying we don't, but *cosmos* doesn't. The greater worlds do not need us to say anything or do anything per se. What they *do* need is for us to get the top off our head, get the bottom off our feet, get the stuff off our sides and show up. But that's not according to any formula, no matter how sophisticated. It's a matter of presence. Fully mobilized presence."

And suddenly class was over.

We had a celebration, music, a party and a play in which Val, Nancy and I satirized our group (I played *Shmilliam Talltale*) and cracked up the room, William most of all. Straight-faced, with my shirt tail sticking out, I improvised replies for spontaneous queries students hurled at me, which lampooned the eccentric way our teacher had of answering questions without answering them. When the satire ended William was red-faced and sputtering, and tears streamed down Sara's face.

The nine-month project was done. Whatever collective organism we'd midwifed was in the world and breathing. As Val and I drove home I was overtaken by a swell of sadness, and longing. Sadness that our cosmic odyssey through *The Book of Destiny* was over, and longing to spread our findings to others.

—13

Bringing the Stars
Down to Earth

A few days later I was freed from my weekly job of transcribing, editing and distributing chapters of *Destiny in Action*. I invited Val to the Oregon Country Fair for her first time, my home away from home since 1979, where I get to play music around the clock and drink in an enormous wealth of tribal spirit with forty thousand others.

The fair is many hundreds of wooden booths of handmade crafts laid over the earth in the path of a huge infinity symbol in the wilds of the northwest, with scrumptious food, beautiful women, and the country's most soulful acoustic music all night long under the stars. The baby grand piano in the intimate outdoor stage at The Ritz sauna and shower booth, by the heart-shaped fire pit, is the sweetest gig I know of.

Just as Harbin Hot Springs is the only place I know that provides guaranteed healing each time I've gone for decades, Country Fair is the only place I know providing guaranteed transformation. Each July I fret, telling myself, 'It can't do it again, can it? It can't change my life again?' . . . And each year the Fair finds some new way to do it.

Part of the reason it works this way, I'm convinced, is because everyone walks around that mystical Brigadoon by the Long Tom River with their belief systems blown open to the premise that Love Rules and Magic Happens. Decades of this collective belief seem to have imprinted the molecules there, creating an Evolutionary Acceleration Chamber where miracles occur, and doorways open. Three days of this catapult me through more musical evolution than a normal year. I see the event as a psychic wetlands, a master link in the mystic transformation chain, which people don't necessarily register, but might notice if the Fair ever dried up or was paved over.

As we prepared to drive north from Santa Cruz in the summer of '92, Val learned that one of her friends owned a funky mobile home up for rent cheap in the woods of southern Oregon.

As usual, the Fair delivered. Val and I soaked it in, emerging emotionally replenished and physically exhausted. On the way back we checked the trailer and I felt a pull, not because it was the perfect place (far from it), but because I was burnt out on Santa Cruz and felt drawn toward a rural environment where life might settle and my spirit could open.

Moving came naturally to me. I'd done it forty times and wasn't even forty years old. But I felt a pang when I considered leaving William and Sara. I was concerned about Sara's healing and didn't want to be left out of the ring of support that was forming around her in response to William's call. Also, group seemed likely to regenerate before long in some new form, and it was hard to think I wouldn't be a part of it. Still, I figured I'd always be welcomed back in the circle. But I began to hanker to quit preaching to the choir and take Star Genesis out of its birthing grounds to the great wide world beyond Santa Cruz. On the ride back, Val and I talked over pluses and minuses of the move and decided to do it.

As a going-away present, William gave me a copy of his comprehensive degree lore, six thick notebooks packed with extensive information on each degree of the zodiac. These were the different-colored binders I'd glimpsed in Ross the day we met.

The zodiac is a circle of three-hundred-sixty degrees. Each of the twelve signs has thirty degrees, and it makes a huge difference whether a planet is at Four Aries, for instance, or Five Aries; Twelve Capricorn or Thirteen. William, who inherited the project of degree interpretation from his teacher Marc Edmund Jones (the previous foremost degree scholar), has become the world's expert, decoding the complex tale of each degree into mini-glimpses of human nature, three-hundred-and-sixty fascinating stories all their own. Once or twice a decade he reformulates all of them. The version he gave me that day consisted of four pages of information on each—1,440 pages in all. At last I had a full lexicon of the wizard's clairvoyant lore to bolster my readings. Now I could fine-tune my comprehension of human beings to a cutting-edge instrument of pinpoint precision, thereby gaining some of the wizard's own advanced mastery.

Driving north along the Pacific outside Half Moon Bay with Val, I recalled my teacher's parting words.

"Did I ever tell you," William said, handing me the binders, "Jones's Sun was at Nine Libra."

"Like mine!"

"Yes."

"Oh. So you're a hamburger," I retorted, "a Taurus cow sandwiched between two Libras with the same Sun! Your main teacher and student share the exact same degree. Hmm . . . I wonder why?"

William threw up his hands. "It's a conspiracy. You guys were out to get me from the start! One coming from the past and one from the future. I had nowhere to run."

I laughed. "I wonder why the gods set it up this way? What are you trying to learn from Nine Libra? What do *I* have to teach *you*?"

He thought a moment. "You know, Jones and Rudhyar were obsessed with the Neptune-in-Libra generation more than any other."

"Those of us born from 1942 to 1956."

"Yes."

"Why?"

"Because Libra has the passion to change the world."

"I should tell you," added Sara, embracing me, "I learned degrees over the course of a year by getting up early each morning and reading the full information for the degree the Sun was passing through that day."

"That's a great idea! I'll do it," I said, hugging her back. "I just want to—" I spoke haltingly. "I wanna thank you for everything you've given me, given all of us. You're my new hero."

She laughed. "Thank *you* for your great work on the chapters. We couldn't have done it without you. And for the Solstice workshop."

"Mmm," I said, recalling the closeness we had all shared that day.

"I hope Oregon gives you what you're searching for."

In the Valley of the Seven Winds, in what Val christened The Ramshackle Palace—a drafty slipshod trailer with extensions cobbled on both ends— I sank into my studies of Star Genesis, including notes from years of personal talks with the mage. I boiled everything down to my "little black book," a slim binder with codes and formulas that's become my main reference for studying charts.

The day we moved in I found the kitchen sink broken. Two days later we drove to Cave Junction, the closest town of any size, for plumbing parts. The town struck me as a sleepy, slightly rednecky/slightly hippie burg between I-5 and the sea. We found a rundown laundromat with stacks of Jehovah's Witnesses' *Watchtower* and *National Geographic*, a pizza place and not much more. Then we bumped into Hammer's Market.

The first thing I noticed at Hammer's were four shelves of Steiner books in a small wooden bookcase greeting everyone who walked in. Spotting the telltale anthroposophic art on the covers, I did a double-take. *Here?* In a backcountry grocery store? Fishing tackle, pocket knives, canned stew, Wonder Bread and *Knowledge of the Higher Worlds*—? I took it as a sign from spirit I hadn't completely thrown my life away by leaving the Bay Area.

With money left from the move I sprang for three books to add to my collection. Steiner is the source of William's metaphysics, and now I had the root of the root to grab hold of in the wilderness. In the Bay Area I'd used Star Genesis to make a living. In Selma I worked it deeper into my pores. I had to. There was little else to do. Along with bears and coyotes and a rare reading, Val and I were on our own in what felt like a haunted house. We heard that a murder had taken place there, and rarely felt alone. Against this stark foreground the mysteries became more primal, a matter of survival in a precarious new existence where everything was as funky as a busted pipe.

One day I stumbled upon a foundational concept of Steiner's that froze me in my tracks:

When tempted to find an imperfection in the universe, you'll make progress if you assume the flaw is more due to your temporary failure to grasp the underlying web of unity that connects all things, rather than an actual imperfection.

I read this over and over until it penetrated me like a healing balm. It seemed the fundamental axiom, a magic formula, the key to existence. I inscribed it in my date book, meditated on it for weeks, until it lodged deeper and deeper into the core of my belief system.

In the first four months in our new home Val and I were squeezed because even though our rent was much less than in Santa Cruz, our nest egg got used up by the move and for daily living. Her attempt to transplant her career teaching singing fared little better than my attempt to transplant my astrology practice. Our idea to remove distractions from our love in order to see what it was made of worked, but we didn't much care for what it was made of. I began to sense the creeping presence of the Void.

We sank to our nadir one rainy morning in early December, scraping the dregs of a peanut butter jar with no help in sight. Later that day the phone rang.

"Is this Mark Borax?" said a woman.

"Yes."

"My name is Judith. I'm a therapist in Port Townsend, Washington. My friend in Santa Cruz can't stop raving about your work. What would it take to get you up here to give me a session?"

"A few others who feel the same way."

"I might be able to do that," she replied. "Would you like the money up-front?"

"At least half, for deposit."

"That can be arranged."

I didn't tell her that without the deposit I wouldn't have gas for the drive.

Judith agreed to put me up, lend me her office and spread word of my availability. In return I promised to give her and her husband free readings.

I drove north the second week of December while Val traveled to Santa Cruz to teach. Our plan was to gather funds and meet back at the Palace for Christmas.

I crossed Hood Canal in snowfall, mesmerized by the way the flakes swirled along the bridge grating, startled when the storm curtain blew open a seawater expanse of the rolling snowcapped Coastal Mountain range in the distance. The sweeping magnitude of the Pacific Northwest shocked me out of my trailer-park blues, delivering the prescient awareness that, once again, I was leaping into the unknown and my life was about to change.

As I pulled into Port Townsend I felt a tug of instant kinship with the place, which had the blustery picturesque appearance of a New England seaport, towering wooden ships harbored along the main road into town.

When I met Judith she handed me birth data and appointment schedules for nine clients, more than I expected, and that number soon multiplied. One of my new clients, Alia, was married to the dean of an acupuncture school in Seattle and knew loads of folks on the spirit path. She sent more clients my way—friends, relatives, co-workers—as the first wave of readings produced a second, then a third, until I was swamped with ample opportunity to test out my new reference material.

Winter Solstice the previous year thrust me into the Capricornian core of my nature: *A student of nature lecturing.* Solstice in Port Townsend thrust me into the core of my work. Each night I stayed awake long after midnight marking up the next day's charts in the shorthand color-coding system I developed to give me something to improvise off of.

Nights were spent studying charts; mornings I rose early to do yoga and snatch a quick breakfast. I was getting little rest but surfing energy waves from client to client.

I bartered readings for meals with a young restaurant owner named Dawn who was short on cash, a three-star chef who left her gourmet concoctions on a silver platter outside my door while I was in session. After scraping peanut butter jars in Selma, salmon meals with rice, veggies and dessert made me feel I'd died and gone to heaven.

P.T. rolled out its red carpet, magnified by the snowy backdrop of Christmastime, and I rose to the challenge. Never had I experienced such readings. Each began at a depth of insight I'd only formerly reached at the end of certain special readings. True to Steiner, I felt a direct ray of higher force streaming through the Solstice right down into me.

The plush furnishings of my Port Townsend office were the most posh showcase of my practice thus far. I felt like a king from the wilderness sitting in that big cushy swivel chair surrounded by exotic paintings and plants. For the first time in my career there was even a waiting room where clients could sit reading magazines until I was done with the previous session, which reminded me of how I'd waited in that office in Ross five years earlier for my first meeting with the mage.

During rare spare moments, I browsed through downtown P.T., buying a snazzy southwestern-style winter coat, music tapes for Val and various homey things to spruce up our wilderness outpost. In the flush of good fortune I was seized with a desire to share the bounty.

I finished my readings and left town three days before Christmas in a much different state than I'd arrived, driving over Hood Canal singing Christmas songs, with an urge to move to Port Townsend. After my time there, prospects in southern Oregon looked bleak.

The moment I pulled into Selma a storm blew in that lengthened to a two-day blizzard, dumping a few feet of snow through Christmas Eve. The forest took on a sparkling shroud that mercifully obscured the blemishes of our battered home. Val was stranded in Santa Cruz so I sank into communion with nature and spirit, as Steiner advised to do at that time—bypass commercialism and go deep within.

I'd returned with supplies I used to transform our bedroom to a sensuous love palace. Previously I'd refrained from decorating because Val had such strong ideas about what she liked and loathed. Normally I was pretty easy-going with these things. But in the afterglow of my success in Port Townsend I forged ahead and redid the room. If there was any part of me that had been holding back the full force of my desire, I wanted to release that and go all the way.

The next day I picked up Val at the Grants Pass bus depot and drove her home. She took one look at the room and said, "Ugh, what happened here?" That disgusted tone of voice, more than anything, told me it was over.

We hacked it out a couple weeks until I decided to part company. I offered to bring Val up north, because even though we wouldn't be lovers, I figured we could still be friends.

She was touched by my offer but decided to remain in Selma, and we had a good cry over the fact I'd taken her out of Santa Cruz, brought her to the wilderness and was dumping her now to go off on my own.

"I'm a Love Train," I said, "picking up women and dropping them in some new life they get to keep while I move to the next depot."

"God, Mark," my lover blurted through tears, "I thought I was bad, but you're a serial monogamist who goes from love to love to love. When will it end?"

Crying, I shrugged and told her I was going to miss my metaphysical study buddy and all her late-night stuffed-animal psychodramas. So she did one last routine for me, using Pinky and Teddy and Leo (three stuffed animals) to act out the feelings of her inner child at the moment of my leaving. I drove away bawling until I felt the good clean cutting away of some abscessed part of my life, some male/female wound that had to bleed freely before it could heal.

Instead of relocating to P.T., though, I decided to move to nearby Whidbey Island, which I'd gone to visit and felt grabbed by. True to Sara's insight, my life was turning out to be composed of things I prepared ardently for that weren't necessarily what I needed, but led me to what I did need. Or so it seemed in the winter of 1993.

My heart, though, began to hanker for some richer culmination that might only come from taking root. Berkeley led to Shasta, Shasta to William, William to La Honda, La Honda to Santa Cruz, Santa Cruz to Selma, Selma to Port Townsend, which led to Whidbey—where would Whidbey lead?

On the island I found a red farmhouse for sale on the road to Langley, which I was able to rent cheap until it sold. From my second-storey bedroom I could see the ships at Langley harbor. That summer, sprinting into yet another new life, I reread *Zorba the Greek*, played guitar, studied Star Genesis, shot pool at the Doghouse, walked the charming streets of Langley village late at night and fell in love with my sexy new female companion, Pooky the Wonder Cat, a small, feisty, irresistible Lynx-point Siamese who was vastly psychic and chased deer through the orchard.

I made friends quickly on the island.

I pitched an astrology column to the local newspaper, *The Island Independent*, telling Drew the publisher I only wanted to do it if I could find a whole new take on Sun Sign columns. He said that's the only way he wanted to do it too, so I came up with *Revolutionary Astrology: Breaking the barriers between us and ourselves.* It was my first attempt to craft a language to translate Star Genesis into something colorful, exciting and accessible to a diverse readership.

I only got twenty bucks for each column but figured it would announce my presence in the Puget Sound and bring in readings. As winter turned to spring, though, readings were scarce and once again I had to scrimp. I began to question my choice to ignore my original instinct to move to P.T., but somehow that didn't feel right either. Then I began to wonder if my practice was inextricably linked to the Bay Area.

But Langley, with its whimsical seaside shops, had so many cool people—pockets of artists, conscious parents, writers and healers—and the land took my breath away with its rolling green hills and beachfuls of bald eagles, such that the romantic in me felt compelled to hang on and eke out a living. If nothing else, I told myself, I was courting a new disaster I could one day use to fuel my literary adventures. *Cosmic Fool Rides Again....*

I moved to Whidbey in early 1993. In July of that year, raw and hoarse and freshly back from the Country Fair, I crashed headlong into a divinely inspired, emotionally volatile Gemini artist named Alex, who resembled Uma Thurman and was in the end stages of a passionless marriage. *This one's different. This'll last. I've never felt this way before. . . .*

For ten years Alex's libido had smoldered underground like magma. The first time we made love was more of a volcanic explosion than anything else. From then on our bodies couldn't stay away from each other, which drove our minds crazy, because even when we weren't getting along later, we couldn't keep fire from the fuse.

It took this fierce lanky primal force in the shape of a woman to release the full force of my lust for the first time in my life. The only thing that infuriated Alex was if I held back. Even if she began to *suspect* I was holding something primal back from lovemaking it was trouble. Unless I plowed in hard enough, long enough, deep enough, often enough, she refused to believe any poetic words I showered her with, and just about bit my head off. Once we made love five times in one day, and when I went to leave that night she followed me to my car and gave me oral sex on the lawn before letting me drive off.

Her other favorite pastime became lying on her back beneath me while I stood straddling her, drumming naked full-force on my booming wooden African djembe, with the bottom of the drum's sound hole positioned directly over her sternum. This mixture of cold island and hot woman drove me back to eating meat, which I'd refrained from for years.

A couple months after we met, Alex and I moved in together, into an adorable yellow cottage with inlaid floors and cabinets, perched on a cliff over the sea on a point jutting out from a remote tip of the island, where orcas spouted and howled like wolves of the sea in front of the big picture window.

In that windblown cottage I was admitted to the inner sanctum of a hand-painting textile goddess who drank my desire like a love-starved teenager and bared her sex to me like a high-paid prostitute. Our blend of fire and ice was dynamic and addictive, as we clung to love and wrested

every ounce of meaning we could from passion. Raw gems of poetic revelation from the depths of our bodies floated up past our descent into an
ocean of lust and dysfunctionality, as the rain fell and the skies darkened and summer turned to autumn.

For six months we clashed and crashed and loved into each other
with fierce abandon until we blew ourselves out of the waters. Once
again I was left stunned, thrown up on the sand like a beached whale
with money problems and love problems and health problems and an
outlook as dark as the impossible weather which had become one big
storm since I moved to the island.

With the idea of placing my hands far enough away from Alex's breasts
to keep me out of trouble, and to scrape up Christmas money, I arranged
to go back on *Seeing Beyond* via telephone, to drum up enough business
to make it worthwhile to drive to the Bay Area and do readings.

Blythe told me group had rekindled in Bonny Doon, though no one
seemed clear on the focus. I also got word the Lonsdales were going to
teach a two-day public workshop in Vancouver, Canada, not far from the
island. Even though we weren't getting along so well, Alex and I drove
up for the event, sponsored by the local anthroposophy society.

The large auditorium was packed. The tenor of William's talk differed
from a California presentation in terms of the staid seriousness with
which his far-out ideas were received, and the well-thought-out questions raised by the audience. Metaphysics seemed more traditionally
woven into society there, unlike the fringe position it occupied in the
States. I saw how legitimately these Canadians regarded our cosmic wildman, how sensibly they approached the supersensible, how pleasantly
normal they appeared.

After the workshop, William invited us to a healing for Sara in a private home they were staying in. We drove up the heights out of Vancouver in late afternoon as a thunderstorm rolled in. Clashing storm fronts
felt like a battle in heaven as we climbed higher and higher into the
clouds. The house was perched on a lightning-spackled cliff overlook-
ing the city and a broad sweep of the sea.

Inside, we gathered on chairs in a circle in the living room. Along with the Lonsdales, Alex and me, five others were present. We settled in without speaking for a long time.

"Thank you all for coming," William said, breaking the ice, sitting to the left of his wife while I sat to her right. "When we set up this event we didn't know the cancer had entered Sara's pancreas, where it's causing tremendous pain."

I looked at her but saw no signs of suffering. Either she'd taken painkillers or was using some psychic technique to distance the agony.

"The purpose we had in calling you here wasn't to cure Sara," the mage continued, "but to clear any vestiges of resistance she may have to totally aligning with her destiny. Tonight I'm not interested in words. We're beyond that. I'm interested in deep process."

I sat beside my friend during the next few hours engaged in a mostly wordless energy healing while the storm howled. I dredged up the-wolf-that-eats-the-darkness, whom I'd met on the slopes of Shasta during the Harmonic Convergence. I'd brought this totem out in men's groups and sacred rituals I'd led over the years, and used him in a handful of shamanic healings for clients. I tapped this reluctantly, and with great care, because it left me drained afterwards.

I sent the wolf down to eat her cancer, a process which broke me out in sweat. It felt similar to sex in that I needed to choose how invasively to psychically enter Sara while maintaining some healthy boundary, which was not easy. Some part of me bared its fangs, warning *if you hold back you'll regret it. . . .*

In the end I wasn't sure what was achieved, and it wasn't the kind of group where they wanted to talk about it.

As the circle disbanded I took Sara to the bedroom and played a song for her on the stereo, which I'd brought to Vancouver for that purpose— "Unbroken Chain" by Paul Kamm and Eleanor MacDonald, which summed up what I wanted to say in case I never saw her again.

We sat on the bed holding hands and listening to this heartfelt impressionistic sketch of mortality and eternity, freedom and bondage. It was sad and sweet for me to silently acknowledge that my most intimate moment with Sara Lonsdale might be my last.

When the song ended Sara let the waves of it wash over, then asked, "How's life on Whidbey Island?"

"Whidbey's amazing," I replied. "I'm not sure if I'm progressing or regressing, though. I seem to have run into my old karmic pattern where things begin with such promise then fall apart. Alex and I are beginning to get wobbly, and my work hasn't got launched in Langley like it did in Port Townsend."

"Could you move *there?*"

I threw up my hands. "Please—not another new start in another strange place! What do they want from me?"

Sara laughed.

"How's group going in Santa Cruz?" I asked.

"We stopped teaching."

"No! Why?"

"You're the only one who learned it."

My jaw fell. Once again, in her understated way, Sara managed to casually drop a bomb that exploded my accustomed reality. Even though part of me must've already suspected the truth of this, Sara's statement took the wind out of me. *Though we went on a wild ride, I'm the only sorceror's apprentice.*

After people said goodbyes, Alex and I were last to go. Sara told Alex she loved the pants Alex had on—a pair of silk pants my lover had hand-painted with her own vibrant tribal art, a flowing viney pattern of elemental fury of dark green, brown, yellow and red. In a twist of the old cliché, Alex gave Sara the pants off her butt, and after a brief heartfelt farewell, we left, Sara's words about me being the only one to learn Star Genesis haunting me all the way to the island.

A few weeks later I got a phone call from Margie: Sara was in the hospital close to death. "She's receiving calls, though. Most people haven't been able to get through, but if you have anything to say, now's the time."

I clicked off then dialed the number. After half a ring she answered.

"Sara!"

"Mark! *Mark!* I have to tell you—" she giggled. "Oh, but you know. *You* know! It's amazing—the light, the *light*—oooh. Ahh."

I waited for more but the silence held. "Yes, Sara," I said, beginning to cry. "I know."

I fought for words. But what could I say? "I wish I could be there," I uttered in a halting voice.

"*Oh Mark,*" she replied, "but you are here! You know that. Remember the light. . . . I've gotta go now."

"Okay," I said, sniffling. "I—I'll remember . . . Sara—."

"*—have to go.*"

"I love you, Sara," I told her for the first time, tears flowing.

"I love you," came the faint reply.

A week or so later Margie phoned again, convulsed in weeping, telling me Sara had just died.

I thanked her and placed the phone in its cradle.

As the pain welled up in my chest it was accompanied by a feminine laugh that rang unmistakably clear in my temples, and the words: *Who are you sad for?*

This message jerked me upright.

I should be sad—I protested.

Shouldn't I? . . .

Who am *I sorry for?*

I saw then that grief can be self-pity in disguise, and I wanted to get through that to some deeper truth that might be down there. *What is death about, anyway—me, or her?*

Go ahead, said the voice, *cry if you need to. Just know whom you're crying for.*

This statement was so commonsensical it made me laugh even as I broke out in tears. I knew only one person who could simplify such metaphysical tangles. Yes, my guts were kicked in that Sara was gone—but it was hard to indulge that while she was beaming messages to me! My laughter and tears fused until I didn't know what I felt. . . . *Remember the light. . . .*

A few days later I drove to an acquaintance's estate in the hills south of Santa Cruz to do readings I'd garnered on radio. From a client, I heard that William was holding a ceremony in two days for family and friends.

After my first day of work I took a sunset walk through the high meadow. While passing a tall stand of pampas grass, my attention riveted to the sky, where a corona of liquid light poured out of the sun, which flared into a huge rose-golden orb with violet and brown streaks behind it. The background deepened while the sun swelled forward three-dimensionally with sculptural precision. I'd never seen a sunset solid as a living engraving, pouring pulsating plasma bursts in scintillating waves like a great banner in the west. The sun streamed into a radiant cross that took up one-third of the sky, growing more and more saturated with depth of field and color until I longed for someone to verify the enormousness of what I was seeing. But with no one there I just watched, staring in wonder, eyes tearing, soaking it in.

It reminded me of years earlier, in my La Honda studio, when I'd seen chakras, except now perhaps I was seeing the jeweled chakra of the sky. Maybe it was one of those nodes my teacher mentioned where greater reality streams in. I stood immobile until the colors faded. From beginning to end the whole thing lasted about forty-five minutes.

After two days plowing through readings, I drove to Bonny Doon for the first time since Val and I moved away a year and a half earlier. Sara's ceremony was at the Baha'i school adjacent to the cottage grounds. About sixty people circled up in the meeting room. I recognized half.

One by one we went around the ring counter-clockwise, in the direction the planets move through the birth chart, giving each person a chance to speak. I learned that a tight inner core of companions huddled close to Sara in her final weeks, helping William maintain round-the-clock vigil. Many people shared heartfelt stories of their experiences at this time. I was surprised to hear others relate inexplicable phenomena surrounding her death—colors in the sky, messages in their head and other telepathic news of her passing.

Apparently, in her final weeks Sara Lonsdale broke through to some rare state of embodiment, which filled her with such fierce radiance that no one could keep up. Doctors and nurses who'd gone to her hospital room before she was released to die at home (one of the doctors was in the circle), expecting to find an emaciated woman, came out shaking their heads in disbelief. Practitioners girding themselves to aid a terminally ill patient ended up testifying how Sara had energized their lives. As more of these tales were told, the circle seemed to swell with life force.

In a light Brooklyn accent my fairy godmother Hina said, "I was one of the last with Sara before she went to the hospital. She was blasting Beethoven out of those huge speakers and dancing away. At the height of it she threw her top off and I took mine off, and she grabbed my hands and we danced and danced until I stopped to catch my breath and I saw blood pouring from her nipples."

A moment later Bhasa added, "I too was there in the final days. At one point Sara had gone to the bathroom. When a lot of time went by I began to get concerned. I heard her cry out and was just about to knock when she said, 'Oh wow! So *that's* what consciousness is!'"

As we laughed I realized that in dying Sara had finally managed to *live.* She'd done it. My friend had really done it. She'd beaten the odds, overcome every obstacle to being fully present in the physical plane, and the power of this event raced around the circle like a spark around an ignition coil.

When my turn came I told of the message I'd gotten within moments of her death, to know what I was sad for, and I mentioned the jeweled chakra in the sky, which others had seen. I shared a couple private moments I'd had with Sara in the past few years, how in that understated way she'd helped me grasp who I was in the greater scheme of things, giving me reflections I was still digesting years later.

And so it went, around the circle until it came all the way to Safiya, William and Sara's closest friend, who stood next to the mage.

"I was the last person with Sara as she died," said the slender angelic-looking woman with pipe-curled auburn hair and large liquid eyes. "But first, I want to say that a few days before this, I came to the cottage to be with her. She was sitting on the front steps and it was very cold. She had nothing but a t-shirt on! I sat next to her and was quiet for a while.

"She'd just had an experience of Christ. It was dark and wet but she didn't feel any cold. A sun was bearing down on her—but not the sun. She was bathed in light. She revealed to me this extraordinary, intimate experience of being completely drenched in Christ light.

"On December fifth, the day of Sara's death, I drove up to the cottage that morning feeling a huge sense of urgency. *'Please please please wait till I get there. Please wait till I get there. Please. . . .'*

"And when I got there our friend Salima said, 'I'm gonna build up the fire.' William went off to do a reading.

"I walked in the room. Everyone else was gone. Sara looked at me. She really, really looked at me. She said, 'Here comes beauty!' and then she shot off like a comet way way up into the sky and took me with her—and then," Safiya's eyes widened as if she were realizing this for the first time, "she came back! She came back in, from *below,* and I realized, 'Oh, so that's where it's coming from now, from *under the earth.'* And then she was gone."

After this William exhaled sharply, shaking his head. Uncharacteristically, he stood chewing his beard and fretting, which made me wonder *what's it like to lose your wife?*

"People talk of isms," he finally began. "Racism, sexism, age-ism. But there's a much deeper 'ism' written into our culture—deathism.

"We're life bigots. We harbor the deep prejudice that it's better to be alive than dead! No one questions this. We marginalize the dead. We pity them. Turn them into second-rate citizens. We shirk contact with death and dying. And so we create yet another barrier between ourselves and everyone wishing to relate with us. It's a lie. The biggest of all.

"Since the moment Sara died, she's been taking me along on her journey through the preliminary death realms. She's using her no-nonsense Virgo sensibility to articulate clearly and concisely, and in picturesque detail, her encounters with others recently dead, and with guardians, spirit beings who preside over these realms. She's rendering such a vivid description of this right now that it's making it impossible for me to stand here and pretend to be normal."

The group hushed. Somebody groped for my hand, and I took their fingers until one by one the circle linked.

William started to add something, swallowed it, then began again. "The dead," he fished for words, working his hands at his sides, "the dead fertilize the living. Sara's onrush into death realms is pumping huge bursts of life force into this land, which she loved. Into me, into her daughter," he nodded at Amy, "exploding every idea I've had of death and dying. And many misconceptions about life."

William's chest heaved. Clearly he was waging some inner battle. "Look—I want to fully express this to you, I really do, but it's excruciating . . . while my insides are being dosed with . . . wave after wave of— [He didn't finish the sentence.] . . . I haven't slept for days . . . but I don't think that's pertinent. . . ." he trailed off.

After steadying himself he added, "I have a lot to say . . . I have to say that I'm in, even for me, such a . . . state from this shared journey that I can scarcely contain myself. For once in my life words fail me." His mouth worked but nothing came out.

I watched eyebrows rise through the room as William's face reflected a plethora of emotion. "I'd love to talk about this. I really would"—he broke into laughter—"*ha-hee!* But to have to say anything at all—*Ha!*— is such a huge distraction from the thing itself that . . . I don't know if I can.

"Let me try again." He blew out his breath. "O, *ah*, me." He straightened like a guilty high school kid stifling stoned giggles. "*Whew.* Okay. Steady, William. You can do this. . . ."

He wiped his mouth with the back of his huge hand. "The truth," he began haltingly, slowly gaining control, "the truth is that Sara and I are more together now than we've ever been. I am totally, excruciatingly, euphorically inside my wife at this moment. And she's inside me. More than ever. And we're both deep within the Earth, in a way that's coming back to me now from my own deaths. Except it's all different—" Again he paused, wrestling for words while the rest of us waited.

"I have to say this one thing at least: Sara died at the most conscious, most awake, most energetic, most alive pinnacle of her life. Of her entire reincarnational cycle. The result is she's funneling a flood of information to me about what she's experiencing, and it's positively fraught with implication, absolutely terrifying and ecstatic."

He took a deep breath. "I realize many folks here, especially Sara's family, have no background in the things some of us have been studying for years. But I won't apologize to you because I can't disown even a fraction of what's going on here. The one in me who used to apologize for such things is gone. Sara blew him away when she crossed over, and I'm not sure he'll be back.

"The truth, which emerged more and more as people spoke, and which she herself ultimately recognized, is that *Sara never came alive until she began dying.*

"All her life, and even long before, Sara was haunted. Some of you know this but many of you don't, and nobody knows the full extent of it, because she carried it unobtrusively, beneath that pragmatic nature of hers, while she went about her business as good old dependable Sara. She didn't know the full truth of it herself, really," he mused, "for a long while.

"Inwardly, though, Sara was tortured by the horrid suspicion that something vital was missing. And something *was* naggingly, torturously missing from her life, from her many lives to that point. What was missing was *her.*

"A little over a year ago, when cancer approached, Sara got to work and used the proximity of death to burn up everything between her and absolute presence."

The circle drew closer in on itself.

"The way she achieved this," continued William, "the way this diminutive bulldog of a woman took up life-in-death with a force nobody dreamed she had inside—was nothing short of miraculous at the outset and from there increased exponentially during her final months, days, weeks, minutes and seconds, until she ignited so much life force at the moment of expiration that she rocketed through the death realms on a blazing journey that has profound ramifications for us all.

"Sara died supremely consciously. And that burst of life-unto-death produced a dimensional splash seen across the world. Reports are still coming in by phone of odd visual phenomena even from people who didn't know her.

"Sara mustered such force of being that she shot through the death realms with a *sploosh* that's absolutely shaking things up over there, infusing the hidden realms with supercharged vitality that she brought from the land of the so-called living.

"But—I'm sorry to have to report—compared to many of the dead, we in this room are barely alive. Yes." William halted and I was struck by the effort it cost him to stay on his feet.

"It's becoming clear to me," he said, coughing into his hand, "that the journey between death and rebirth has at least as many phases as the journey between birth and death, probably more, to such an extent that my entire worldview is being demolished in a process I'm not likely to recover from any time soon.

"Sara's experience, which she's sharing with me even as I speak, is so astonishingly lucid and vivid, gripping me with such force, that I can scarcely contain myself. The man I was, as recently as this morning, is falling away, falling away, even as I'm gaining compassion to see him through the eyes of the newly dead, to see why he was the way he was, that odd stuffy fellow . . . why he inhabited that half-assured, half-stultified existence when there was always so much more . . . so much more."

My teacher removed his glasses and rubbed the bridge of his nose.

Unsteadily, a moment later, he slid them back on. "I'm being taught by this experience what it means to be living with another human being in the most graphically intimate terms possible, including everything you could ever imagine such a thing between two lovers could include, to the degree where I'm being filled with such inward potency that I can scarcely breathe, let alone describe this coherently, or see anything ever again as cut off from anything else.

"The truth," he said, pulling himself together, "is that our love is more alive now than ever. So," he cleared his throat, "I'm using the power of this circle to devote myself to honoring our bond now and for the rest of my life, whatever that turns out to mean. I'm remarrying Sara the way I should've the first time."

After a collective gasp there were shrieks of laughter, *oohs* and *ahs* and scattered clapping, which William stood there taking in.

His voice steadied. "I just want to share one final thing, the primary thing Sara and I have been doing. We bridged worlds and we bridged time zones. This was our real work, beneath all our other work, through the years.

"We opened lines of communication between Earth and other realms in preparation for this journey. Since six years ago at Harmonic Convergence, every tap-in we did was the set-up for what's happening now. Because of this, Sara's able to inhabit and report a full-spectrum death journey, which most people only get to partly experience. The same way many of us on this side were impacted by the sheer force of her aliveness as her journey through life ended, so it's happening, even more, on the other side, where her journey's just beginning. And what this adventure bodes for the world has me captivated to the point where I don't think I can say anything more except *Hallelujah!*"

The group burst into rousing applause, which gave way to laughter and tears.

During subsequent months and years William continued to receive elaborate letters from Sara until there were more than two hundred thousand pages. Sara became Theanna, the name William told us she had when they'd known each other in Atlantis. A fraction of these letters were published in 1994 by Frog Ltd. as *The Book of Theanna: In the Lands that Follow Death*. One of the most grueling narratives of modern metaphysics, it narrates Sara's arduous passage through realms more convoluted than those described by Dante. Even today my teacher is busy transcribing messages from Theanna.

A few days after the memorial I drove north. Shortly after, my relationship blew up. Each time I opened my heart to Alex she slammed the door in my face. In our yellow cliffside cottage I felt marooned at the end of the world in a recurring nightmare. Once again love imploded, leaving me raw and wounded and very confused as to who had done what to whom.

My time on Whidbey turned out to be the darkest, wettest twelve months on the island for decades. The sun only came out twice for more than two days in a row, and, even apart from my lovesick blues, it was a wrenching battle for anyone to raise health and spirits in such cold, waterlogged darkness. *One big shit storm.*

At the lowest point of my life, I sank prone to the kitchen linoleum, much as I'd done on the slopes of Shasta. With Alex off island, I was stricken with a sickening urge to be done with the whole thing. If I could've wished myself out of existence, I might have. But I couldn't begin to realistically consider suicide because of what it would do to my mother. Besides that, Pooky needed me, as she reminded me, pushing her warm nose in my face on the cold floor. From her point of view, I thought, this might even be a positive move—me finally sinking to her level to visit her in the place where she gets fed, that's normally hers alone. As Pooky licked my nose it dawned on me that she was far and away my most faithful companion, which made me cry even more.

I was fed up with getting chewed by the same karma over and over, like Nietzsche's Chamber of Eternal Return. But then I was struck with the realization that the urge for suicide may actually be the cry of a past dead self seeking release from the weight of another round of the same karmic battle. Maybe it wasn't *me* that wanted out, I realized, but *that dude.* Sara's fight to conquer her own demons had equipped me to deal with mine. The subself that had been haunting me since before I could remember was close enough now that I could sense his toxic presence, even if I couldn't see him.

This is what Love's been trying to show me, I realized, flooded by the poisonous shadow that underlay each love. It wasn't me that wanted his life to be over, it was someone in me who was dying to be freed from the Void. This revelation shot me off the floor and gave me back to life. How many times would I have to die before I could live?

Now maybe I could get somewhere. But where?

Within weeks of my kitchen-floor epiphany, in a vindictive hurricane of emotion Alex and I split. I fled the cottage and a month later realized that for my career, health and sanity it was time to head back to Santa Cruz.

William had stopped teaching but was doing readings and plowing deeper into *The Book of Theanna.*

It was April 1994, the seventh year of my apprenticeship. I'd been on Whidbey one year on the day I packed Pooky and my things into the Volvo and drove south, determined to resuscitate my practice. I'd arranged to stay temporarily in a tiny trailer on my friend Barbara's land in Ben Lomond, adjacent to Bonny Doon, which I called the gypsy wagon because it reminded me of Professor Marvel's trailer in *The Wizard of Oz.*

In my forest home I pushed myself to do yoga, eat well, clear my head and launch a whole new life, whatever it took.

Fleeing the Puget Sound gloom gave me a boost, but I wrestled with the details of starting another new beginning in a life of nothing but. What most people think of as transition describes my entire existence, I reflected sardonically. *If you could ever get to something stable,* that *would be a transition.*

Despite the fallout of another break-up, and another new start, I felt mounting promise at the prospect of re-launching my astrology career. *You have a great reputation in the Bay Area,* I told myself. *People trust you and believe in you. You're not a stranger. You belong to something. You don't have to start from scratch.*

So I made plans to go on *Seeing Beyond* and set up my astrology materials on the narrow Formica table of the gypsy wagon.

In early May, as William's birthday approached, I enlisted Jade, Rob and Margie as co-conspirators to rustle up a posse of former students to ambush him. I knew if the gang showed up on the wizard's doorstep asking to resuscitate mystery school, he'd be hard-put to refuse.

On the afternoon of his birthday we carpooled to the cottage unannounced, which added a special thrill because of William's penchant for privacy. None of us had ever been so bold as to drop in on him before. On the way through Bonny Doon, Margie said she heard he'd changed his name. When he answered the door we sang:

Happy birthday to you,
Happy birthday to you,
Happy birthday, dear William-or-whatever-your-new-name-is—
Happy birthday to you!

He stood there mouth agape for a good long while, then shook his head in disbelief.

I stepped into the breach and announced, "We're giving you the birthday present of asking you to teach us! We want to start group again. Have you changed your name?"

After a moment, he nodded. "Yes. I've taken the name I had in Atlantis, which goes with Theanna. I'm Ellias." He pronounced it *EH*-lee-yoss.

Jade said, "Will you think about starting class again?"

Surrounded by each of us hanging on his response, what else could he say? "Yes. Can you give me a day or two to get back to you?"

As he said this, my teacher looked so forlorn—as if we might remain on his porch until we got an answer—that I had to laugh.

"Okay," I said, hugging him. "Happy birthday—*Ellias!*"

"Have some *fun* today!" Margie called over her shoulder as we walked away, leaving him shaking his head and sputtering.

Within two weeks Ellias took us up on our offer and launched a study group based on the Theanna letters. I felt that, as fascinating as the new material was, the sessions lacked the breakthrough power of the Destiny classes which (I saw even more with hindsight) had undoubtedly been the peak of my apprenticeship and a climactic moment in world astrology.

Since then, metaphysics hasn't grabbed me so powerfully. Since then I've practiced my craft diligently, doing hundreds of Soul Level Astrology readings. Since then I've turned to the master for advanced lessons, but those years of apprenticeship in the cottage beneath the trees ring out through the decades as a sterling moment in my life which impacted me so deeply that I am still sifting through the layers to sort it all out. To be sure, I've written this book for myself as much as for anyone else. I'm still trying to make sense of what happened on Comstock Lane.

Certain things can only happen when a rare confluence of people and events occurs. Those Destiny classes created such openings in so many of our lives, which cannot be duplicated but need to be mined and regenerated, even as we offer them to others. And the supercharged intensity of those times is something, I often have to remind myself, that lives in each us now. Rather than depending on Ellias to restore the unique power of those days, I'm striving to mine my own magic.

Still, it felt good to be studying with the mage again.

In the spring of 1994 I went on *Seeing Beyond* and announced I'd moved to the Bay Area after a two-year absence and was available for readings. I was stunned by the amount of listeners who called in to thank me for returning. Many mentioned how I'd touched their lives since way back at the 1989 earthquake.

As if my listening audience were a collective organism that sensed my need for reassurance, callers testified as to how much they'd been touched by the depths of my work. A few revealed that even though they'd never met me or gotten a reading from me, they felt encouraged and inspired by my voice, and were glad to be able to hear it again.

Bonnie and I soon realized we had a different kind of show on our hands. The extension lines on the studio phone never stopped flashing. During a commercial break before the final segment of the program I exclaimed, "How am I ever going to do all this work from a tiny trailer in the mountains?"

"Put it out there," my hostess retorted. "Ask for what you want."

So when we went back on the air I appealed directly to listeners and ended up securing four offices, which I used during the next few years, in San Francisco, Oakland, San Jose, and Carmel. By the close of the show I'd booked seventy sessions, far more than ever. This expanded client roster and months of bookings came as a tremendous relief and powerful positive augury on which to begin my new life.

I moved into a jungle-like, custom-built, freeform collage of domiciles linked by catwalks on the suburbanized west side of Santa Cruz, near the university. My new group home was on Spring Street, which I took as a good omen.

During previous months I'd racked up bills, and also needed funds to settle into my new place, so my first weeks of income were spoken for as I traveled through the Bay Area meeting old and new clients.

In Carmel one afternoon I had a revelation. After spending eleven days conducting four or five ninety-minute sessions a day, I was psychically tuned, emotionally raw, physically exhausted-energized and buzzing. I felt utterly grateful to be back in the swing of things, out of the gloom, single, strong, healthy, contributing to the well-being of the world, holding my head up high, listening to people's dreams, getting paid doing something I loved.

When my day's work ended I walked around town enamored by the little alleys, restaurants and shops. I love the tidy feel of Carmel, the colorful flowers and breezy landscaping, the quirky cottages, and fresh smell of the sea. I was elated to be doing powerful work and to have the next two days off. It was California spring after a year of cold dark rain, a pure pleasure just to breathe the velvety air.

Even though I didn't feel I had money to spend, I indulged in a glorious window-shopping spree, strolling along, trying on shirts, jackets, pants and hats just to see how they looked. I hefted shoes and belts just to feel their weight in my hands. I relished the scent of fresh clothes, the sense of new life inherent in each, and sauntered through the streets and alleys of the little European-like town feeling on top of the world.

At one shop I found an elegant pullover sweater, made of thickly woven cotton, adorned with sturdy different-colored patches of leather—a coat of many colors—but I left it untouched and walked by. *It's too something.*

After ten minutes or so I ran out of things to try and was about to leave when I remembered the sweater. Timidly, I approached the rack. I saw it was the only item of its kind. I ran my fingers over it, picked it up, smelled it. Then I pulled it on.

I walked past the sock department, past shoppers, salespeople and accessories, stoned on life just to be in Carmel with the shop door open and all of spring unfolding before me. I ducked into the fitting room and reviewed myself in the mirror while Ray Charles belted out a soulful rendition of Leon Russell's "A Song for You" on the house stereo.

When the tune ended and I emerged from the chamber I was struck by the sense of everyone zooming mindlessly past fabrics, colors, and moments. I felt a pang. I wanted to slow the world down and point out the exquisiteness of everything.

Everyone I saw looked as though they had much higher incomes than me. Yet here I was indulging in unabashed revelry of the senses. The material plane was a waterfall of beauty pummeling me in waves that I longed to share.

I stood in the midst of the store adorned in my coat of many colors, pierced by the sheer joy of life, beaming well-being and abundance toward everybody I saw. But no one seemed to notice.

I observed the hurried cast of faces, the pricey clothes, rings and watches. I sensed the pressures these Carmel people were under. I seemed invisible. It struck me as ironic that here I was in one of the world's wealthiest towns, and who was enjoying the wealth? Everyone seemed to be on the way to somewhere else.

I realized then that being rich has nothing to do with the amount of money you have. You get rich the moment you recognize that you have so much more to give to this world than you'll ever need to take from it.

Afterword

This book is intended to be read on several different levels. On the surface, it portrays the true story of my mystical apprenticeship to the world's greatest astrologer. One level deeper, it paints a new Creation Story to explain what humanity is doing on Earth. Another layer creates a shamanic journey in which, if you let the poetic images wash over you and go to work on an intuitive level, the sound of the words can conjure an initiation into your own core nature. The final level is a zone in which the book was written through me, and is weaving some message that I don't yet understand myself.

The main story portrays a young man's search for answers to the Big Questions: Are we all part of a Grand Design? What on Earth are we doing here anyway? What's the resounding need of our time? What happens when we die? How can I stop sabotaging myself and become the person I *really* am? What are love and sex all about? Where must we go to bring on the optimal future of our species?

Though I'm not so young anymore I still grapple with many of these issues to get to the bottom of them. I'm still working to bring on the future.

In recent years it's become fashionable to be skeptical about the fate of humanity, to succumb to numbness, fatigue, or apathy, to feel as though the world juggernaut has steamrolled beyond our control. We scramble around maintaining day-to-day existence while leaving the big picture in someone else's hands. My story posits the theory that we were born for so much more than this—that we're connected to a potent inner dimension we can draw upon to make all the difference; and the future, to a large extent, is in each of our hands.

Our mystery classes were many-layered and multidimensional, with much hidden between the lines that I'm still trying to get at. Our queries ranged through time and space but always came back to the premise that cosmos can best be found right here on Earth, and most of what you need to know can be discovered in the depths of your own nature, if you know where to look.

Our iconoclastic professor has a mad passion for inspiring people to find their own truths, and this book is my attempt to carry on that tradition. By encouraging us to expand our everyday awareness, by challenging the most fundamental beliefs about our place in the universe, and by introducing us to a great source of power and creativity buried within the human soul, the Lonsdales equipped us to use the current time as a bridge to a viable future for our world.

As I write these words it's December 2007, and 2012 is much closer than it was when we studied that year in the wizard's cottage. It's been twenty years since I began my apprenticeship the day I met Ellias in December 1987, year of Harmonic Convergence. The world has changed since then, and it hasn't. Mystery school was in my thirties. I'm fifty-three now, and it's become clearer than ever what a rare combination of people and ingredients came together in Bonny Doon, a remarkable convergence of timing, personalities and circumstances that won't happen again. And that future we studied is getting closer by the minute.

What do I *think* is going to happen at 2012?

I agree with other cultural visionaries who feel the world is ending. But I'm very optimistic about the end of the world. *Because that world I used to know is already gone.* The world I grew up with has been subsumed by an enigmatic new planet I strive each day to find my place in. Terms like "sustainability," "green building," "polar thaw," "biodiesel," "ozone hole," "Patriot Act" and "global warming" have entered our vocabulary. We don't have to wait for 2012 to see the death of the past—evidence is quite clear already that the old world is sinking fast. The question is less whether the world is ending, and more: *what do we wish to replace it with?*

You won't find any doom-and-gloom scenarios here, though. I don't envision 2012 as the righteous comeuppance for a species gone mad, nor as fate-like fulfillment of historic prophecies carved in stone. Conversely, I don't see it as utopia, either.

I see 2012 as a huge crossroads in history, a key choice point in evolution, a rare window of opportunity that appears to have been forecast in ancient days. The choice is: Will we emerge from the dark ages to write a new ending to humanity's countless variations on short-sightedness, self-sabotage and greed? Will we quit pretending to be so much less than we are? Will we step up to fulfill our awesome potential as a species? Will we seize this unique moment and finally haul ourselves toward something infinitely more satisfying than replaying the same historical mistakes over and over?

Yes, it's true that every moment in history, not just our own, is also a choice point. But there may be key periods, crux points, destiny crossroads where history becomes more malleable and we tap a larger stream of development. There may be fluid time zones where a greater portion of future is at stake. Choices made at such times could have more impact than normal.

Even by normal reckoning, though, so many massive challenges face us today—global climate change, droughts, floods and food shortages, the preservation of natural resources, the erosion of human rights—that we seem to be at a crux point in world evolution no matter how you look at it. And this crossroads, for perhaps the first time in history, doesn't seem to be the provincial dilemma of one nation or locality, but the complex quandary of the whole global village. It's easy to see why futility sets in, because these dilemmas cross all borders, yet we have no world council capable of putting aside its differences to unite the disparate factions and come up with viable longstanding solutions.

Yet there is still hope.

In recent years I've sensed a bright spirit rising all around me, a nascent spark of a kind I haven't seen since the 1960s, a yearning to challenge the status quo and refashion basic existence, a need to quit pretending to be so much less than we are and get on with something *real*.

Anyone paying attention to the youth of today is likely to notice that many of them are not even bothering with the stuck world I spent so much of my life railing against. They're already *in* the future.

As world events darken, in fact, this revolutionary impulse only seems to quicken. It's as if the strange lies and distortions of our "leaders" had to get so patently absurd that the old system could finally become a caricature of itself, which we can cast aside in order to usher in a whole new way to be.

But for the new to be truly innovative it has to come inside-out. For civilization to transform, human nature itself has to change. We must become hungrier for miracle than limitation; more addicted to transformation than repression. We must break the Trance of Normalcy, challenging presumed distinctions between "us" and "them," between the living and the dead, between all polarities striving to find each other after centuries of separation.

In the Age of Aquarius our commonality leads us forward. Now is the time for the genius sleeping in mass consciousness to awaken and turn the tide on centuries-old karma of the corrupt few lording over the many. Therein lies the crux of my story, because the overarching bias of our mystery school was that something marvelous is contained in the core of even the most unassuming human being, that we each have massive soul force to turn the world around, and that every moment offers us a gateway to a fuller inhabitance of our true nature, our lives and our planet.

And if the predictions turn out to be true and humanity *is* transforming on an unprecedented scale, then my little tale may inspire you to contact something magical, transformative and profound inside your own story. And if enough of us do that, who knows, maybe the world *will* change. . . .

2012

Acknowledgments

Heartfelt thanks to Marcella, my redheaded passion muse who materialized out of the warm pool at Harbin during the home stretch of writing this book, and has been an unflagging source of inspiration and constructive criticism.

Special thanks to Rich Noel, Bill Fedorko, Jeff Wignall, Chris Cohn, and Peter Selgin who, over four decades, never stopped believing in my writing and helped me keep the hearth fire burning.

Thanks to Susan and Susanne for going up the mountain with me.

Much love to Dana and Sky for getting me through lean hungry years of composition.

A special nod of appreciation to the hundreds of people all over the world in the last forty years who had no doubt of my future as an author—your confidence helped me believe in myself.

Thanks to my literary godfather Ray Bradbury for collaborating with me in my younger years, and being so clear about my talent.

Another kind of thanks to bosses, teachers, parents of friends and girlfriends, who treated me like I'd never amount to anything—your negativity put enough fire in my belly to prove you wrong.

Deep gratitude to three people at North Atlantic Books: my publisher Richard Grossinger, who saw the vision of this book at an earlier stage when the manuscript was a jumbled mess and I couldn't see it myself; my superb editor, Kathy Glass, who suggested the preface and afterword and did a great job helping me polish the story; and Hisae

Matsuda, my project editor, who contributed excellent editing and positive faith.

Hina and Bhasa, my Brooklyn-born fairy godmothers—thank you so much for sponsoring my ability to transcribe all our mystery school chapters way back when, which, years later, became the source material for this book.

Also, thanks to all who passed through Comstock Lane circa 1991–93: Alissa, Val, Barbara, Bhasa, Blythe, Bonnie, Bruce, Carol, Chellema, Cheryl, Dana, Dean, Dylan, Elizabeth, Frances, Gaia, Gaila, Gwen, Helaine, Hina, Ian, Jack, Jim, Kayla, Kenny, Larry, Lauriel, Lee, Margie, Maria, Marie, Marsha, Megra, Melanie, Merriem-Kathleen, Michael, Michele, Nancy, Paul, Renee, Rob, Robert, Rochelle, Rosa, Safiya, Sandra, Sharon, Susannah, Susie, and so many others whose names I can't recall.

Most of all, thanks to the Lonsdales for opening the doors of the mystery school that are now being opened to a wider audience. May the sacred circle we started beneath the redwoods grow and grow.

My heartfelt thanks go across the veil to Jade Redmon, who didn't live to see this book, but whose presence informs every word.

Finally, regarding two others on that side, I am so grateful to my parents and have never forgotten my mother saying when I was five years old, "My son is going to write the Great American Novel."

Look, mom and dad—I did it!

About the Author

Mark Borax has been a nomadic poet his whole life. In the late seventies he traveled the U.S. and Canada performing and selling his poetry. In the mid-eighties, Mark was befriended by his adolescent idol, Ray Bradbury, who became his literary godfather, believing in Mark's writing even though it was taking forever. In 1984 he became a comic book writer and the managing editor of *Comics Interview* magazine. In 1998 Mark rode his Harley Davidson Low Rider halfway around the world, through the U.S. and Europe, stopping for a year in the Tuscan countryside of Northern Italy.

Mark is an accomplished body worker, pool shooter, percussionist, singer and guitarist, and a trained actor and director who has produced performances on the east and west coasts of the U.S. He has worked more than a hundred jobs, but the thing he's proudest of is being the father of his five-year-old boy, Sky, who's the light of his life.

In 1987 Mark created Soul Level Astrology as a means of using the birth chart as a window to the soul, and in 1995 was invited to write the preface to *Inside Planets,* Ellias Lonsdale's first visionary astrology book. Since then he has helped thousands of people all over the world get in touch with their soul purpose. Mark is currently a practicing astrologer doing private readings. He can be contacted via his toll-free number: 1 888 SKY SOUL, or via his website, markborax.com and is available for public speaking and workshops. This is Mark's first book.

Also available from North Atlantic Books/Frog Books

THE BOOK OF THEANNA
In the Land that Follows Death

Ellias and Theanna Lonsdale

$16.95 / $20.95 in Canada, paper, 978-1-88319-37-3, 344 pp.

INSIDE DEGREES
Developing Your Soul Biography Using the Chandra Symbols

Ellias Lonsdale

$16.95 / $20.95 in Canada, paper, 978-1-55643-241-5, 190 pp.

INSIDE PLANETS

Ellias Lonsdale

$16.95 / $20.95 in Canada, paper, 978-1-55643-212-5, 328 pp.

INSIDE STAR VISION
Planetary Awakening and Self-Transformation

Ellias Lonsdale

$16.95 / $20.95 in Canada, paper, 978-1-55643-324-5, 208 pp.